Language Learning and the Mother Tongue

Innovative and interdisciplinary in approach, this book explores the role of the mother tongue in second language learning. It brings together contributions from a diverse team of authors to showcase a range of Francophone perspectives from the fields of linguistics, psychology, cross-cultural psychiatry, psychoanalysis, translation studies, literature, creative writing, the neurosciences, and more. The book introduces a major new concept, the (M)other tongue, and shows its relevance to language learning and pediatrics in a multicultural society. The first chapter explores this concept from different angles, and the subsequent chapters present a range of theoretical and practical perspectives, including counselling case studies, literary examples, and creative plurilingual pedagogies, to highlight how this theory can inform practical approaches to language learning. Engaging and accessible, this book offers readers new ideas and methods to adopt for their own thinking and practices, whether their background is in language and linguistics, psychiatry, psychology, or neuroscience.

SARA GREAVES is Associate Professor of twentieth- and twenty-first-century British poetry, translation studies, and creative writing. She has published a book on James Fenton (2016) and was co-winner of the Mustela Prize in social pediatrics for a Plurilingual Creative Writing Workshop in a Medical Centre (2014).

MONIQUE DE MATTIA-VIVIÈS is Professor of English linguistics. She has widely published in the field of free indirect speech, and one of her books was awarded the *Prix de la recherche* by the SAES in 2006. She has recently published three grammar books for advanced students of English (2018, 2019).

T0381917

Language Learning and the Mother Tongue

Multidisciplinary Perspectives

Edited by

Sara Greaves

Aix Marseille Univ, LERMA, Aix-en-Provence, France

Monique De Mattia-Viviès

Aix Marseille Univ, LERMA, Aix-en-Provence, France

Translations by

Sara Greaves

CAMBRIDGE
UNIVERSITY PRESS

Shaftesbury Road, Cambridge CB2 8EA, United Kingdom

One Liberty Plaza, 20th Floor, New York, NY 10006, USA

477 Williamstown Road, Port Melbourne, VIC 3207, Australia

314–321, 3rd Floor, Plot 3, Splendor Forum, Jasola District Centre, New Delhi – 110025, India

103 Penang Road, #05–06/07, Visioncrest Commercial, Singapore 238467

Cambridge University Press is part of Cambridge University Press & Assessment, a department of the University of Cambridge.

We share the University's mission to contribute to society through the pursuit of education, learning and research at the highest international levels of excellence.

www.cambridge.org
Information on this title: www.cambridge.org/9781009014243

DOI: 10.1017/9781009029124

First published 2022
First paperback edition 2024

A catalogue record for this publication is available from the British Library

Library of Congress Cataloging-in-Publication data
Names: Greaves, Sara, editor. | De Mattia-Viviès, Monique, 1965– editor.
Title: Language learning and the mother tongue : multidisciplinary perspectives /
    edited by Sara Greaves, Monique De Mattia-Viviès.
Description: New York: Cambridge University Press, 2022. |
    Includes bibliographical references and indexes.
Identifiers: LCCN 2021050124 (print) | LCCN 2021050125 (ebook) |
    ISBN 9781316516416 (hardback) | ISBN 9781009014243 (paperback) |
    ISBN 9781009029124 (epub)
Subjects: LCSH: Second language acquisition. | Language and languages–Study and
    teaching–Foreign speakers. | Native language and education. | BISAC: LANGUAGE
    ARTS & DISCIPLINES / Linguistics / General | LCGFT: Essays.
Classification: LCC P118.2 .L3647 2022 (print) | LCC P118.2 (ebook) |
    DDC 418.0071–dc23/eng/20220217
LC record available at https://lccn.loc.gov/2021050124
LC ebook record available at https://lccn.loc.gov/2021050125

ISBN   978-1-316-51641-6   Hardback
ISBN   978-1-009-01424-3   Paperback

Yamma

When she is happy, her voice is high, like a harp, like staccato. *Yamma mahala! Ya habibi!* To hear her voice like this makes my heart swell, knowing that this is her voice, that this is the truest joy she can express. When she answers the phone, or narrates the videos she sends of the cats. *Willec* Matilda (the cat), *laish rubic me way ha. Yamma.* She calls me *ya buttah*, my duckling, *ya habibi*, my love.

When she is angry, her voice is fast; it squawks like a bird, it crashes like piano chords. *Willec laish rubic awaj?* – why is your god crooked? And it is in these moments that I feel something like sorrow. I realize I will only ever know her through a thin veil of English. I cling to these moments where the veil is thinnest, where I can reach out and know her, know the outline of her soul like a blind man knows another's face.

Samantha West, Yamma

Contents

List of Contributors and Their Works

Boris Cyrulnik is a neuropsychiatrist, a psychoanalyst, the former director of research in clinical ethology at the hospital of Toulon/La Seyne-sur-Mer, and the director of studies in human ethology at Toulon-Var University. He is a well-known public figure and the author of an extensive interdisciplinary bibliography, including the following:

Mémoire de singe et paroles d'homme. Paris: Hachette, 1983.

Sous le signe du lien. Paris: Hachette, [1989]; Paris: Fayard/Pluriel, 2010.

The Dawn of Meaning. New York: McGraw-Hill, 1993. [*La naissance du sens*. Paris: Hachette, 1991.]

Les nourritures affectives. Paris: Odile Jacob, 1993.

De la parole comme d'une molécule. With Émile Noël. Paris: Seuil, 1995.

Un merveilleux malheur. Paris: Odile Jacob, [1999] 2002.

Dialogue sur la nature humaine. With Edgar Morin. La Tour d'Aigues: Éditions de l'Aube, [2000] 2010, 2015.

Vilains petits canards. Paris: Odile Jacob, 2001.

The Whispering of Ghosts: Trauma and Resilience. New York: Other Press, 2005. [*Le murmure des fantômes*. Paris: Odile Jacob, 2003.]

Talking of Love on the Edge of a Precipice. New York: Viking, 2007. [*Parler d'amour au bord du gouffre*. Paris: Odile Jacob, 2004.]

De chair et d'âme. Paris: Odile Jacob, 2006.

Autobiographie d'un épouvantail. Paris: Odile Jacob, 2008. (Renaudot essay prize)

Je me souviens... Paris: Odile Jacob, 2010..

Mourir de dire: La honte. Paris: Odile Jacob, 2010.

Quand un enfant se donne 'la mort'. Paris: Odile Jacob, 2011.

Resilience: How Your Inner Strength Can Set You Free from the Past. Translated by David Macey. London: Penguin, 2009.

Sauve-toi, la vie t'appelle. Paris: Odile Jacob, 2012.

Les âmes blessées. Paris: Odile Jacob, 2014.

Psychothérapie de Dieu. Paris: Odile Jacob, 2017.

La nuit, j'écrirai des soleils. Paris: Odile Jacob, 2019.

Monique De Mattia-Viviès is a professor of English linguistics, psycholinguistics, and grammar at Aix-Marseille University, the head of the English
Studies Department, and a former assistant director of the LERMA research
centre. Her publications include an award-winning book on free indirect
speech in English, along with her recent groundbreaking three-volume
grammar manual:

Le discours indirect en anglais contemporain: Approche énonciative. Aix-en-
Provence: Publications de l'Université de Provence, 2000.

Le discours indirect libre au risque de la grammaire: Le cas de l'anglais. Aix-
en-Provence: Publications de l'Université de Provence, 2006. (SAES/AFEA
Research Prize, 2007, ex aequo)

*La grammaire et le style: Domaine anglophone. Numéro spécial du Bulletin de
la Société de Stylistique Anglaise 30.* Monique De Mattia-Viviès (ed.).
Paris: Atelier Intégré de Reprographie, Université de Paris-X
Nanterre, 2008.

'Les déconnexions forme/sens et la syntaxe dite mensongère'. *E-rea,* 9.2,
2012. Monique De Mattia-Viviès (ed.). https://journals.openedition.org/
erea/2651

'Entrer dans la langue ou dans les langues: de la langue maternelle à la langue
mat-rangère'. *E-rea,* 16.1, 2018. https://journals.openedition.org/erea/3613[1]

*Leçons de grammaire anglaise, Volumes 1, 2, et 3: De la recherche à
l'enseignement.* Aix-en-Provence: Presses Universitaires de Provence,
2018–19.

Nathalie Enkelaar is a psychoanalyst specialising in children and adolescents,
a member of the International Lacanian Association, and the author of the
following:

'Quand le service de placement fait crédit aux parents: Le cas d'Alexandre'.
Cahiers de PréAut, 5.1, 2008. www.cairn.info/revue-cahiers-de-preaut1-
2008-1-page-143.htm

'Ohé, l'adolescente qui ne parle pas'. In *Vivre le multilinguisme: Difficulté ou
richesse pour l'enfant?* Marika Bergès-Bounes and Jean Marie Forget
(eds.). Toulouse: Éditions Érès, 2015.[2]

Alain Fleischer is a writer, a film director, a photographer, and an artist, as
well as the founder of Le Fresnoy National Studio of Contemporary Arts in
Tourcoing He is the author of an eclectic bibliography and filmography,
including the following:

L'Accent: une langue fantôme. Paris: Éditions du Seuil, 2005.[3]

---

[1] Translated by Sara Greaves as Chapter 1 of this volume.
[2] Translated by Sara Greaves as Chapter 5 of this volume.
[3] An extract from this essay appears here as Chapter 6, translated by Sara Greaves.

Simon Hantaï, vers l'empreinte immaculée. Lille: Éditions Invenit, 2011.

Conférenciers en situation délicate. Paris: Éditions Léo Scheer, 2012. (short stories)

L'impératif utopique: Souvenirs d'un pédagogue. Paris: Galaade éditions, 2012.

Britten, Quilter, Warlock. Arles: Actes sud, 2013.

Alma Zara. Paris: Grasset, 2015. (novel)

Effondrement. Paris: Grasset, 2015. (novel)

Retour au noir. Le cinéma et la Shoah: Quand ça tourne autour. Variations XXX. Paris: Éditions Léo Scheer, 2016. (essay)

Valeurs sûres. Le Fresnoy/La Pomme à tout faire (coproduction), 2007. (film)

Morceaux de conversations avec Jean-Luc Godard. Serge Lalou (producer), 2007–9. (film)

Le frivole et le complexe: La dentelle d'Alençon. 2008. (film)

Antony Caro, la sculpture comme religion. 2008. (film)

Georges-Arthur Goldschmidt is a writer, an essayist, and a translator, as well as a member of the German Academy for Language and Literature. He has translated authors including Walter Benjamin, Georg Büchner, Franz Kafka, Peter Handke, Friedrich Nietzsche, and Adalbert Stifter, and is the author of the following (a selection):

La traversée des fleuves. Paris: Éditions du Seuil, coll. 'Points', 1999.

Le poing dans la bouche. Lagrasse: Verdier, 2004.

Le recours. Lagrasse: Verdier, 2005.

Quand Freud voit la mer: Freud et la langue allemande, Volume I. Paris: Buchet/Chastel, [1988] 2006.[4]

Quand Freud attend le verbe: Freud et la langue allemande, Volume II. Paris: Buchet/Chastel, 2006.

Celui qu'on cherche habite juste à côté: Lecture de Kafka. Paris: Verdier, 2007.

La joie du passeur. Paris: CNRS éditions, 2013.

Un destin. Paris: Éditions de l'éclat, 2016.

Sara Greaves is an associate professor of poetry, translation studies, and creative writing at Aix-Marseille University, the head of the ECMA master's degree (Cultural Studies on the Anglophone World) at Aix-Marseille University, and in charge of the LERMA research group 'Language and Languages: From Disorder to Therapy'. Her publications include the following:

---

[4] The first chapter of this book appears in this volume as Chapter 7, translated by Sara Greaves.

Côté guerre, côté jardin: Excursions dans la poésie de James Fenton. Aix-en-Provence: Presses Universitaires de Provence, 2016.

'Transcultural Hybridity and Modernist Legacies: Observations on Late Twentieth- and Early Twenty-First-Century British Poetry'. In *Modernist Legacies*, Abigail Lang and David Nowell Smith (eds.). New York: Palgrave Macmillan, 2015.

'Étudiants d'anglais langue seconde et autotraduction'. With Marie-Laure Schultze. *E-rea*, 13.1, 2015. https://erea.revues.org/4769

'Un atelier d'écriture pour les exilés: Une question de statut'. *E-rea*, 14.2, 2017. https://journals.openedition.org/erea/5666

'Traduction et traduction interne chez Stephanos Stephanides, poète chypriote de langue anglaise'. In *Littératures migrantes et traduction*, Alexis Nuselovici, Crystel Pinçonnat, et Fridrun Rinner (eds.). Aix-en-Provence: Presses Universitaires AMU, 2017.

'Sloughing Off Empire: "Multi-monolingualism" in Daljit Nagra's *British Museum*'. In *No Dialect Please, You're a Poet: English Dialect in Poetry in the 20th and 21st Centuries*, Claire Hélie, Elise Brault-Dreux, and Emilie Loriaux (eds.). Abingdon: Routledge, 2019.

Jean-Jacques Lecercle is an honorary professor of English literature, linguistics, and philosophy at Paris Nanterre University. He is the author of numerous influential works on the philosophy of language, including the following:

Philosophy through the Looking Glass. London: Hutchinson, 1985.

Frankenstein, mythe et philosophie. Paris: Presses Universitaires de France, 1988.

The Violence of Language. London: Routledge, 1990.

Philosophy of Nonsense. London: Routledge, 1994.

Le dictionnaire et le cri: Carroll, Lear, et le nonsense. Nanterre: Presses Universitaires de Nanterre, 1995.

Alice. (Ed.). Paris: Gallimard, Collection Autrement, 1998.

Interpretation as Pragmatics. Basingstoke: Macmillan, 1999.

Deleuze and Language. Basingstoke: Palgrave, 2002.

The Force of Language. Basingstoke: Palgrave, 2004.

Badiou and Deleuze Read Literature. Edinburgh: Edinburgh University Press, 2010.

De l'interpellation: Sujet, langue, idéologie. Paris: Éditions Amsterdam, 2019.

Yoann Loisel is a psychiatrist, a psychoanalyst, and the director of outpatient care at the Institut Mutualiste Montsouris in Paris. He is the author of the following:

La bobine de Louis-Ferdinand: Louis-Ferdinand Céline, le négatif et le trait d'union. Paris: MJW Fédition, 2018.

Le complexe traumatique – Fonctionnement, limite, et trauma: La réalité rejoint l'affliction. Paris: MJW Fédition, 2018.

Pratique des médiations corporelles à l'adolescence. Yoann Loisel, Maurice Corcos, and Marc Gumy (eds.). Paris: Dunod, 2019.

Samuel Beckett. D'une langue à l'autre: L'outre-verbe. Paris: MJW Fédition, 2020.

Marie Rose Moro is a professor of child psychiatry at Paris Descartes University, the director of La Maison de Solenn, Hôpital Cochin, Paris, and a research director at the Institute of Health and Medical Research (INSERM), Unit 1018. She has published extensively on transcultural psychiatry; the following works are particularly pertinent to this volume:

Parents en exil: Psychopathologie et migrations. Paris: Presses Universitaires de France, [1994] 2011.

Enfants d'ici venus d'ailleurs: Naître et grandir en France. Paris: La Découverte et Syros, [2002] 2017.

Nos enfants demain: Pour une société multiculturelle. Paris: Odile Jacob, 2010.

Grandir en situation transculturelle. Bruxelles: Temps d'arrêt, 2013.

La violence envers les enfants, approche transculturelle. Bruxelles: Temps d'arrêt, 2015.

Bien être et santé des jeunes. With Jean-Louis Brison. Paris: Odile Jacob, 2019.

Rahmeth Radjack is a child psychiatrist at La Maison de Solenn, Hôpital Cochin, Paris, and a researcher at the Institute of Health and Medical Research (Inserm), Unit 1018. She has contributed to the following publications:

'Devenir parents, faire famille en situation transculturelle'. With Marie Rose Moro. *Sud/Nord*, 28.1, 2019. www.cairn.info/revue-sud-nord-2019-1-page-173.html

'"Je suis sans papiers, donc je n'existe pas": Filiation et affiliations impossibles des jeunes étrangers exclus de la protection de l'enfance'. With Fiammetta Nincheri and Alice Titia Rizzi. *Empan* 133.1, 2019. www.infomie.net/spip .php?article4653

'Se raconter à l'autre et se construire à travers des objets: Une médiation intéressante pour les jeunes isolés étrangers'. With Laure Woestelandt, Fatima Touhami, Jonathan Lachal, and Marie Rose Moro. *La psychiatrie de l'enfant*, 61.2, 2018. www.cairn.info/revue-la-psychiatrie-de-l-enfant-2018-2-page-393.htm?contenu=resume

Acknowledgements

First, we would like to thank all our contributors for their thought-provoking and inspiring work, to which this book pays tribute. Second, we would like to thank our students, past and present: those who have contributed materially (see the Epigraph and Chapter 3), and all those who over the years have shared our enthusiasm for language and literature and fuelled our thinking on the Mother tongue. Third, we thank the LERMA research centre of Aix-Marseille University for enabling our research over the past years, and the CAMSP Salvator medical centre for our fruitful partnership. We are grateful to the French publishers Buchet/Chastel, Érès, le Seuil, and the online journal *E-rea* for permission to print translated versions of their publications, and to Penguin Random House for Noor Unnahar's poem. Special thanks go to Jean Robert for his invaluable expertise in text formatting and for his infectious love of language, and to Professor Jean Viviès for his precious advice and unwavering support. We offer many thanks to Tamsin Greaves for her discerning ear, and to Dr Simon Greaves for his close reading of Chapter 8. With regard to Cambridge University Press, we would like to thank our commissioning editor, Rebecca Taylor, for her fabulous guidance and Isabel Collins, for her unstinting help and advice.

Introduction

Sara Greaves and Monique De Mattia-Viviès

This book springs from an ongoing reflection on the role of the Mother tongue in second language learning. It draws on nearly thirty years of teaching English linguistics, literature, and translation at the university level in France, observing the diversity of ways in which students progress and studying the difficulties they encounter. It is the fruit of our quest for theoretical insights to help interpret these difficulties, and adapt our teaching methods accordingly, in particular by means of creative pedagogic practices. Our objective here is thus twofold: to present our research on the residual, sometimes inhibiting presence of the Mother tongue in second language learning, and to showcase a selection of essays by Francophone authors whose thinking on language and the Mother tongue has influenced, reinforced, furthered, or expanded our own. These contributors, most of whom have not so far been published in English, work in a variety of fields: philosophy of language, literature, child psychiatry, psychoanalysis, translation studies, plurilingualism, and neuropsychiatry.

With this book, we wish to introduce Professor Monique De Mattia-Viviès's concept of the *langue mat-rangère* or '(M)other tongue'.[1] This term conveys the way the second language always comprises, as a constitutive component, an *in-matrie* dimension, 'within the bounds of the mother': a regressive, sensory, physical dimension that underlies speech in a foreign language. Indeed, speaking a foreign language is also an act involving the body. To develop this thesis, this volume focuses on two second language learning situations: the foreign language taught at school, usually starting at about eleven years old, a language the child's parents may or may not be familiar with; and the second language that is grafted onto the original language in a context such as migration, although other contexts exist too. Both situations may lead the learner to acquire a 'second Mother tongue', and the diverse approaches presented here do not oppose these two language learning contexts but reveal a common denominator between them: the central role played in

---

[1] In De Mattia-Viviès's article in which this concept is introduced (see Chapter 1 in this volume), the French portmanteau word 'mat-rangère' is composed of two adjectives, *maternelle* (mother) and *étrangère* (foreign, here translated as 'other').

1

second language learning by the original Mother tongue, the language of the mother, in its most archaically emotional, sensory, and bodily dimension. The Mother tongue establishes the foreign language as other, as situated 'outside the bounds of the mother', while at the same time constantly drawing the foreign language back to it during what can sometimes be an ecstatic – if painful – language learning experience.

This volume falls into three parts: 'The Mother Tongue and Second Language Learning', 'From the Mother Tongue to the Second Mother Tongue', and 'The Second Mother Tongue as a (M)other Tongue and the Return to the Body'. Part I comprises three chapters by English studies academics: Professor Monique De Mattia-Viviès, Honorary Professor Jean-Jacques Lecercle, and Associate Professor Sara Greaves. These studies explore the Mother tongue from linguistic, literary, psycholinguistic, sociolinguistic, psychoanalytical, plurilingual, and pedagogical perspectives, and while concerned with early childhood, plurilingual literature, the plurality of the linguistic subject, or creative writing, they provide detailed discussions of the importance of the Mother tongue in second language learning in young adults. Part II, which includes chapters by child psychiatrists Professor Marie Rose Moro and Dr Rahmeth Radjack, by psychoanalyst Nathalie Enkelaar, and writer, photographer, film director, and artist Alain Fleischer, is concerned with the second Mother tongue needed by children and adolescents in order to succeed at school and to develop healthily. These chapters envisage adolescent psychopathological contexts and engage with the urgent demands of multicultural society, ending on an autobiographical portrayal – a joyful celebration – of lived plurilingualism in an exiled family. Part III embraces chapters by writer and translator Georges-Arthur Goldschmidt, psychiatrist and psychoanalyst Dr Yoann Loisel, and neuropsychiatrist and clinical ethologist Dr Boris Cyrulnik. The role of the body in the Mother tongue and the body's underlying presence in the second language traverse this book, but in Part III the question comes into the foreground in three distinct ways. Chapter 7 focuses on a nation's relationship to its language and traces the origin of Freudian psychoanalysis to the body-oriented nature of German grammar; Chapter 8 demonstrates how Samuel Beckett seeks a return to the body in his literary writing through the intermediary of the second language or (M)other tongue; and Chapter 9 places the body at the heart of its account of the crucial role of relating – beginning with interuterine vibrations – in the development of language in the brain.

In gathering these diverse essays under a single heading, we aim to draw attention to the theoretical pertinence and pedagogic potential of this multidisciplinary approach to the Mother tongue in language learning. By anticipating what can be framed as a return of the repressed in second language learning, we hope to help more students acquire less a foreign language than a second Mother tongue. This volume thus promotes multidisciplinarity (bringing diverse disciplines to bear on a research object) and interdisciplinarity (diverse disciplines work together and interact) as progressive forces enabling theories and practices to converge fruitfully.[2] Thus, the overall volume is multidisciplinary and our individual approaches are interdisciplinary, as evidenced in Sara Greaves's creative pedagogy (poetics, creative writing, and translation studies, as well as plurilingualism and psychoanalysis) and in Monique De Mattia-Viviès's combination of linguistics, psychoanalysis, psycholinguistics, and sociolinguistics to study the progression from the Mother tongue to a foreign language composed of an ever-increasing share of the maternal dimension: the (M)other tongue.

Above all, we are convinced of the impact and benefits of approaches such as these in education and child and adolescent psychiatry. Their insights into the power of attachment of the Mother tongue and its enduring sway throughout adult life, brought to bear on relationships with languages and cultures in multicultural societies, are in our view crucial. Tensions due to divided loyalties and an uncertain sense of legitimacy, as experienced by children of migrant families and second language learners alike, can be alleviated and transformed, and parental or individual authority restored. Such is our conviction.

The Mother Tongue and Second Language Learning

In 'Entering into Language and into Languages: From the Mother Tongue to the (M)other Tongue', Monique De Mattia-Viviès provides the principal theoretical foundation to the didactic approach set out in this book with her presentation and definition of the (M)other tongue. It draws on psychoanalytical theory, in particular the conceptual framework of attachment theory, and the bodily imprint on the psyche, as elaborated by John Bowlby,[3] and on examples taken from French or English literature, such as Louis Wolfson's *Le Schizo et les langues*.[4] Her research focuses on the language learning process in early childhood and its repercussions later in life in second language learning. It is rooted in her lecturing experience at Aix-Marseille University and her lifelong engagement with psychoanalysis, reinforced by a research experiment in a children's clinic during which she attended psychiatric

---

[2] Frédéric Darbellay and Theres Paulsen (eds.), *Au Miroir des Disciplines: Réflexions sur les pratiques d'enseignement et de recherche inter- et transdisciplinaires/Im Spiegel der Disziplinen: Gedanken über inter- und transdisziplinäre Forschungs- une Lehrpraktiken* (Bern: Peter Lang, 2011).

[3] John Bowlby, *Attachment and Loss, Volume 3: Loss. Sadness and Depression* (Croydon: Pimlico, [1980] 2006).

[4] Louis Wolfson, *Le Schizo et les langues* (Paris: Gallimard, [1970] 2009).

consultations with small children suffering from speech impediments, and their parents.

While steeped in French psychoanalytical theory, among others the Lacanian school (with its focus on the father as the principal facilitator of language, through his role in enforcing the incest taboo, the *Non/Nom du père*, the No/Name of the father), Monique De Mattia-Viviès's interest in second language learning has led her to investigate the processes of separation in early childhood, and thus to explore Bowlby's maternal deprivation theory, which is better known in Anglophone psychiatric circles than in France. In this chapter, she provides an account of the hybrid nature of the Mother tongue, analyses the social and linguistic tensions experienced by children caught between the 'interior' languages (the Mother tongue is already divided) of their family circle and the 'exterior' language spoken at school 'beyond the bounds of the mother'. When these experiences produce trauma, their reactivation in adulthood by the attempt to speak a foreign language can prove an inhibiting force.

In the following chapter, drawing on linguistics, literature, and philosophy, a complementary perspective on the plural nature of the Mother tongue in relation to language learning is offered, and teaching foreign languages is strikingly envisaged through the lens of subjective aesthetic appropriation. The foreign language is envisaged as 'an increased Mother tongue' that draws on 'interpellation' and the creation of a 'fictitious past' in the new language, so as to acquire a style in it.

Jean-Jacques Lecercle is an intellectual mainstay of English studies in France, whose thinking on language and literature has inspired and stimulated generations of students and colleagues. We would like to mention two passages from his seminal work, *The Violence of Language,* to which this book is indebted. One concerns the persistence of the Mother tongue and its 'possession' of the subject: 'One cannot escape one's Mother tongue, the tongue of one's memories and desires, a tongue that possesses the subject to such an extent that it is always in excess of any attempt to force it within the boundaries of rules';[5] the other is a reflection on the contrasting ways in which we respond to agrammatical formulas according to context. Quoting a phrase from Somerset Maugham's *Cakes and Ale*: 'I'm not so young as I used to was', Jean-Jacques Lecercle comments as follows: 'Were I to read this in a student's paper, I would underline the last word in petulant red. As a reader of fiction, I enjoy the sentence'.[6]

---

[5] Jean-Jacques Lecercle, *The Violence of Language* (London: Routledge, 1990), 22.
[6] Lecercle, *The Violence of Language*, 7.

His reflection in 'One Mother Tongue – or Two?' takes off from Jacques Derrida's *Monolingualism of the Other or the Prosthesis of Origin*.[7] The chapter then proceeds by assessing the hesitant answer given by Barbara Cassin in response to a question from the audience (can we ever learn a second language to the level of our first?) at the end of a lecture entitled 'More Than One Language'.[8] Her answer is on the whole negative, and she evokes Hannah Arendt's attachment to her native German. From these points of departure, the chapter presents the paradoxical and plural nature of the Mother tongue, with particular reference to Monique De Mattia-Viviès's diachronic account of the three stages of the language learning process (cf. Chapter 1). This construction over time of an individual Mother tongue suggests a number of propositions: the Mother tongue isn't a unitary entity; its construction is the result of a continued process of linguistic interpellation of the speaker; it is therefore the product not so much of an individual as of a social relation.[9] Two detours, through Lucien Sève's Marxist anthropology and the 'tetraglossic' theory of Henri Gobard,[10] supported by Gilles Deleuze, help account for this individual-cum-social construction of a speaking subject.[11] The acquisition of a second Mother tongue – meaning the construction of a second version of Gobard's four 'languages' – can then be envisaged. Each of these languages may be acquired, it is argued, in a process that duplicates the acquisition of the original Mother tongue, thus giving a positive answer to the question addressed to Barbara Cassin.

The following chapter takes its cue from Jean-Jacques Lecercle's concluding call for teachers of foreign languages to teach students 'not a means of communication but ways of acquiring a style'. The creative writing workshops presented here, through their appeal to the body and to affect, designed as they are to create or revive or simply revitalise a semiotic link to the body that is frequently lost sight of in the rule-bound, highly codified foreign language, are a means to that end.[12]

Sara Greaves has developed an interdisciplinary approach to teaching and research, infusing her academic teaching with creative, plurilingual practices. In 'Embracing the Bilingual Overlap in Creative Second Language Learning', she presents some of her creative courses or workshops at Aix-Marseille

---

[7] Jacques Derrida, *Monolingualism of the Other or the Prosthesis of Origin*, translated by Patrick Mensah (Stanford, CA: Stanford University Press, 1998).

[8] Barbara Cassin is a French philologist, Hellenist, and philosopher.

[9] Cf. Chapter 9 of this volume.   [10] For a definition of this term, see Chapter 2, note 32.

[11] Lucien Sève is a French Marxist philosopher. Henri Gobard is a French linguist.

[12] As a reminder of the challenge this represents, cf. Péter Medgyes's claim that non-native speakers 'are by their very nature, norm-dependent'; 'Native or Non-Native, Who's Worth More?', *English Language Teaching Journal* 46.4 (1992), 343, https://doi.org/10.1093/elt/46.4 .340.

University and in a local medical centre, as well as a new action research project in creative pedagogy with Monique De Mattia-Viviès.

She became aware of the pleasures – along with the stresses and strains – of thinking and writing between languages when studying English poetry for her PhD in French, as well as of the negotiation of the cultural and conceptual mismatches between the discourses of English poetry criticism and French academia, and between interior and exterior languages but with a crossover effect: a language of intimacy from which one was estranged by distance, a language of exteriority in the immediate environment.[13] Having always been struck by the creative energy of language learning – noting, for instance, the pleasure certain learners take in savouring the phonetic materiality of foreign words – and in the hope of bridging the learning gap in first-year literature classes, she took a university diploma in facilitating creative writing workshops at Aix-Marseille University, going on to develop a pedagogical approach in English studies designed to include what Yoann Loisel calls, in Chapter 8 of this volume, the 'maternal side of language'. She references Julia Kristeva's *chora* to convey the way creative translation and plurilingual creative writing workshops offer the possibility of playing with new 'ways of [writing]', new 'manners of being', in the words of Marielle Macé, reinforcing self-confidence and encouraging risk taking, so as to break with determining, limiting identities and try out a new, plural 'Skin-voice' (a concept developed from French psychoanalyst Didier Anzieu's 'Skin-Ego').

Throughout Part I, then, language learning in infancy is discussed in relation to second language learning in adulthood. But there are, of course, situations in which the second language must be learnt in early childhood, which is the situation presented in Part II. When this process goes smoothly and the children's social and cultural assimilation is harmonious, the result is a 'second Mother tongue', a term also used for the 'first' language of children whose parents have not spoken to them in their mother tongue. Part II thus concerns plurilingual families and the importance of the preservation of a linguistic filiation in the acquisition of a second language: the valorisation of the language of origin as a condition for the harmonious learning of the second language.

From the Mother Tongue to the Second Mother Tongue

In 'Language Diversity: Time for a New Paradigm', Marie Rose Moro and Rahmeth Radjack discuss the urgent need for contemporary multicultural societies to reassess their attitudes towards language. This will enable children

[13] Cf. Sara Greaves, *Poésie, poïétique, traductologie: parcours interdisciplinaires*, Synthèse d'Habilitation à Diriger des Recherches, Paris, Université de Paris III, 2017 (unpublished).

from multilingual families to learn the second Mother tongue that is crucial to their assimilation, on which their healthy growth and development depend. This chapter focuses on the children of migrant families who are afflicted by an 'aporia of transmission', leading to premature school leaving and in some cases separatism, whereas the cultural wealth of such children should be acknowledged and allowed to be of benefit to them and to society at large.

While French language policies have remained broadly monolingual (e.g., in preschool children's medical centres, plurilingual parents are still frequently advised to use French in their homes, even when neither of the parents is a native French speaker), and the use of interpreters in hospitals is generally underdeveloped, Marie Rose Moro has followed in the footsteps of Georges Devereux, the founder of ethnopsychiatry, and his disciple, Tobie Nathan, to open up child psychiatry to a transcultural approach.[14] Placing the Mother tongue at the centre of the therapeutic protocol at the Maison de Solenn, a new discipline called 'parent–child ethnopsychology' has been established, its clinical success bringing new arguments to the controversy surrounding the monolingual language policy prevalent in French schools. The authors offer a clinical perspective on the problems some children and adolescents face, deprived of their heritage or torn by a conflict of loyalty between disparate languages and values, forced to negotiate two modes of belonging: filiation and affiliation. They make a strong case for reinforcing the Mother tongue to engender or rekindle in such children a desire for language, a desire to relate.

The following chapter provides a clinical illustration of what Moro and Radjack call an 'aporia of transmission'. Like so many children, Ohé, the adolescent girl presented here, has been propelled directly into the 'second' Mother tongue, bypassing the primary foundation in the 'first' Mother tongue and suffering from her mother's 'untranslatability' in French.

Nathalie Enkelaar's case study, 'Ohé, the Silent Teenager', is a moving account of a course of treatment in psychotherapy. It references French psychoanalyst Jean-Paul Hiltenbrand's work on untranslatability in situations of migration and bilingualism – the impossibility to experience certain pro- found emotions in the second language. Silent and depressed, Ohé, a thirteen- year-old who is the third daughter of a Korean mother and a French father, was brought for counselling by her mother, who, it transpires during the therapy, learnt French at university upon arriving in Paris and chose to speak to her daughters only in her 'host language'. The therapy sessions focus increasingly on the analyst's intuition that something is lacking in the adolescent's Mother tongue, leading to the hypothesis that the daughter's difficulties might be related to the mother's 'untranslatability' in certain crucial areas of experience

---

[14] Georges Devereux, *Basic Problems of Ethnopsychiatry* (Chicago: University of Chicago Press, 1980); Tobie Nathan, *L'Étranger ou le Pari de l'autre* (Paris: Autrement, 2014).

(e.g., mourning). The therapist observes language and behavioural patterns in the adolescent and, in keeping with Lacanian theory, lets the signifier 'play'; – in this case pinpointing the word 'décalage', meaning a discrepancy or a shift in space or time (translated here as 'time lag'). This is related to the adolescent's passion for Japanese cartoons; to Ohé, it seems, Japanese has come to represent a kind of halfway house, a language in which the maternal dimension can be retrieved, between the second Mother tongue and the first (albeit absent) Mother tongue.

The ensuing chapter pursues this discussion of languages in childhood but from the perspective of a plurilingual speaker. Through metaphorical language, it describes the emotional dimension of accent and envisages its meaning as a sign of belonging – and non-belonging. Although we usually think of accents as foreign, they naturally derive from the Mother tongue, and Alain Fleischer's comparison of accent with a ghostly presence hovering over the spoken language is a telling image of the way the Mother tongue holds sway in second language speech.

Alain Fleischer's 'Accent: A Ghost in the Language', comprises the opening pages of an essay and an autobiographical fragment presenting his mixed-origin multilingual family, his 'small family Tower of Babel'.[15] The short final section, 'Border Tax', extracted from a later chapter of the same essay, reflects on power relations strategies and the high economic and political stakes of multilingual verbal interaction. The economic metaphor of border tax to convey the idea of accent as the price to be paid for speaking a foreign language is striking as a reminder of the material, hybrid character of language: linguistic transparency and purity, as well as sharply delimited bilingualism, are delusions.

Fleischer's musical ear, studies in linguistics and anthropology, and subsequent career in the visual arts are all brought to bear on the strangely sensitive phenomenon of accent in second language speech, and this rich family tableau opens numerous paths of enquiry. Accents are described as markers of belonging and of distance; they are shown to an attuned ear to convey fine nuances of identity, to carry with them distant or lost worlds that can be suddenly revealed to the imagination, and sensitivity to them leads to unsuspected dimensions of human expression. Languages are seen to serve diverse functions: they can be commandeered as a form of refuge from other members of the family or flaunted as a means of self-assertion and community-belonging even within the family circle. In contrast with the usual perception of accent as something to be erased, Fleischer prizes accent as a remanence of the past in the present, or of far-off places in the here and now. A foreign

---

[15] Alain Fleischer, *L'Accent: une langue fantôme* (Paris: Seuil, Collection La Librairie du XXIe siècle, Maurice Olender (director), 2005).

accent is a residue, an index of continuity spanning fragmented personal and family histories.

Fleischer's family Tower of Babel is a microcosm for our plurilingual world (in the broad sense of the term, embracing the plurality of the Mother tongue and the dialectical nuances of region and class, in which language unites and divides, enhancing belonging and inflicting exclusion). His essay is a love letter to language, especially as modulated musically by the lingering presence of a foreign accent. On reading his chapter, we are reminded that the price to be paid to speak a second language 'without an accent' can be a high one, and as teachers we may be cautioned not to set our sights too high for our students, as we cannot know how high the price will be for them. Helping students reach an awareness of what their own language barrier 'border tax' might consist of could prove more effective in the long run.

The ghostlike presence of a foreign accent is thus suggestive of the idea running through this volume that the languages an individual speaks are not distinct territories but overlapping entities. The conception of the second language as a second Mother tongue – or, better, as a (M)other tongue that has retrieved or repaired its links with the body – underpins Part III. Chapter 7 provides a teleological account of Freud's psychoanalysis, locating its source in the presence of the body in the German language. Chapter 8 is devoted to Samuel Beckett, whose choice of a foreign literary language (French) is related to the possibility it offered of recapturing the 'maternal side of language', thereby voicing the lost *infans*. In Chapter 9, the perspective of ethology and the neurosciences is brought to bear on language learning, emphasising the ways body and mind converge in the formation of language circuitry in the brain.

The Second Mother Tongue as a (M)other Tongue and the Return to the Body

Georges-Arthur Goldschmidt's 'The Sea of Language' is the first chapter of Volume 1 of a work entitled *Quand Freud voit la mer: Freud et la langue allemande* (*When Freud Sees the Sea: Freud and the German Language*). Written as most of Goldschmidt's works are in his second Mother tongue, French, which enabled him, through a return to the body, to find his way back to his native German.[16] It paves the way for Goldschmidt's highly original study. Deploying his learned and highly sensitive French/German bilingualism, he explores the German language and reveals how the founding tenets of Freudian psychoanalysis are not concepts that happen to have been framed in

[16] Cf. Georges-Arthur Goldschmidt, *La traversée des fleuves* (Paris: Éditions du Seuil, Collection Points, 1999), and other autobiographical texts.

German, but were derived from the way German parts of speech are rooted in the body, and thus grounded in the language itself. The chapter opens with an extended metaphor comparing languages to the sea, drawing poetic and historical parallels, such as the concomitance in the late nineteenth century of the first explorations of the seabed and Freud's new perspectives on the human mind. This leads to a visionary yet precisely conceptualised study whereby the sea's ebb and flow, bodily rhythms such as breathing in and out, and the spatial coordinates of German grammar seem held in a state of fusional interconnection, which seemingly naturally gives rise to Freudian theory. The German language is thus not a language of abstraction, as French admirers of German philosophy tend to believe, but of the body in space and in motion; it is not a language of scholars, but of the common people going about their everyday life. This is not idealised or romanticised, however, and Goldschmidt's brief study here of the character or essence of German takes him from poetry to philosophy to the 'ultimate perversity': the language of the Third Reich, which he briefly envisages as a return of the repressed within the German language, possibly intuited by Freud.

Goldschmidt's is the subjectivity of an exile who has had to 'translate himself',[17] of a decentred subject capable of observing at a high level of refinement and nuance his own relationship with his languages.[18] Through his analysis of German, he illustrates to a poignant degree how the character of a language can lend itself to perverse manipulation, and how individuals can find themselves rejected by the Mother tongue that had so far nurtured them. Goldschmidt's work is testimony to language's shaping powers in the private and public spheres, in certain cases with the yoke embracing them being twisted out of shape, even broken.

Yoann Loisel has written books on Louis-Ferdinand Céline and Samuel Beckett, both writers who push back the limits of literary writing. In 'Samuel Beckett's Change of Literary Language: An Apparent Severing of Links to Continue Writing on the Maternal Side of Language', he writes: '*Molloy*, especially, exhibits fury of staggering intensity throughout the novel – a degree of rage more or less unprecedented in the history of literature so far'. Most critics writing on Samuel Beckett's bilingualism take exophonic writing and self-translation as their starting point, but Yoann Loisel focuses on this 'extreme degree of rage' to view Beckett's change of literary language 'from underneath'.[19] He brings his specialist knowledge of adolescent care to bear on

---

[17] Salman Rushdie, *Shame* (London: Vintage, 1995, 29).

[18] One is reminded of Freud in *The Psychopathology of Everyday Life*, translated by Anthea Bell (London: Penguin, [1901] 2002).

[19] A wealth of publications can be found on the subject, including Michaël Oustinoff, *Bilinguisme d'écriture et autotraduction: Julien Green, Samuel Beckett et Vladimir Nabokov* (Paris:

his subject and explodes some of the myths surrounding it, such as the famous 'no style' of French and the idea that for Beckett, French was a 'counter-language' to ward off the '(s)Mother tongue'. Loisel thus makes a convincing case for Beckett's use of French as a paradoxically regressive move. It allows him to live 'in exile within exile', to set up the conditions of 'nostalgia' by putting the distance of the foreign language to the service of a risky regression to infancy in search of the body, in search of sensory perception and archaic aggressivity: a language 'beyond-the-verb'.

From a language learning perspective, this research deepens our awareness of the psychic stakes at play. It cautions us as language teachers against intellectualising our approach to language didactics, and to ponder the Mother tongue's origin in the body and in the prelinguistic *infans*. It can alert us to what may lie behind our academic exercises and incite us to tread more carefully when correcting students' work and perhaps to reappraise language errors, to envisage the possibility that they might in a sense be symptoms.

Finally, in 'Language, the Brain, and Relating', Boris Cyrulnik gives an interdisciplinary account of language through the lens of ethology and the neurosciences. An interdisciplinary researcher influenced by Konrad Lorenz and John Bowlby,[20] a highly esteemed populariser of the concept of resilience, Boris Cyrulnik interweaves diverse scientific discourses that complement and illuminate each other. Using phylogenetic and ontogenetic accounts, he describes the transition from sensory perception to symbolic representation in animals and humans, and the way neural circuitry of language coalesces through relating, through taking an interest in another's thoughts and agreement between two brains. He thus maps the processes and trajectories of the 'word-making machine', corroborated by studies of sensory or institutional deprivation or of illness, abuse, or accidents. Studies carried out on plurilingual speakers recovering from aphasia reveal that the Mother tongue, the most deeply imprinted language, is the one that comes back first. Experiments with newborn babies confirm the origin of the Mother tongue in tactile interuterine stimuli, which are later recognised by the newborn in the lower frequencies of the mother's voice, creating 'a reassuring bond of familiarity'. The progression through the determining strata in the development of the Mother tongue, from the neurological to the emotional to the sociocultural, recalls the diachronic transition observed by other contributors to this book from an interior language to an exterior one, a progression that is repeated and at the same time pursued from the Mother tongue to the (M)other tongue.[21] Thus, this interdisciplinary approach drawing on ethology and neuropsychiatry sheds light on the

L'Harmattan, 2001), and Rainier Grutman, 'Beckett and Beyond: Putting Self-Translation in Perspective', *Orbis Litterarum*, 68.3, Special Issue on Self-Translation (2013).
[20] Cf. Chapter 1 of this volume.   [21] See Chapters 1 and 2 of this volume.

embedding of language in the body and confirms the overarching concept around which this book coheres: the enduring imprint of early language formation in the brain.

It thus emerges from the diversity of approaches that make up this book that the Mother tongue, in its inherent plurality and corporeality, occupies a central place in the learning of a foreign language; rather than a polarization between the two, the foreign language is a filial continuation of the Mother tongue.

We argue that it is only by valuing and preserving a strong relationship with the Mother tongue, or by trying to retrieve or restore it (e.g., through creative writing), that one can access a form of plural identity very often sought after by learners of a second language. This implies a necessary phase of fusion and interplay between the two languages, composed of accepted deviations from the norm and accepted interference of the Mother tongue: a necessary phase of hybridization leading to bilingualism as a consequence of harmonious learning. And even when the foreign language is a counter-language (a way of escaping from the Mother tongue), clinical experience reveals the persistence of a regressive attraction for the figure of the mother through the foreign language, an unconscious desire to reconstruct an archaic experience, both corporeal and emotional, that has gone wrong. The foreign language, being a language, distinguishes itself both as other ('beyond the bounds of the mother') and (M)other ('within the bounds of the mother'): *other* in the separation from the Mother tongue that its learning induces, and *(M)other* in the return to archaic experiences its learning entails.

This, approached from different angles, is what this multifaceted book is about.

The Mother Tongue and Second Language Learning

Part I defines and analyses the Mother tongue as plural (it is composed of three or four linguistic stages, or registers), reflecting upon its enduring hold over us – as is revealed in second language learning in adolescence or adulthood. In Chapter 1, language learning – or entering into language – is related to attachment theory, which sheds light on instances of developmental delay in childhood; this early language-learning experience, whether a smooth transition or otherwise, is then brought to bear on second language learning. Chapter 2 asks whether it is possible to master one's second language as well as the first, and it sees in a regressive detour via *lalangue* and inventing a past history in the second language a possible way forwards. The bodily dimension of language being frequently overlooked in language teaching, Chapter 3 discusses pedagogical strategies designed to tap into the creative potential of this regressive moment – which in some cases can lead to a kind of second chance.

1   Entering into Language and into Languages

From the Mother Tongue to the (M)other Tongue

Monique De Mattia-Viviès

> To my student Miriam, whose mother does not speak French.
> To all the students whose mothers do not speak their (M)other tongue.

This study begins with an observation based on thirty years of teaching English linguistics in higher education.[1] For many students, learning to speak English, and especially mastering the phonetics of English, is a fairly smooth process; for others, however, it is highly challenging or almost impossible, to the extent that some students abandon the prospect of becoming English teachers, even though that was what they initially set out to do. Poor marks given for oral exams as undergraduates, which can be levelled out by written assignments, leave almost no hope of success when attributed for spoken English in French schoolteachers' competitive exams (the English CAPES and *agrégation*).[2] While the majority of native Anglophones no longer speak phonologically standard English, it is nevertheless this variety of English that persists – or 'insists', to borrow a term from linguistics philosopher Jean-Jacques Lecercle[3] – at least in the French system, which values it very highly.

Confronted with the variable results of traditional approaches to remediating these difficulties (e.g., long stays in English-speaking countries, intensive listening to programmes in English, all-English experiences of various kinds based on the idea of immersion and presumed to guarantee significant progress), I began to wonder whether they might be rooted in something other than, for some students, an always too brief exposure to the sounds of English.

---

[1] This chapter was originally published as follows: Monique De Mattia-Viviès, 'Entrer dans la langue ou dans les langues: De la langue maternelle à la langue "mat-rangère"', *E-rea*, 16.1 (2018), https://journals.openedition.org/erea/6502, https://doi.org/10.4000/erea.6502. Translated by Sara Greaves and reproduced by kind permission of *E-rea: revue électronique d'études sur le monde anglophone*. I give many thanks to Eilish McNamara, Mohamed Lamine Mariko, and Clémentine Garcenot for their personal contribution to my thinking, and to Samia Ounoughi for our fruitful discussions.

[2] The *CAPES* and the *agrégation* are two national competitive examinations for recruiting secondary school teachers in France. The *agrégation*, of a higher level, is a prestigious qualification that is also often held, in literary disciplines, by university lecturers.

[3] Jean-Jacques Lecercle, 'A global language is not a language', Unpublished lecture, Padua University, 15 February 2013.

15

Might it not be worth studying how children learn to speak, in order to observe whether the difficulties encountered when learning a foreign language are, up to a certain point, of a similar nature to those encountered in the mother tongue when a child enters into language ... or fails to?

1.1   The Research Experiment

During a three-year period (2014–17) of half days on a weekly basis, I sat in on the medical appointments of Dr Jean-Luc Di Stefano, child psychiatrist and head of the Centre for Early Infancy Socio-Medical Action (CAMSP) at Salvator Hospital in Marseille, at which a clinical psychologist was also present, either Julia Maraninchi or Myrto Rapti. The children admitted for consultations in this facility, accompanied by their parents, all have difficulty speaking and are developmentally delayed in various ways that affect more than speech.

It appeared that the most frequent causes for these difficulties were fairly directly related to problems of separation, although other influences should be considered as well.[4]

1.1.1   Child–Mother Separation

- This can be rendered problematic by, first and foremost, insufficient presence on the part of the father, thereby placing the mother in a position of emotional and relational predominance, for various possible reasons:[5]
  – the father is frequently absent for professional reasons;
  – the parents have separated, and the father has left the family home;
  – the mother fails to 'make room' for the father; or
  – the father is physically there but his linguistic presence is sketchy, either because he is taciturn or speaks too sparingly or because the linguistic space allowed him is insufficient, thus making the mother–child separation, via language, problematic; as is well known, the words of the father are responsible for severing, little by little, a fusional prelinguistic experience with the mother.
- An impossibility exists for the mother to let go of her child, for reasons related to her own life story. This fusional state may sometimes be revealed by the way she addresses her child, for instance, by calling the child not by

---

[4] This notion is distinct from that of 'attachment patterns', which are more common in English-language psychology.
[5] The term 'caregiver', frequently used in the English-speaking world, is not appropriate here, as will become apparent (translator's note).

their name but by the word 'mummy', with the result that, linguistically speaking, mother and child are one and the same.

- An accident at birth has transformed the child into an object of constant attention, thereby encouraging fusion and making it harder for the child to gain access to articulated language. When this accident has become a family secret that has not been explained to the child, including and especially in terms of its emotional impact on the parents, there is an added degree of complexity.
- A preterm birth (moderate to late) has occurred.

1.1.2   Enforced Separations due to Abuse or Inadequate Care

Traumatic situations such as these, making what should be a natural bond unnatural, delay all the essential learning processes, starting with language. The child is not protected, is only perceived in terms of the worry he or she is the cause of, and is insufficiently loved and taken care of and immersed in perplexity and guilt ('if I am treated this way, it must be my own fault'[6]), thus maintaining the child in a pre-verbal state. Such lack of care and maternal guidance means that the infant is not in a position to envisage separation from an initial state, as they have no experience of that state's fusional nature and the security it provides.

1.1.3   Separation from an Original Language That Is Hidden
             or Disparaged

For some migrant families, French is a foreign language, and a child's diffi-culty in learning to speak (French) may stem from the fact that the parents perceive it confusedly as the language of their enforced separation from their original language. It may even be perceived as the language of their renounce-ment (out of the desire for assimilation) or of social domination, producing a rift or reticence that is not conducive to the child's successful language learning, whether French or the often-underrated original language – assuming the parents continue to use it in the home. Generally speaking, people who have experienced exile, who are 'exiles', are faced with a foreign language that they are forced to use, even if they do not completely abandon their Mother tongue and continue to use it amongst themselves. The world, especially the linguistic one, of the family and the developmentally delayed child no longer coheres. Exiles are 'foreigners' in the strictest sense of the term, as they are

---

[6] See Ronald Fairbairn, *Psychoanalytic Studies of the Personality* (London: Routledge, [1952] 1994).

foreign to themselves, and a child who has lacked homogenous structuring in an original language is not even foreign in that sense, for they have no identity at all but are trapped between the country of origin and the host country, between two languages, of which neither can easily become their own. A gap is opened up in the filial relationship.[7]

As a rule, exile, just like early separations, delays the entrance into language and confines the infant in a position of pre-verbal fusionality, preventing them from developing out of infancy and interacting with others.

1.1.4   *Separation from the Mother Tongue through Learning a Foreign Language*

Some parents wish for their child to learn a foreign language from birth, in general, English, even though neither of the parents are native Anglophones. Rather than address their child in their Mother tongue, they speak a language that is not their own and which often lacks fluency and is phonologically stilted, thus shutting the child out of the bonding language, the language of affect, which is also that of the family circle. In so doing, they replace this language with a language devoid of their own life stories – but which is the vector of a fantasy project of self-generation, of 'filial dissolution' or of 'de-generation' – thereby producing a hiatus in transmission and making all organic processes unnatural (e.g., language learning, potty training, walking).

1.1.5   *Language Variations*

Language variations within the family are another source of difficulty when one parent attempts to have the linguistic advantage over the other. For instance, this occurs when one parent speaks one language (e.g., French) and the other parent speaks another (a foreign language), and one tries to dominate the other linguistically. Or perhaps the mother has had a university education and the father has not (or the other way round), and she tries, consciously or unconsciously, to impose her value system on the father. Interlingual or intralingual discrepancies can in such cases create conflicts of loyalty that prevent the child from finding their place in language. Language variations within a family can give rise to disorder when they go hand in hand with power struggles. The variation known as intralingual variation occurs when there is a usually unconscious underlying intention, which can delay a child's development.

---

[7] Cf. Chapters 4 and 5 of this volume.

1.1.6 Other Possible Causes

- Choosing a child's name is not a neutral act. When a child is given a foreign name (e.g., a name heard in an American TV series or a name linked to a country of origin in the case of exiles) and the meaning of this act has not been explained to the child, it isolates them in a filial descendancy that is different or rooted in the past. Such children may sometimes be invested in a project of self-generation, of severance from the parents' origin, which prevents them from taking up their natural filial position and entering the parents' language, out of uncertainty as to the legitimacy of this language for the parents.
- The parents' separation, especially if violence is involved, may generate difficulties. To avoid taking sides between father and mother, the child attracts attention by contracting a whole series of pathological conditions and developmental delays that can extend to aphasia.
- Excessive parental expectations can leave no place for the child as an individual. The child becomes uncontrollable ('a nightmare!'), always out of line with respect to what is expected of them. Proving incapable of being loved for what they are and compelled to follow strict requirements, they develop theatrical behaviours staging non-conformity to the parents' desire and, through language learning difficulties, the impossibility of communicating with them.
- Taboos and secrets prevent the child from learning language harmoniously, as if the act of speaking could have uncontrollable, or even tragic, consequences.

Thus, learning one's own language is not necessarily an automatic process, but one that is affected by psychological and emotional complexes, which, if they are obstructed, can in some cases delay or even obstruct a child's language development. If speaking means separation (i.e., separation from a primary, pre-verbal, and fusional state), then any entrance into language is traumatic – all the more so when this initial state of fusion has not occurred, when there is neither no *paradise lost* nor any paradise to lose. In such cases, the child has not received their due, and this can lead to delays in gaining access to other pleasures, such as those less body oriented and more symbolic.

Let us return now to the reasons that led me to carry out this experiment. Why is it that certain students – who may perform brilliantly in other areas and have mastered English grammar and vocabulary with ease – cannot assimilate the sounds of the English language? To answer this question, it appears necessary to return to the Mother tongue. The clinical experiment shows that to learn language harmoniously, certain psychological and emotional conditions must be fulfilled for a child to take the risk of, or consent to, a separation from an early phase in their attachment to primary carers, in particular the mother. Born of her body, that primary relationship is expressed essentially through the body and through sound, which means that the mother's role is unique. It is first and foremost from her that the child must part, by means of language, with the father playing the role of separator in this process, associated as he is with the entrance into articulated language. Hence, we see the importance of his role, or of any figure with parental responsibility, in facilitating the gradual termination of a state of mother–child fusion.

My hypothesis here is that learning a foreign language reactivates this primary phase of separation, namely, the child's accession to articulated language. Even when it proceeds smoothly, this phase comprises a primary severance, a primary traumatism, that is attenuated, or, on the contrary rendered more problematic, by a more or less favourable emotional context. When difficulties have arisen at this stage, it is possible that they will be reactivated when a second language comes to be learnt. Ultimately, the impossible appropriation – far more so than where syntax or vocabulary are concerned – of the *sounds* of another language, which are bound up in the body and in this pre-verbal phase that the infant goes through before language, would seem to be rooted in the Mother tongue and in a number of early positive or negative experiences that have resulted – to put things very broadly – in the child being able to speak or not.

But the concept of the Mother tongue and what it embraces is not self-evident.

1.2   The Mother Tongue and Loss

Learning a foreign tongue, a language 'beyond the bounds of the mother', to borrow Michel Foucault's coinage,[8] and beyond the bounds of the family history, or even learning one's Mother tongue can never be taken for granted, as it is a learning process that implies loss.

What is it *exactly* that is at stake, or at stake all over again, in the process of learning a second language? The terms 'Mother tongue' and 'foreign tongue' are set in opposition to each other, but is it not true to say that any language is at first foreign when a child enters its sphere? What fundamental experience is it that is reactivated in foreign language learning that distinguishes it from all other learning processes? Should we content ourselves with explanations in terms of 'errors', resulting from lack of work, lack of time spent abroad, and so on? Of course, these factors should not be overlooked, but is there not something more fundamental in this difficulty to assimilate, to embrace the

---

[8] Michel Foucault, 'The Flight of Ideas'. In Jean-Bertrand Pontalis et al. (eds.), *Dossier Wolfson ou l'affaire du schizo et les langues* (Paris: Gallimard, 2009), 123.

sounds of the Other? What is it that gets in the way? Could it be that this fundamental factor is the Mother tongue, which the would-be linguist must consent, at least in part, to leave behind?

Speaking, to be sure, requires separation from the mother, but only up to a certain point, for when this separation takes place the child enters the sphere of the *Mother tongue*, which is of a symbolic order where her presence can still be felt. This is what prompted Jean-Jacques Lecercle to declare that the Mother tongue possesses the subject to such an extreme extent – being the language of affect, memory, and desire – that it is no doubt illusory to think that one can discard it completely.[9] The Mother tongue is the place of fusional memory, the place of a state of bliss that is lost yet constantly regained, indirectly, through its intermediary.

Ultimately, what is it that gets in the way of learning a foreign language, preventing it from ever becoming a Mother tongue – could it be the Mother tongue itself? What is lost in learning one's own language, and what is lost or gained in acquiring a foreign one? To borrow a phrase from Michèle Vierling-Weiss, what does the (foreign) language force us to part with?[10]

Hannah Arendt spent part of her life in exile in the United States and never lost (or wanted to lose) her German accent. 'Nothing can replace the Mother tongue', she said.[11] What remains is the Mother tongue. She felt an unwavering sense of loyalty to the German language, and her exile was not so much from a country as from a language. Moreover, she did not define herself as German, but as Germanophone.

The Mother tongue seems, therefore, to be one of the fundamental factors at stake when learning another language, whether as a help or a hindrance, or sometimes a bit of both.

1.3   Defining the Mother Tongue

However, the Mother tongue is not one language. It is a plural, divided entity, corresponding to phases in the evolution of the child. In other words, the Mother tongue is by nature plural, and we are all plurilingual within the same language, without necessarily being aware of it.[12]

---

[9] 'One cannot escape one's Mother tongue, the tongue of one's memories and desires, a tongue that possesses the subject to such an extent that it is always in excess of any attempt to force it within the boundaries of rules'. Jean-Jacques Lecercle, *The Violence of Language* (London: Routledge, 1990), 22.

[10] Michèle Vierling-Weiss. 'Que reste-t-il ? La langue maternelle'. *Che vuoi*, 26.2(2006), 11–21.

[11] Hannah Arendt, 'A Conversation with Günter Gaus', *The Last Interviews and Other Conversations* (New York: Melville House, [1964] 2013).

[12] Cf. Sara Greaves, *Poésie, poïétique et traductologie, parcours interdisciplinaires: Synthèse d'habilitation à diriger des recherches* (Paris: Université de Paris III, 2017, [unpublished]).

Indeed, a transition takes place from *lalangue* (a concept borrowed from Jacques Lacan[13]), passed on to the infant by the mother, by the body of the mother, to articulated language. Mother and child share this *lalangue* until the child learns constituted language ('*Lalangue* is that private language that the mother and child share, the language of that primary erogenous bodily contact', writes Michèle Vierling-Weiss;[14] it is that initial state of fusion between two beings through *lalangue*, which is a fusioned signifier: 'a form made of *body thought language*', in the words of Yoann Loisel[15]). Articulated language performs the mother–child separation while remaining the language of the interior,[16] internal to the family, even if it is in contact with the outside world; this *interior language* is not necessarily homogenous, as it may bear traces of other languages (e.g., Spanish, Italian, and Arabic, while nevertheless remaining French), but its principal characteristic is to comprise the child's language of identity, the language of their close circle and primary emotional identity.[17]

This interior language meets the language of the exterior (the one spoken amongst friends, at day care and then school), from which it differs to varying degrees. In some cases, there is a sociological discrepancy with the language spoken at school, which is positioned therefore at a further remove from what is remembered of the primary *lalangue* as well as from the language of the interior. In fact, all children are at least bilingual, and most often trilingual within their Mother tongue, which can be broadly subdivided into three categories:

- *lalangue*, body and sound oriented, a private language shared by mother and child;
- *language of the interior*, articulated language, at once sociolect, idiolect, and language of affect, the language of the child's close family circle, of their people; and
- *language of the exterior*, including the language used at school, of varying degrees of sociological and idiolectal discrepancy with the interior language.

---

[13] Jacques Lacan, *Encore: Le séminaire-livre XX*. (Paris: Éditions du Seuil, Collection Points Essais, 1975), 174.
[14] Vierling-Weiss. 'Que reste-t-il?'.
[15] 'Écho de l'ego, du monde des choses: La rencontre Keaton-Beckett'. An unpublished lecture, 'Écriture et arts du soin'. A study day co-organised by Sara Greaves and Jean-Luc Di Stefano. Timone Hospital, Marseille, 17 March 2017.
[16] The concepts of *language of the interior / language of the exterior* are also used by Marie Rose Moro. 'Passer d'une langue à l'autre, le cas des enfants migrants' (2014). www.youtube.com/watch?v=WwcGUuCpzXs.
[17] Julia Kristeva, 'L'amour de l'autre langue' (2014). www.kristeva.fr/la-traduction-langue-de-l-europe.html.

The language of the exterior is still, to be sure, the Mother tongue, but no longer entirely so. It comes into varying degrees of conflict – especially the language spoken at school – with the interior language if the latter is socio-logically distinct and devalued by the very people who speak it. For the child, two levels of legitimacy then come into conflict: an emotional legitimacy ('I speak my home language at home, not school language, as I would risk losing my rightful place in my family circle') and a social legitimacy ('I speak school language in the classroom, but not my home language, for if I were to, I would lose my rightful place in the classroom, in the language used at school'). Later, under the influence of the two languages, interior and exterior, with one no doubt dominating the other, the adolescent forges their style, which is to say an exterior language of their own, in which *lalangue* neverthe-less remains present, unconsciously remembered, assimilated by the body. These different points of contact come together to generate style, or the relationship that each person has with language and that is their own. Generally speaking, this language has moved away from the realm of intim-acy; it is at once more personal and invested by a kind of norm to be respected (school language), sometimes at odds with the interior language, which may be sociologically devalued.

The aphasic child, whatever the reason for the aphasia, must therefore turn their back on the affect- and body-oriented monolingualism of *lalangue* (which Lacan calls elsewhere the *One*, the same[18]) to progress towards bilingualism (interior language) and then trilingualism (exterior language), multiplying in this way the separation phases. The Mother tongue, *lalangue*, which they find it so hard to let go of so as to embrace the interior language, will one day itself become exterior. There are three levels of loss in this. As Rajaa Stitou writes, 'Such is language, born of the mother "*lalangue*" [...]. The latter should not be confused with codified language, but it is attached to it and their connection can never be erased'.[19]

So we are all plurilingual, and at the same time monolingual, according to the would-be paradox in Jacques Derrida's famous formula in *Le Monolinguisme de l'autre, ou La prothèse d'origine*,[20] defined in two ways:

We only ever speak one single language – or rather one single idiom.
We never speak one single language – or rather there is no pure idiom.

---

[18] Lacan, *Encore*, 174.
[19] Rajaa Stitou, 'Épreuve de l'exil et blessures de la langue', *Cahiers de psychologie clinique*, 18.1 (2002), 159–70.
[20] Jacques Derrida, *Le monolinguisme de l'autre ou La prothèse d'origine* (Paris: Éditions Galilée, 1996).

That is indeed what it amounts to: we are plurilingual and at the same time monolingual through the memorising of *lalangue* and our practice of the language of the interior, which makes our relation to language a unique one. At the same time, while each of us has a unique relationship to language, language is nevertheless common to a given entity. The Mother tongue, therefore, both is and is not private property, nor is it a homogenous entity. It is at once personal and psychically invested, and always already there. It evolves with time, but what does not change is the initial experience of *lalangue*.

Derrida's acceptation of the word 'monolingualism' is a highly singular one, derived from his personal life story in Algeria. His Mother tongue is French. However, he is deprived of legitimacy in this language because this Mother tongue has its roots elsewhere, outside Algeria. 'For us all, the French language was supposedly a Mother tongue, but one whose origin, norms, rules and law hailed from elsewhere. They harked back to another country. [...] The monolingual speaker I refer to speaks a language of which they are *deprived*'.[21] Derrida is thus deprived of one of the dimensions of his own tongue, the exterior language, which has no legitimacy within the historical context in which he finds himself, whereas more frequently it is the interior language that is devalued and the exterior one that is legitimate. In Derrida's case, the delegitimization of the exterior language affects the interior one, to such an extent that the emotional roots of his relationship with language are called into question. This is how I understand the word 'deprivation'.

1.4   The Experience of Exile as Constitutive of the Mother Tongue

Generally speaking, all children, even those born to a homogenous environment, are in reality exiles from the moment they enter into language, in the sense that they have experienced the exile of separation, the severance from *lalangue*. According to Rajaa Stitou:

Speech is what prevents us from becoming confined within our language and invites us to recognise that all speaking beings are exiles from language-as-all (which is to say, *lalangue*). It is this exile from language-as-all that enables the subject to find their style and to acquire speech, in other words to enter the sphere of misunderstanding, of the hiatus between the word and the thing.[22]

This is all the more true of the child whose interior and exterior languages are at variance with each other, and who is an exile within their own language. Barbara Cassin asserts that more than one language is needed for an experience

[21] Derrida, *Le monolinguisme*, 72.
[22] Stitou, 'Épreuve de l'exil', paragraph 21. www.cairn.info/revue-cahiers-de-psychologie-clini que-2002-1-page-159.htm.

of exile to occur.[23] But exile is always already there; it can be intralingual when the discrepancy is too great between the language of one's family circle and the language of the outside world and of school.

Learning a foreign language, especially one phonologically very different from French such as English, may reactivate that initial exile – fraught as it was with an intermingling of pain and pleasure – the transition from *lalangue* to language, from the bliss of the body and of sound (*lalangue*) to that of words and meaning (language): an exile founded upon an initial renouncement that is necessary for accession to a symbolic order, which bears a tenacious trace of that renouncement. Michèle Vierling-Weiss is right to emphasise the fact that the word *exile* (from the Latin *ex(s)ilium* derived from *ex(s)ul*: 'living in another country, banished', or from *ex(s)ilere*: 'to leap outside') has the same etymological root as the word *exulter* (from the Latin word *exultare*: 'to leap').[24]

1.5   Why Learn a Foreign Language?

If the Mother tongue is the place of primary bonding, what can explain the appeal of a foreign language or, on the contrary, the forms of resistance it gives rise to? Similarly, what can explain the fact that some people sever all links with their interior language for the sake of a foreign language (or extra-erior language, one might say) or, on the intralingual level, for the sake of the language used at school, the exterior language? This brings us back to the question asked above: 'What does a (foreign) language force us to part with?'[25]

1.5.1   *The Foreign or 'Extra-erior' Language as* Anti-destiny

The foreign language (or exterior language when totally at variance with the interior language) is a means of escape from the language of origin, experienced as stiflingly familiar, and – to borrow a phrase from André Malraux concerning art – the foreign tongue can be seen as an *anti-destiny*.[26] Being the only one to be fluent in an idiom – as if it were a private language of one's own, with no one else in the family circle able to speak it – provides acute narcissistic pleasure; it thus becomes possible to undertake the effort of moving away from the original interior language and to sidestep the conflictual

---

[23] 'Hannah Arendt et les langues de l'exil'. Radio 'France Culture' (2011). www.franceculture.fr/conferences/ecolenormale-superieure/hannah-arendt-pour-etre-confirme-dans-mon-identite-je-depends.

[24] Vierling-Weiss. 'Que reste-t-il?'.   [25] Vierling-Weiss, 'Que reste-t-il?'.

[26] André Malraux, *Les voix du silence* (Paris: NRF/La galerie de la Pléiade, 1951).

traumatism between interior language, the language of the rift, and exterior language, the language used at school. The foreign tongue offers a way to bypass this conflict through a return to the intense pleasure of *lalangue* that this experience of learning another language – perceived, as Catherine Coquio argues, as 'good', as a 'counter-language' – makes it possible to reactivate.[27] Here are a few examples to illustrate this.

1.5.1.1   *When Exterior Language Is Adopted to Counteract Interior Language: Edouard Louis – Being Excluded from One's Own Language*

The real name of Edouard Louis, a young writer born in 1992, is Eddy Bellegueule. He claims to have struggled against a language that is doubly hostile, both the language of his family circle (interior language) *and* the language used at school (exterior language, that of the 'bourgeoisie' and his chosen idiom), which was unwittingly antagonistic towards his home environment. To highlight his choice, he changed his name and wrote an auto-fictional narrative, *En finir avec Eddy Bellegueule* (*To See the Back of Eddy Bellegueule*).[28] Making a clean break with one's experience involves a change of words and name. It is not he who has rejected his social class and the language of his family circle (interior language), but his family who have rejected him, refusing his new language, which contrasts so sharply with theirs. The exterior language he uses is foreign to his community and has made him a stranger to them. He no longer speaks as they do, and his family no longer 'recognise' him. He, on the other hand, has reinvented himself and his book is a plea 'not to be what we have been made into', 'for before I took exception to the world of my childhood, that world took exception to me. Very early on I became, for my family and other people, a source of shame and even of disgust. I had no other choice but to run away.'[29] Very early on, he had to part company with his emotional self in order to put everything into words. One may then wonder what is left, in his case, of *lalangue*, the sphere of affect, if the interior language that came after it and in which it remains present has rejected him and has had to be abandoned. Can it be that writing with the words of the exterior language has produced a kind of self-generation and given rise to a *foster* mother, another primary fusional experience that is more abstract than the former, another *lalangue* that is more solitary and less body oriented, and has come to replace the original *lalangue*?

---

[27] Catherine Coquio, *La littérature en suspens. Écritures de la Shoah: Le témoignage et les œuvres* (Paris: L'Arachnéen, 2015).

[28] Edouard Louis, *En finir avec Eddy Bellegueule* (Paris: Éditions du Seuil, 2014).

[29] Edouard Louis, *Les matins de France Culture*. Radio 'France Culture' (2014). www .franceculture.fr/emissions/les-matins/quand-lecriture-de-soi-devient-un-acte-de-revolte-avec-edouard-louis-auteur-de.

As Julia Kristeva points out, 'There is matricide in the abandoning of a native tongue'.[30] Edouard Louis has not abandoned his native tongue, which is French; he has abandoned a substantial emotional dimension of that Mother tongue (his interior language) into which *lalangue* is incorporated. He has thereby – at least so it would seem – lost his original *lalangue*, which is to say his early affects.

1.5.1.2   When a Foreign Language Is Adopted as a Counter-Language: Louis Wolfson and 'Counter-Language' For some, the foreign language is a means of protection from the other language, in this case the Mother tongue, which is perceived as predatory. It offers a means of escape from the incest of *lalangue*, from that initial body-to-body experience that has been incorporated into the interior language, and of seeking refuge in it as an exterior language in the fullest sense of the word, as a counter-language. It offers a means to protect oneself from the affect of the Mother tongue, to make a cleaner break with the body of the mother, to re-engender oneself outside of one's life story, 'beyond the bounds of the mother'. Moreover, during a lecture on Beckett in Marseille in June 2017,[31] Yoann Loisel alluded to the attraction of anorexics for foreign languages.

Let us briefly consider the case of Louis Wolfson.

The 'language student', as he refers to himself in a book entitled *Le Schizo et les langues*, of which he is the author, cannot bear to hear his mother speak.[32] He fears that 'through the intermediary of words the bad maternal object will enter [his] body'.[33] He therefore sets out to learn languages (mainly four: French, German, Russian, and Hebrew) so as to translate the English words she uses into foreign ones, and to learn these languages without the help of English, through the intermediary of interlanguage dictionaries. Wolfson's plan is to destroy his Mother tongue so as to avoid being mutilated by it. To borrow from Gilles Deleuze, 'Translation, involving a phonetic dismantling of the word, and without transference into any single language but into a magma composed of all languages against the Mother tongue, is a deliberate destruction, [. . .], a de-boning, since consonants are the bones of language'.[34]

---

[30] Kristeva, 'L'amour de l'autre langue'.
[31] 'Écriture et arts du soin' (Writing and the healing arts). A study day co-organised by Sara Greaves (LERMA) and Jean-Luc Di Stefano (IDEC), La Timone Hospital, Marseille, June 2017.
[32] Louis Wolfson, *Le Schizo et les langues* (Paris: Gallimard, [1970] 2009).
[33] Michel Foucault, 'La fuite des idées' et 'Les trois procédés' (Dits et écrits [1958–1988]; Vol. II, 1976-1988; Paris: Gallimard, 2001). In Jean-Bertrand Pontalis et al., *Dossier Wolfson ou l'affaire du Schizo et les langues* (Paris: Gallimard, 2009), 125.
[34] Gilles Deleuze, 'Schizologie', préface de *Le Schizo et les langues* (Paris: Gallimard, [1970] 2009) 10.

This extreme undertaking goes hand in hand with an eating disorder: Wolfson refuses the food provided by his mother, and when she is out he gorges himself, greedily swallowing the contents of tin cans whose English labels he forbids himself to read, thereby putting himself at risk. 'The equivalence thus runs deep between the unbearable maternal words and venomous or soiled foodstuffs'.[35]

However, at the end of the book, it seems that a form of relief has been found. The mother 'consents', as Wolfson puts it, to speak increasingly in Yiddish, his father likewise, and his stepfather in French. Is it, Deleuze asks, this wordplay based on similarities both 'of meaning and of sound between the English words and the foreign ones, his Mother tongue, that of his family circle' that has made English more bearable to him? Is it the story of this destruction through the writing of the book *Le Schizo et les langues* and the progressive diminution of the role of English in the speech of his family that have had a therapeutic effect on him? Is it the renewed bond with another Mother tongue, his mother's Yiddish, that allows a kind of reconciliation with English, with, as Foucault writes, 'the enraged idiom of his mother'?[36]

While most experiences are not as extreme as Wolfson's, learning a foreign language may stem from a desire to escape maternal omnipotence, which can only be tolerated by learning one or several counter-languages to counteract it.

1.5.2   Beckett and the Forbidden Mother Tongue

Samuel Beckett had a slightly similar experience, although considerably less spectacular. He used the expedient of French, which he learnt at the age of about fifteen, for his writing, so as to be able to speak in the first person, which he was unable to do in his native Irish-English. He could only truly be the subject of his utterance, a subject-enunciator, in a foreign language. As Michèle Vierling-Weiss puts it, 'For others, the foreign language provides a body that they can then inhabit, far from the incestuous suffocation of the Mother tongue, as we see for instance in the case of Samuel Beckett, for whom Irish-English was too close for him to be able to sustain an enunciative position'.[37] It was only after his mother's death that Beckett undertook to translate his works into English, and that for him, finally, the 'I' of enunciation in English was no longer out of bounds. In some cases, for someone who has been dispossessed of it, the Mother tongue must die through the body of the mother for it to become a reality at last.[38]

---

[35] Deleuze, 'Schizologie', 13.   [36] Foucault 'La fuite des idées', 123.
[37] Vierling-Weiss, 'Que reste-t-il?'.   [38] See also Chapter 8 of this volume.

1.5.3   The Foreign Language as a Way Back to the Mother Tongue

Learning a foreign tongue sometimes amounts to a detour allowing a return to the self. Using the expedient of the outside as a way back towards the inside is for some an indirect way to return to the origin of trauma. What is more, it is not unusual for a traumatic experience to be approachable only in a foreign language due to the protective screen it provides, the distance from the events, whereas in the Mother tongue they are impossible to put into words. Another language of intimacy, the adopted foreign tongue, makes it possible to escape the incestuous intimacy of the original language.

Georges-Arthur Goldschmidt, for instance, had an experience of this sort.[39] The foreign tongue, in this case French, enabled him to reconnect with his original language, German, which he considered to have gone insane – perverted by Nazism – and which he was prohibited from speaking when he came to France as a refugee during the Second World War. He was only able to re-engage with his Mother tongue thanks to French. The language of the social codes (French) made it possible to return to the language of the body (German), which was even more emotionally charged as it had for a while been forbidden and deformed by Nazism. The Mother tongue only exists through its opposition to other languages. When Goldschmidt was a child he was able to use a counter-language, which ultimately enabled him to keep his Mother tongue.[40]

1.5.4   The Foreign Tongue as a Way Back to Lalangue

Conversely, learning a foreign language can mean being able to re-enact the experience of exile as a source of elation, the experience of separation as a source of liberation – even without abandoning the Mother tongue, although gaining a slightly less fusional one than *lalangue*. The initial transition from *lalangue* to language, with the renouncement it implies, is also a moment of intense satisfaction for the child: there is a great sense of achievement as, beneath their parents' admiring gaze, they understand the meaning of what is being said and say their first words. It is this that makes learning a foreign language so pleasurable. In other words, learning a foreign language can maintain the fusional bonding with the mother in another form – by learning a language that she does not speak but which she holds in high esteem. In this case, the foreign tongue allows for a gentler separation, with the mother's approval and with the child's fulfilling at one and the same time their own

---

[39] Cf. Chapter 7 of this volume.
[40] Cf. Georges-Arthur Goldschmidt *La traversée des fleuves* (Paris: Éditions du Seuil, Collection Points, 1999).

desire and the mother's personal project, the two being difficult to distinguish. This foreign tongue is thus a language of desire, which allows both mother and child to reconnect with the forgotten language, *lalangue*. The fact that this foreign language learning is granted value in the mother's discourse guarantees the avoidance of conflict between the Mother tongue (the interior) and the acquired language (the exterior); however, the situation is of limited scope, for as the foreign language is mastered with increasing proficiency, so the divide between mother and child increases and the separation grows more acute, producing the very conflict that it was hoped would be avoided, the tug-of-war between interior language and exterior language.

Thus, despite the pleasure derived from the other tongue, the Mother tongue maintains its hold and will not let go – for one always ends up being confronted in the acquired language with the limits experienced in the Mother tongue.

What can be done to make the foreign language into another body-oriented language, even when the maternal phase of *lalangue* has not taken place? What can be done to make it into a language of invention, as the Mother tongue can be, a language inhabited by the body? What can explain the failure of a stay abroad for a language student who, once separated from their Mother tongue, 'in exile', must come back to France for unexpected health reasons?

Why is it, despite its attraction, that the foreign tongue is sometimes a screen concealing what cannot be said in one's own language, generating failed attempts to run away?

1.6   The Mother Tongue or Impossible Separation

Miriam M., one of my students, once told me at the end of a mock English competitive exam, for which I was one of the assessors and which had not gone very well (her spoken English was found wanting: numerous displaced word stresses, improperly pronounced vowels, excessively soft plosives, etc., which at a few days from the exam left her with little hope of success): *my mother does not speak French.*[41] Given the emotion of the student when she said this, it was clear that this was not an attempt at self-vindication but something running far deeper and that reached beyond her performance that day or even her own life story. With these words, she was justifying her own difficulties with the English language and in particular with English phonetics, as becomes immediately apparent: *if my mother does not speak French, then I cannot speak English.* While foreignness stands for hope (being in France means the chance of another life story, another language, another life...), it

---

[41] The first name and the initial of the surname have been changed.

can also connote the disappointment of that hope if learning the language of the country of this new life has proved, for one reason or another, impossible. If the mother does not speak French, the daughter will not be able to speak English. The experience of unattainable foreignness is re-enacted as a learning failure, revisiting an impossible separation from the country of origin. The mother cannot forget her Mother tongue in her inability to speak French. The daughter will be unable to relinquish hers, which is double, as *lalangue* and the interior language are Arabic while the exterior language is French. It will therefore prove impossible for her to acquire that other 'extra-erior' foreign language, English.

The Mother tongue, therefore, seems to be deeply enmeshed in the possibility of learning a foreign language, whether as help or hindrance. In the case of this young woman, learning English meant re-enacting a failed attempt on her mother's part to learn French. Her experience of exile, charged with an enforced separation from her origins, had been absorbed spongelike by the child, now a student, and was being acted out in her difficulty to learn another language.

What are the subjective effects of a rift, chosen or imposed, from language? What future paths are caused by forgetting, losing, censuring or even repressing it? Does this affect the body in any way? The language? Can one speak of mourning in relation to the effects caused by the loss of the Mother tongue? A separation ... that seems never to come to an end.[42]

In this case, while the separation was impossible for the mother, it was achieved by the daughter (who speaks French), but only within certain limits: she will not be able to succeed in another language (not academically at least, without distancing herself from this personal life story), thereby reconnecting herself with her mother's life story. That is indeed what she seems to have tried to do with these words: *my mother does not speak French*.

1.6.1 *French, an Exterior Language, Experienced as a Foreign Tongue*

Sometimes it is French itself, the exterior language – especially school language – that is felt by the child to be foreign because there is too great a discrepancy with respect to the interior language, the language of the family circle. When a child is immersed in a working-class or foreign interior language, distinct from the language spoken at school, how can they speak that school language, learnt beyond the bounds of the family? How can they fail to perceive this acquired language as a language that delegitimizes and debases the language of the family circle, or simply as a language of division

---

[42] Vierling-Weiss, 'Que reste-t-il?'.

that makes of the child an enemy to their parents, an enemy to themselves? How can this inner immigration – which some adopted children are extremely sensitive to – be dealt with? How can the sociological dimension of this rift be negotiated, by which I mean the conflict between the language of the oppressed (the family language) and the language of the oppressors (that used at school, the 'legitimate' language)? It seems likely – when the school environment is felt to be antagonistic to the family one – that this discrepancy can give rise to numerous 'conflicts of loyalty' between the spoken language and the acquired one, sometimes leading to language and behavioural difficulties in the divisive relationship that it produces with respect to authority. How can this confrontation between two legitimacies, one emotional, the other social, be avoided? How can one attempt to solve this seemingly unsurmountable division through language, in which the division itself is rooted? Annie Ernaux describes this phenomenon very poignantly:

Can it be that I – the small girl from the grocery shop in the rue du Clos-des-Parts, brought up as a child and adolescent in a working-class dialect, a working-class world – intend to write and choose my mentors in the acquired, learnt, literary language, the language that I teach in my present role as a French literature teacher? Can it be that I – without batting an eyelid – intend to write in the literary language that I have broken into like a burglar, in 'the language of the enemy' as Jean Genet put it, by which he meant the enemy of my social class? From the beginning I have been torn – caught in a crossfire even – between literary language, the language I have studied and loved, and the language of my origins, of home, of my parents, the language of the oppressed, the language I have since felt ashamed of, but which will always be part of me. Deep down the question is: how can I write without betraying the world I come from?[43]

What if learning a foreign language were a way to reactivate that initial divide between the interior language – which the interior itself holds in poor esteem (thereby overriding all possibility of speaking the exterior language, or a foreign language, without conflict) – and the exterior language, the only legitimate one, valued but eliciting a feeling of betrayal or of conflict, of exclusion from the first language, which is disparaged? True, the foreign tongue can perhaps be viewed as a means to surpass this conflict, as a form of self-generation, but only within certain limits.

Having witnessed the difficulties encountered by certain children for whom language is a foreign tongue with respect to *lalangue*, thus producing a rift, it seems to me highly unlikely that learning a foreign tongue can be a neutral process: human beings speak the language of their own people. Changing languages amounts to losing that naturalness. Hannah Arendt stressed this point:

---

[43] *Retour à Yvetot* (Paris: Éditions du Mauconduit, 2013), back cover text.

I refused to lose my Mother tongue and kept a certain distance from English [. . .]. The German language is the only thing that has remained.[44]

Language contains *lalangue*; it contains forgotten affect. This is why some people take so much pleasure in speaking a foreign tongue, with the learning process reactivating *lalangue* that recalls both the rift and the primary pleasure shared with the mother, whereas others are confronted with almost insurmountable difficulties because something relating to an-Other scene – a scene of trauma – is reactivated.[45]

1.6.2   Hypotheses and Conclusion

This research project is in progress, and I advance my hypotheses at this stage with caution.

First, I would contend that in order to move from one language to another, one needs to have confidence in one's Mother tongue and to feel that it is highly valued, for it is this language that has made speech possible.[46] Miriam was unfortunate in this respect; when the value of the Mother tongue, the language of one's family circle (Arabic in this case), is not acknowledged, it then becomes very hard to venture into a foreign tongue with a light heart. This 'other' language reactivates the initial suffering of the mother – which Miriam has clearly taken upon herself – that emotionally charged environment in which she spoke her first words, first in Arabic, which was discredited by the family circle, and then in French, which her mother never learnt to speak. Miriam already speaks one language (French) that is foreign to her mother; speaking English, a language in a sense doubly foreign, would mean taking the risk that her mother herself would appear a stranger to her.[47] Thus, there are psycho-emotional limits imposed by one's linguistic family history, in this case by the mother's relationship with French, and more broadly with foreignness.

It is likewise my contention that there exists in every acquired (foreign) rather than transmitted (Mother) tongue a *remainder* of the Mother tongue, notwithstanding the fact that the foreign tongue lies, as Foucault puts it,

---

[44] Hannah Arendt, 'A Conversation with Günter Gaus' [1964]. In *The Last Interviews and Other Conversations* (New York: Melville House, 2013). www.youtube.com/watch?v= dVSRJC4KAiE, minute 38.

[45] This concept is borrowed from Octave Mannoni, *Clefs pour l'imaginaire ou l'autre scène* (Paris: Points, Collection Points Essais, 1985).

[46] Cf. Marie Rose Moro, 'Passer d'une langue à l'autre, le cas des enfants migrants' (2014), www .youtube.com/watch?v=WwcGUuCpzXs, and 'De l'importance des langues maternelles pour la cohésion' (2015), www.youtube.com/watch?v=9asuUem0rGs. See also Ellen Bialystock, 'On Bilingualism and the Middle Way' (2017), www.youtube.com/watch?v=XwRr_74YkEQ.

[47] Jacques Hassoun, *Fragments de langue maternelle* (Paris: Payot, 1979).

beyond the bounds of the mother. It nevertheless remains true that within this *beyond-the-bounds-of-the-mother* language, there lies what I would call a *within-the-bounds-of-the-mother* dimension, which seems to transpire in one's speech, in spite of oneself, in another language. This occurs to varying degrees, of course, sometimes to the point of hindering all other language acquisition; a within-the-bounds-of-the-mother dimension might perhaps be worth making room for and valuing during the learning process, with the aim either of attempting to escape its influence, at least in part, if only through being aware of it, or simply of coexisting with it, by speaking an English within the bounds of the mother and acknowledged as such. This would amount to a compromise of sorts, allowing for a possible reconciliation with the trauma of the forgotten separation, of the transition from fusional *lalangue* to language proper.

Can the idea be countenanced that this Mother tongue in which memories and desire inhere, this *lalangue*, might be expressed through the intermediary of the foreign tongue? That what is within the bounds of the mother is a necessary constituent of what lies beyond those bounds? If, instead of presenting Miriam M. with a poor mark, we had told her that at this stage her English was as yet strongly imbued with French, but that that was inevitable and in no way her fault, would we have increased this student's chances of success in the competitive exam she wished to take? If we had explained to her that in order to teach English, her own plurilingual life story would prove an asset, but that her pupils would need her to move a little closer to the English language if she was to set a phonological example offering guaranteed authenticity, would we have increased her chances of success?

If the maternal *remainder* is indeed always present, why not legitimize it? Don't students need to have transmitted to them something more than an illusorily perfect code? Can a speaker be transformed into a subject-enunciator – a difficult position to attain in a foreign language (except perhaps for Beckett…) – without venturing to include *lalangue*? Is it not this dimension that is so often lacking in the foreign tongue? Might it not therefore be the case that *consenting to speak imperfectly* is a necessary prerequisite for learning another language? Some people manage to sever as far as possible the ties with their language of origin by going to live abroad, but in most cases, for those who live in France, what is left of the acquired language? What we should perhaps aim for is to cease excluding the language of the mother, of the body, from the foreign tongue – to allow it to return, to allow it to inhere, so as to avoid speaking a disembodied language, a pure code, devoid of affect. Or even, in certain extreme cases, not speaking at all.

With this in mind, here are a few suggestions:

– a semiology of language disorders could be established, to be taught with
   the aim of tackling English-language learning difficulties according
   to their relation to the Mother tongue;

- students could be encouraged to accept the idea of speaking an imperfect English, to accept an inevitable remainder due to the traces *left* by the Mother tongue, by alerting them to the role it plays in second language learning;
- students could be made aware of what takes place psycho-emotionally during the childhood language-learning process – in particular, the fact that learning a language immediately thrusts you to the heart of your and your family's relation to that language, to the heart of things that remain unspoken or are forgotten;
- plurilingual creative writing workshops could be set up, with the aim of valuing the Mother tongue so as to facilitate foreign-language learning;[48]
- students could be taught about language disorders, which would be useful both to language students and to future language teachers; and
- we should abandon the normative approach, which produces feelings of guilt and denies the role of affect in language learning. Why not speak a *(M)other tongue*, at once *within* and *beyond the bounds of the mother* – without going so far as to distort the foreign tongue, but letting a residue, reminiscent of its link to *lalangue,* settle there, such that for a given speaker the foreign tongue is invested bodily, thus standing a better chance of *sounding authentic*?

Jean-Jacques Lecercle makes the following distinction between *insistence* and *existence*: 'Standard English does not exist, but it insists. What exists is what it ignores and represses – idiolects, dialects, registers and style'.[49]

In light of these few hypotheses, one could therefore let standard English insist, but without either the idiolect or the Mother tongue being denied.

Bibliography

Anzieu, Didier. *Beckett*. Paris: Seuil-Archimbaud, [1992] 2004.

Arendt, Hannah. 'What Remains? (Full Interview with Günter Gaus),' 1964. https://www.youtube.com/watch?v=dVSRJC4KAiE.

Bhugra, Dinesh, and Kamaldeep Bhui. *Textbook of Cultural Psychiatry*. Cambridge: Cambridge University Press, [2007] 2019.

Bialystock, Ellen, and Kenji Hakuta. *In Other Words: The Science and Psychology of Second-Language Acquisition*. New York: Basic Books, 1995.

Bowlby, John. *Attachment and Loss. Volume 3: Loss. Sadness and Depression*. Croydon: Pimlico, 2006.

---

[48] See Chapter 3 of this volume.

[49] Jean-Jacques Lecercle, 'A global language is not a language', unpublished paper given at Padua University, 15 February 2013.

Canetti, Elias. *The Tongue Set Free*. Croydon: Granta, [1977] 1979.

Coquio, Catherine. *La littérature en suspens. Écritures de la Shoah: Le témoignage et les œuvres*. Paris: L'Arachnéen, 2015.

Danon-Boileau, Laurent. *L'enfant qui ne disait rien*. Paris: Calmann-Lévy, 1995. *The Silent Child*. Translated by Kevin Windle. Oxford: Oxford University Press, [1995] 2007.

De Mattia-Viviès, Monique. 'Entrer dans la langue ou dans les langues: De la langue maternelle à la langue "mat-rangère"'. *E-rea*, N° 16.1, 2018. https://journals .openedition.org/erea/6502

Deleuze, Gilles. 'Schizologie' [preface]. In Louis Wolfson, *Le Schizo et les langues*. Paris: Gallimard, [1970] 2009, pp. 5–23. *Critique et clinique*. Paris: Éditions de Minuit, 1993.

Derrida, Jacques. *Le monolinguisme de l'autre ou la prothèse d'origine*. Paris: Éditions Galilée, 1996.

Diamantis, Irène. *Les phobies ou l'impossible séparation*. Paris: Éditions Flammarion, 2003.

Ernaux, Annie. *La place*. Paris: Gallimard, Collection Folio, 1983. *Retour à Yvetot*. Paris: Éditions du Mauconduit, 2013. *Le vrai lieu: Entretiens avec Michelle Porte*. Paris: Gallimard, Collection Folio, 2014.

Fairbairn, Ronald. *Psychoanalytic Studies of the Personality*. London: Routledge, [1952] 1994.

Foucault, Michel. 'La fuite des idées' and 'Les trois procédés'. (Dits et écrits [1958–1988]; Vol. 2: 1976–1988. Paris: Gallimard, 2001.) InJean-Bertrand Pontalis, Pierre Alféri, François Cusset, Paul Auster, Max Dorra, J.M.G. Le Clézio, Michel Foucault, and Piera Aulagnier, *Dossier Wolfson ou l'affaire du schizo et les langues*. Paris: Gallimard, 2009.

Goldschmidt, Georges-Arthur. *La traversée des fleuves*. Paris: Éditions du Seuil, Collection Points Essais, 1999. *Quand Freud voit la mer: Freud et la langue allemande, Volume 1*. Paris: Buchet/ Chastel, [1988] 2006.

Greaves, Sara. *Poésie, poïétique, et traductologie, parcours interdisciplinaires*. Synthèse d'Habilitation à Diriger des Recherches. Paris: Université de Paris III, 2017 (unpublished).

Green, André. *'Le double et l'absent'. La déliaison: Anthropologie, psychanalyse et littérature*. Paris: Hachette, Collection Pluriel, [1973] 1992. *Associations (presque) libres d'un psychanalyste*. Entretiens avec Maurice Corcos. Paris: Albin Michel, Collection Itinéraires du savoir, 2006. *Du signe au discours: Psychanalyse et théories du langage*. Paris: Éditions d'Ithaque, 2011.

Grosjean, François. *Bilingual: Life and Reality*. Cambridge, MA: Harvard University Press, 2010.

Hassoun, Jacques. *Fragments de langue maternelle*. Paris: Payot, 1979.

Lacan, Jacques. *Encore: Le séminaire-Livre XX*. Paris: Éditions du Seuil, Collection Points Essais, 1975. *Séminaire III. Les Psychoses*. Paris: Éditions du Seuil, 1981.

Lecercle, Jean-Jacques. *The Violence of Language*. London: Routledge, 1990.

La violence du langage. Paris: Presses Universitaires de France, [1990] 1996.

'A global language is not a language'. Unpublished lecture, Padua University, 15 February 2013.

'One mother tongue – or two'. Chapter 2, this volume.

Loisel, Yoann. 'Écho de l'ego, du monde des choses: La rencontre Keaton-Beckett'. Unpublished lecture, 'Écriture et Arts du soin'. Study day co-organised by Sara Greaves and Jean-Luc Di Stefano, Timone Hospital, Marseille, 17 March 2017.

Louis, Edouard. *En finir avec Eddy Bellegueule*. Paris: Éditions du Seuil, 2014.

Histoire de la violence. Paris: Éditions du Seuil, 2016.

Malraux, André. *Les voix du silence*. Paris: Nouvelle Revue Française/La galerie de la Pléiade, 1951.

Mannoni, Octave. *Clefs pour l'imaginaire ou l'autre scène*. Paris: Points, Collection Points Essais, 1985.

Moro, Marie-Rose. *Parents en exil: Psychopathologie et migrations*. Paris: Presses Universitaires de France, 2001.

Nos enfants demain: Pour une société multiculturelle. Paris: Odile Jacob, 2010.

Nassikas, Kostas, Emmanuelle Prak-Derrington, and Caroline Rossi. *Fabriques de la langue*. Paris: Presses Universitaires de France, 2012.

Pontalis, Jean-Bertrand. *Dossier Wolfson ou l'affaire du schizo et les langues*. Paris: Gallimard, 2009.

Stitou, Rajaa. 'Épreuve de l'exil et blessures de la langue'. *Cahiers de psychologie clinique*, Vol. 18, n° 1, 2002, pp. 159–70. www.cairn.info/revue-cahiers-de-psychologie-clinique-2002-1-page-159.htm

Szpacenkopf, Maria Izabel Oliveira. 'Maud Mannoni: Apprendre une autre langue'. *Figures de la psychanalyse*, Vol. 20, n° 2, 2010, pp. 163–76.

Vallas, Sophie, and Viviès, Jean. 'Jean-Jacques Lecercle ou le philosophe insistant: De l'héritier à l'enseignant-chercheur heureux'. *E-rea*, N° 14.2, 2017. https://journals.openedition.org/erea/5876

Vierling-Weiss, Michèle. 'Que reste-t-il ? La langue maternelle'. *Che vuoi*, Vol. 26, n° 2, 2006, pp. 11–21.

Wolfson, Louis. *Le Schizo et les langues*. Paris: Gallimard, [1970] 2009.

Online Lectures and Radio Programmes

Bialystock, Ellen. 'On Bilingualism and the Middle Way', 2017. www.youtube.com/watch?v=XwRr_74YkEQ

Cassin, Barbara. 'Hannah Arendt et les langues de l'exil': Radio 'France Culture', 2011. www.franceculture.fr/conferences/ecole-normale-superieure/hannah-arendt-pour-etre-confirme-dans-mon-identite-je-depends

Goldschmidt, Georges-Arthur. 'A-t-on déjà vu un fleuve avec une seule rive?' Radio 'France Culture', 'Talmudiques'. Presented by Marc-Alain Ouaknin, 2016. www.franceculture.fr/emissions/talmudiques/eprouver-lalterite-22-se-trouver-en-langue-etrangere

Kristeva, Julia. 'L'amour de l'autre langue', 2014. www.kristeva.fr/la-traduction-langue-de-l-europe.html

Louis, Edouard. 'Les matins de France Culture.' Radio 'France Culture', 2014. www
    .franceculture.fr/emissions/les-matins/quand-lecriture-de-soi-devient-un-acte-de-
    revolte-avec-edouard-louis-auteur-de

'J'ai deux langages en moi, celui de mon enfance et celui de la culture', 2014. www
    .telerama.fr/livre/edouard-louis-j-ai-deux-langages-en-moi-celui-de-mon-enfance-
    et-celui-de-la-culture,114836.php

Moro, Marie-Rose. 'Passer d'une langue à l'autre, le cas des enfants migrants', 2014.
    www.youtube.com/watch?v=WwcGUuCpzXs

'De l'importance des langues maternelles pour la cohésion', 2015. www.youtube
    .com/watch?v=9asuUem0rGs

2   One Mother Tongue – or Two?

Jean-Jacques Lecercle

2.1   Trauma

At the heart of Derrida's *Monolinguisme de l'autre*, we find the following paradoxical statement: I have only one language and yet it isn't mine.[1] The source of the paradox is well known; it originates in the trauma Derrida experienced when in 1940, as a Jewish adolescent in Algeria, he was expelled from school under the racial laws of the Pétain regime – a school where he was studying French language and literature, through the medium of the French language (the vast majority of the Algerian population spoke Arabic, yet that language was only an optional subject that hardly any student took).

We understand the strength of his feeling of exclusion: the language that was his Mother tongue, his only real language (he did not speak Arabic, and his family had given up the Jewish dialect of their ancestors), was now in a strong sense forbidden to him. And we understand the distance from his own language that was thus imposed upon him: this is my only language and yet it is no longer my language, as I am no longer allowed to practise it at school, nor am I any longer granted the citizenship that normally goes with it. And yet his text may be read as a love letter to the French language, to the extent that he seems to adopt an extreme form of purism: he claims to be the last defender of the purity of French, a stickler for the rules of French grammar, who confides his hostility to the regional variations of the language, particularly regional accents. He is proud of having lost his *pied-noir* accent,[2] of not being linguistically recognizable as such.[3] In the course of the argument, we even find a strange assassination of René Char, a poet much admired by Heidegger: Derrida found his poetry unbearable when uttered by the poet himself in his decided Southern accent.[4] So the language that was no longer his by rights is still the language not only of his daily expression, but of his affects. In other

---

[1] Jacques Derrida, *Le monolinguisme de l'autre* (Paris: Galilée, 1996), 15.
[2] This is the accent of Algerian-born French citizens.
[3] Cf. Chapter 6 of this volume, which is an essay on accent.   [4] Derrida, *Le monolinguisme*, 78.

words, the French language, in spite of the trauma of exclusion, has remained his Mother tongue.

However, Derrida's plight cannot be accounted for solely in terms of a psychic, and therefore individual, trauma. After all, he was not separated from his mother or his family and he was not sentenced to exile, which may entail the traumatic separation from the Mother tongue and an enforced monolingualism in a foreign language, as was the case of so many Jewish refugees the world over (one thinks of Walter Benjamin, Theodor W. Adorno, or Hannah Arendt) – he went on speaking his Mother tongue as his only language. His trauma was mainly a political one, focussing on the political question of language: the practice of his Mother tongue no longer involved citizenship, that is, membership of the *polis*, a right to use one's language to take part in political deliberation (we remember Aristotle's definition of man as a political animal insofar as he is a speaking animal). Hence, the first paradox (how can this still be my Mother tongue, my only language, if it no longer gives me access to the political community that it defines?) produces a second paradox: *on ne parle jamais une seule langue, on ne parle jamais qu'une seule langue*[5] (we never speak only one language, and yet we only ever speak one language).

We do not speak only one language, not only because of the Babel of tongues that surrounds us, and that certainly surrounded an adolescent in Algiers in 1940 (French with a regional slant in his immediate surroundings, Arabic and Berber in the street, the classical languages and a modicum of modern languages at school, perhaps even shades of the Ladino of his ancestors),[6] but because of the lack of unity and stability of our very Mother tongue, as Derrida's 'Mother tongue' involved the *pied-noir* dialect of French (not only a pronounced regional accent but also idiosyncrasies in vocabulary and syntax, in the same relation to standard or literary French as Wenglish is to standard English) as well as sociolects, technolects and jargons, slang and generational or family dialects, down to each and every speaker's idiolect (what might be called his or her idiosyncratic style of French). What we call 'French', that Mother tongue of which Derrida claims to be the last paladin, is an abstraction. So that his second paradox does not only express what he calls 'the law of translation' but also 'the law *as* translation', a law, he adds, that is slightly mad – a law (in the strictest sense, the racial laws of the Vichy regime) that both forbids and imposes, that restricts the uses of the Mother tongue but imposes its limits on the speaker, thus introducing *within the Mother tongue* a

---

[5] Derrida, *Le monolinguisme*, 21.
[6] Ladino or Judeo-Spanish is a Romance language of Spanish origin spoken in North Africa and the Near East by the descendants of Jews expelled from Spain in 1492.

distance that is the distance of translation, the necessity of moving outside it and the concomitant impossibility of doing so.[7]

The passage from a specific law to 'the law' in general does suggest that Derrida's linguistic trauma should be generalised to all speakers. We do not speak only one language because our 'language' is only an abstraction, subsuming a vast variety of phenomena. And yet we only speak one language because our Mother tongue not only inscribes our affects but also constrains what we are able to say by imposing limits on what can be said (the limits of vocabulary and syntax); in a sense, our Mother tongue speaks us. Hence, a third paradox emerges, as translation is both inevitable and impossible. Derrida's formulation of his second paradox is a perfect example of this. In an obvious sense, it *can* be translated into English since I have provided a translation. But the fact that I first gave the French formulation is not irrelevant, as only in the French language can the semantic inversion that constitutes the paradox be provoked by the mere insertion of a single grammatical word, *que*, which has no immediate apparent meaning – a grammatical tag, what Aristotle called a syncategorematic word, with a plethora of meanings. Nor is this the only way in which the formulation of the paradox thrives on the idiosyncrasies of the French language: it depends on the abstract generality of the pronoun *on* (a *locus classicus* in elementary lessons on translation from French into English), and on the ambiguity of *jamais*, a fine example of what Freud means by the opposite meanings of primitive words, as it means both 'ever' and 'never'. We understand Derrida's declared passion for the subtleties of the French language, as well as the recurrent problems the translation of his works into English encountered.

Derrida's three paradoxes (my only language is not mine; we never/ever speak only one language; translation is both indispensable and impossible) turn around the question of the Mother tongue. In this respect also, his statements have the flavour of paradox, as he states, against the evidence provided by his very text, that he could never consider French as his Mother tongue: 'such words do not come readily, they cannot be spouted forth by my mouth'[8] – he may not be actually speaking them, but he is certainly writing them. And he immediately adds that this is the reason why his culture is fundamentally political. The question of the Mother tongue is inextricably personal and political.[9]

At this point a question emerges that is also a potential solution to Derrida's paradoxes: whether or not my original Mother tongue fails me (and fortunately, Derrida's political trauma can hardly be generalised), perhaps, since my Mother tongue isn't a datum of nature but a social and political construction,

---

[7] Derrida, *Le monolinguisme*, 25.   [8] Derrida, *Le monolinguisme*, 61.
[9] Cf. Chapter 7 of this volume.

I could learn another language as my 'second Mother tongue'. This may be a solution to Derrida's paradoxes, provided I can show that the phrase is not an oxymoron, the experience an impossibility. For how can my Mother tongue be unique and dual?

2.2   Question and Answer

In 2012, Barbara Cassin, the editor of what is commonly known as the *Dictionnaire des intraduisibles*,[10] gave a lecture in the Paris suburb of Montreuil for an audience of schoolchildren and their parents. The title of the lecture was 'More Than One Language';[11] she underlined the necessity of learning other languages in order to acquire a critical distance towards one's own.[12] Such a distance is welcome in order to go beyond the limits imposed by our Mother tongue, limits that are not merely grammatical – there is more to a language than a grammatical system. One is reminded here both of Antonio Gramsci's statement that a language is a 'conception of the world'[13] and of Wittgenstein's words, *'the limits of my language* mean the limits of my world'.[14] At the end of her lecture, she answered questions from the floor. One question was as follows: is it possible to learn a language to such an extent that this language becomes our second Mother tongue?[15] Such a question cannot be indifferent to one who, like me, has spent his life trying to teach English as a foreign language, and one fondly hopes that the answer might be positive. Cassin's answer, however, was in the negative, although in a rather hesitant manner: 'I don't know', she said, 'I don't believe so, or rather, it all depends'. Her embarrassment was made manifest by the fact that she proceeded to invert the terms of the question, when she stated that one can never escape from one's Mother tongue, that it resists, insists, or persists – there can be only one Mother tongue, as it is the language of our own mother.[16]

The bulk of her answer (which takes several pages in the printed version) is devoted to evoking the experience of Hannah Arendt, who, in an interview with a German radio channel, expresses her attachment to her native German. What remains for her of the Europe she left in 1933, she says, is the German

[10] Barbara Cassin (ed.), *Vocabulaire européen de la philosophie* (Paris: Seuil/ Le Robert, 2004). Cf. *Dictionary of Untranslatables: A Philosophical Lexicon*, translated by Emily Apter, Jacques Lezra, and Michael Wood (eds.) (Princeton, NJ: Princeton University Press, 2015).
[11] Barbara Cassin, *Plus d'une langue* (Paris: Bayard, 2019).
[12] Cf. Chapter 7 of this volume, in which we have a brilliant demonstration of such critical distance at work.
[13] Antonio Gramsci, *Quaderni del carcere*, Vol. 1 (Turin: Einaudi, 2007), 401.
[14] Ludwig Wittgenstein, *Tractatus Logico-Philosophicus* (London: Routledge and Kegan Paul, [1921] 1961), § 5.6.
[15] Cassin, *Plus d'une langue*, 60.
[16] Cassin speaks of the 'resistant singularity of the Mother tongue', *Plus d'une langue*, 60.

language ('You may be sure I don't regret Europe before Hitler. What remains of it? Well, the language remains').[17] She goes on to say that she always took care not to lose her Mother tongue and that, although for years she had written her books in English, there was always a distance with what was merely an acquired language (a language she 'had', as Derrida said, but that was not her own). In a sense, she adds, the Mother tongue is never acquired, it is 'a given', a gift – and she mentions the German poems she still knew by heart, which stood at the centre of her cultural memory. This suggests that only the Mother tongue is creative for the speaker and that the foreign tongue reduces speech to the level of the cliché. She went on to proudly state that she spoke English with a strong German accent and knew few idiomatic phrases. At this point, one is reminded of the fact that attachment to the German language is one of the reasons why Adorno, after the war, decided to return to Germany.

All this is bad news for the teacher of English as a foreign language. However, there is a historical and cultural specificity in the experience of Hannah Arendt. Because the trauma of exile is political and ethical as well as psychic, she experienced (a form of double bind) both the necessity of relinquishing her Mother tongue – especially after the shock of learning about Auschwitz, as the German language had become the language of mass murder[18] – and the impossibility of it. Unlike a number of her fellow exiles, she never did relinquish it (after all, she says, it isn't the German *language* that has gone mad and 'besides, nothing can replace one's Mother tongue'), and she tells us of the sheer exhilaration, during her first visit to Germany after the war, of once again hearing German spoken in the street.[19] Fortunately, that traumatic experience is neither mine nor that of the vast majority of my students. Consequently, it may be possible for us not to fall victim to such a linguistic double bind, but experience it as a positive paradox by accepting both sides of it: on the one hand, keeping our Mother tongue, which we cannot relinquish and which nothing can replace, and on the other hand, attempting to acquire another language as a supplementary (but not a substitute) Mother tongue.

2.3   The Language of Affect

It is easy to understand why Arendt states that nothing can replace the Mother tongue. It is the object of our first experience of language, an experience that begins in the womb, and it is from the first charged with affect, as the Mother tongue is the language of the mother and as such the language of desire. The

---

[17] Hannah Arendt, *La langue maternelle* (Paris: Eterotopia, 2015), 34.
[18] Arendt, *La langue maternelle* (Paris: Eterotopia, 2015), 34–5.
[19] Arendt, *La langue maternelle*, 37.

experience of loss and return that Freud's granddaughter expresses in the famous *fort-da* episode is inextricably linked with German words and German phonemes.[20] The primal interpellation of the etymological infant who is destined to become a speaker is auditory as indeed is any primal form of interpellation. In Althusser's 'primitive scene' of interpellation, when the policeman blows his whistle or hails an individual ('Hey, you, there!') and the individual, sensing that *he* is being interpellated, turns round and, Althusser says, by that rotation of 180° becomes a subject, it is the sounds of hailing, before any mental computation or even any full consciousness may occur, that interpellate him. Althusser does state that the interpellated individual *turns round* and therefore is unable to see the policeman who hails him.[21] The process of interpellation – the process that makes subjects of us, and first and foremost speaking subjects, is what the French language calls a *prise de corps*, a bodily capture, and that capture is auditory. The Mother tongue is first a collection of specific sounds of phonemes, hence the importance of accent as a mark of belonging and a test of recognition. When the unfortunate Ephraimites tried to cross the River Jordan after their defeat, the Gileadites made them pronounce the word 'shibboleth', which they uttered with the wrong accent ('for he could not frame to pronounce it right'), thus betraying their identity, upon which they were slain, to the number of 42,000.[22] We understand both Arendt's joy at hearing German spoken in the street and Derrida's indignation at hearing Char's poetry spoken with the wrong accent.

The Mother tongue is an oral dialect before it is a proper *logos* in the Greek sense, where language is coextensive with reason. In order to understand the *prise de corps* it exerts on the infant, we might make a detour through Monique De Mattia-Viviès's concept of the three successive layers that finally constitute what we call our Mother tongue. She analyses the multilingualism of her students in terms of the languages they successively, in their lives as speakers, acquire: first comes what Lacan calls *lalangue*, the language of the intimate relationship between the infant and her mother; then comes the 'interior' language, the language of the family, the acquisition of which marks the passage from the etymological infant to the full-fledged speaker, the moment in which the subject appropriates a system that is interior and exterior to her – such acquisition is practical and is not the object of explicit teaching and learning; last comes the 'exterior' language, the language of the subject's social environment, acquired by a process of nurture at the centre of which is the school. Those three successive strata of language, one merging into the next, constitute what we call our Mother tongue, through three successive processes of interpellation. The first is indeed oral: from the baby's babble,

---

[20] Cf. Chapter 7 of this volume.   [21] Louis Althusser, *On Ideology* (London: Verso, 2008), 48.
[22] Judges 12:6 (quoted in the King James version).

what the French language calls *lallations* (a case of imitative harmony), to the proto-language of her first verbal exchanges with her mother, to the lullabies (another case of imitative harmony) that are sung to her. This is what insists, persists, and resists, what cannot be replaced: the sounds and rhythms of our infant language, as inscribed, for instance, in the ditties we heard and endlessly repeated, and later in the poems that, like Arendt, we learnt by heart. What is important in this theory is that it treats the Mother tongue not as a unitary entity but as a construction over time, from *lallations* to lullabies, from the idiosyncratic family vernacular to the social language of television, and finally to the standard version of the language that is inculcated at school, in layered strata (as the work of Renée Balibar showed, there is a class divide between the language of elementary school and the language of the grammar school and later of university)[23] and commonly practised in later life.

2.4   The Paradox of the Mother Tongue

The Mother tongue is primarily oral, but its orality is eventually supplemented by other types of language. This means that it is both highly individual (I shall never forget the sounds and rhythms of my linguistic infancy – the elementary sensory interpellation or *prise de corps*, charged with affect, that allowed me to move on and become a competent speaker) and collective or rather social, as what captures me as a speaker is not only the meaningless babble of my earliest sounds but also a social system, a *langue* in the sense of Saussure, the constraints of which are what Judith Butler calls 'enabling constraints', constraints that impose limitations on what I may say but at the same time allow me to speak the language as a full-fledged speaker.

I wish to suggest that this paradox is in fact a contradiction, in the Marxist acceptation of the term – to put it briefly, the contradiction between social system and individual style, in which the social system is the dominant and the individual style the dominated pole. In order to understand the function and nature of this linguistic contradiction, which is a special but significant case of a more general contradiction between interpellation (of subjects by ideology and its apparatuses) and counter-interpellation (by the interpellated subject, of the institutions that interpellate her), we may make a short detour through the Marxist anthropology of Lucien Sève.

Sève's point of departure is the famous sixth thesis on Feuerbach ('The human essence is no abstraction inherent in each single individual. In its reality it is the ensemble of social relations'),[24] and his anthropology develops along

---

[23] Renée Balibar, *Les Français fictifs* (Paris: Hachette, 1974).
[24] Karl Marx and Friedrich Engels, *The German Ideology* (London: Lawrence and Wishart, 1965), 652.

the five Marxian concepts of *Tätigkeit* (activity, or practice), *Vermittlung* (mediation, that is, means of labour – *moyens de travail*, in other words, tools and machines – and of communication, in other words, signs), *Vergegenstandlichung* (objectivation), *Aneignung* (appropriation), and *Entfremdung* (alienation).[25] Thus, language is a form of practice (a material, social, and historical practice); it is a means of mediation between human beings and the world in which they live – with its signs, it allows them, as tools do, to interact with it; the practice is objectivised and cumulative, generation after generation (the result of such a process is what we call a natural language, like English); it has to be appropriated by each new speaker, being exterior (objectivised) and anterior (cumulative) to her; lastly, in class societies, language is not only a means of appropriating the world around us but also a source of alienation, as not all interpellation is enabling – or, rather, this is merely another formulation of our contradiction that language qua system is both alienating and liberating (it imposes its constraints upon the speaker, and it allows her to speak her own mind).

In the contradiction, the social pole is dominant, but the dominated individual pole shows activity and resilience (in my theory of interpellation, this is expressed by the maxim: no interpellation without its consequent counter-interpellation).[26] Sève's other point of departure is a passage from Marx's letter to Annenkov: 'The social history of human beings is nothing but the story of their individual development, whether they are conscious of it or not'.[27] Language, in the form of the Mother tongue, is a privileged point where the social and the individual combine. As the French language says, *la langue fait société*,[28] but it does so through individual relationships, mediated by the family, as the first institution through which the individual speaker is socialised. In other words, an essential component of the Mother tongue, before it takes the form of a standard idiom, based on a grammatical system, is what the Italian writer Natalia Ginzburg, in the title of one of her autobiographical texts, calls *lessico famigliare*,[29] of which she provides the following illustration:

We are five brothers and sisters. We live in different towns, and some of us live abroad – and we do not write often. When we meet, we may be, one towards the other, indifferent or distracted. But, between us, one word is enough. One word, or one sentence: one of those old sentences, heard and repeated thousands of times when we were children. It is

---

[25] Lucien Sève, *'L'homme'?* (Paris: La Dispute, 2008).

[26] Jean-Jacques Lecercle, *De l'interpellation* (Paris: Amsterdam, 2019).

[27] Karl Marx and Friedrich Engels, *Études philosophiques* (Paris: Éditions Sociales, 1961), 149.

[28] *La langue fait société* can be translated as 'language enables society'. It constitutes the interface between the individual and the collective.

[29] The expression *lessico famigliare* refers to the dialect spoken in the family circle and that is part and parcel of the Mother tongue.

enough to say: 'We haven't come to Bergamo to run a campaign' or 'What does sulfhydric acid stink of?' to immediately recover the old emotional ties of our childhood and youth, which are indissolubly linked to those words and sentences. One of them would be enough for us to recognize each other in the obscurity of a cave, or among myriad people. Those sentences are our Latin, the vocabulary of days gone by, like the hieroglyphs of the Egyptians or Babylonians, the testimony of a vital nucleus that has ceased to be but has survived in its inscriptions, saved from the fury of waters and the corruption of time. Those sentences are the basis of our family unity, which will be preserved as long as we live, being recreated or resuscitated in various points on the earth. When one of us says 'Mr Lipmann, honoured sir', we shall hear the impatient voice of my father bellowing: 'That's enough with that story! I've heard it too many times!'[30]

Such family dialect is a component of each individual speaker's Mother tongue – it provides a transition from the one-to-one linguistic relationship between mother and child to the socialised idiom practised at school. What the notion of Mother tongue involves is a diachronic polyglottalism, which Monique De Mattia-Viviès captures under the concept of *(M)other tongue* (in French, she expresses this *via* a portmanteau coinage: *la langue mat-rangère*, both *maternelle* and *étrangère*): the Mother tongue is neither a single system nor a unitary entity but a composition of dialectal strata, with overlap and opportunities for clash.[31]

2.5   A Polyglottal Mother Tongue

Monique De Mattia-Viviès's concept is diachronic – it follows the linguistic development of the child into an adult speaker. But the end product, the adult speaker's Mother tongue, recapitulates this diachronic development in synchronic polyglottalism. When we speak our Mother tongue, we speak several languages at the same time: the native speaker is a polyglot. To develop this idea, I shall make another theoretical detour, through the tetraglossic theory of Henri Gobard.[32]

Henri Gobard taught English as a foreign language at the university of Vincennes in Paris. He is the author of a book, *L'aliénation linguistique*, devoted to what he calls (this is the subtitle of his book) *l'analyse*

---

[30] Natalia Ginzburg, *Lessico famigliare* (Milano: Mondadori, [1963] 1974), 23.

[31] Monique De Mattia-Viviès, 'Entrer dans la langue ou dans les langues: De la langue maternelle à la langue "mat-rangère"', *E-rea* 16.1 (2018), https://journals.openedition.org/erea/6502. Translated for Chapter 1 of this volume by Sara Greaves.

[32] 'Tetraglossic' theory, of which Henri Gobard is the author, assumes that language conveys a certain worldview and that, being the pivot point between the individual and the collective, it takes shape – within a given culture – in four different ways, resulting in four different languages within the Mother tongue.

tétraglossique.[33] The book has a preface by Deleuze, in which the philosopher welcomes the tetraglossic theory, although, in the very last sentence of his text, he suggests the author may well belong to the category of *fous littéraires* (and it is true that a good portion of the book is devoted to a settling of accounts within the English Department at Vincennes).[34] Gobard suggests that, in a given cultural area, four different 'languages' are used, whatever the natural language in which they are inscribed: (i) A *vernacular* language is the language not so much of communication as of communion, in other words, the language of affect and personal relationships. This language is said to be 'local', meaning restricted to the use of small and close-knit groups, the family lexicon of Ginzburg, or the dialect of a village. Gobard adds that only such language may be called *une langue maternelle*, a Mother tongue. (ii) A *vehicular* language is used for social communication, typically spoken in cities (as opposed to villages), used in a regional or national idiom, and, Gobard adds, 'learnt out of necessity' – Monique De Mattia-Viviès's exterior language, or part of it. (iii) A *referential* language is 'concerned with cultural traditions, whether oral or written', in charge of the transmission of cultural values, for instance, by reference to the great works of the past (thus, English is the language of Shakespeare, and Italian the language of Dante). (iv) A *mythical* language is the language of *le sacré*, that is, of religion, in that religion is etymologically what ties together the members of a social group (English is not only the language of Shakespeare but also the language of King James's Bible).[35]

That there are problems with Gobard's theory is obvious. The term 'language' he uses is vague (one might wish to talk of dialects or registers instead), and the boundaries between the four languages are rather blurred (e.g., between the language of Shakespeare and the language of the authorised version). The interest, however, is that Gobard suggests that every speaker in a linguistic community, whether she speaks one natural language or more, is polyglottal. I wish to suggest that such synchronic polyglottalism characterises the speaker's relationship to her Mother tongue (even if Gobard restricts the Mother tongue to one of his languages, the vernacular). Thus, a Sicilian speaker will use the Sicilian dialect as her *vernacular* (the lullabies of her childhood are in dialect – in an anthology of *ninne nanne*, the Italian lullabies, the texts are all in various dialects and have to be translated into standard Italian for the average reader).[36] As her *vehicular* she will use the standard

---

[33] Henri Gobard, *L'aliénation linguistique* (Paris: Flammarion, 1976).
[34] The term *fous littéraires* is used to refer to authors who have not achieved academic recognition and whose books deal with subjects that are sometimes deemed quirky.
[35] Henri Gobard, *L'aliénation linguistique*, 34.
[36] Tito Saffioti (ed.), *Le ninne nanne italiane* (Turin: Einaudi, 1994).

Italian she has learnt, if not within her family, at least at school – a version of Italian nowadays tainted with English, the language of globalisation. Her *referential* language will be literary Italian, the Italian of Dante and Manzoni and of the Italian equivalent of the German poems Arendt learnt by heart in her childhood (and we remember that national Italian was first a literary form of the language, extracted from the Tuscan dialect – 'standard' Italian is *literally* the language of Dante). Lastly, her *mythical* language will probably, in that deeply Roman Catholic culture, still be a form of church Latin, in spite of the linguistic *aggiornamento* of the Church.[37]

Such tetraglossic competence is the result of what Sève calls *Aneignung*, an appropriation, as the subject is captured by the successive ideological state apparatuses that linguistically interpellate her (an interpellation, as we have seen, both alienating and enabling): first comes the vernacular, the language of the family; then, in whatever order, comes the vehicular, the referential, and the mythical, inculcated at school and in church. We understand why Gobard wishes to restrict the term 'Mother tongue' to the vernacular register – because it comes first, and it comes first because it is the language of affect, of desire, of the primal relationship between the child and her mother. But this relationship, highly individual as it is, is nevertheless a social relationship, the first stage in a social process of construction of subjectivity: a subject is the sum total of her interpellations over time, not merely in her psyche but in her language – the Mother tongue that her interpellations construct.

My initial question (One Mother tongue, or two? Or again, may we acquire another language to the same level as our initial Mother tongue?) thus becomes this one: may I 'appropriate' a foreign language so that it becomes part of my tetraglossic competence? May my interpellation by a linguistic system at first foreign to me be internalised so that the new language becomes a second Mother tongue – which naturally implies going far beyond the common and garden learning of a foreign language at school? As a first answer to those questions, let us look at a case history.

2.6   Meneghello's Mother Tongues

Luigi Meneghello is widely recognized as an important author in contemporary Italian literature. But he is not a novelist: each of his books is a fragment of an autobiography, from his infancy and childhood in Malo, a small town near Vicenza in northern Italy (*Libera nos a malo* and *Pomo pero*), to his secondary education during the fascist *ventennio* (*Fiori italiani*),[38] his participation in the

---

[37] *Aggiornamento* means 'to update the church'.
[38] The term *ventennio* designates the Fascist double decade, which spans Benito Mussolini's grab for power in 1922 to the end of his dictatorship on 25 July 1943.

resistance (*I piccoli maestri*), his short militancy after the war in a small left-wing party (*Bau sete*), and lastly his settling in England, where he made his career at the University of Reading, ending up as chair of the Italian Department (*Il dispatrio*).[39]

Yet, if in his books we are looking for a proper, continuous autobiography, we shall be disappointed, as what we are offered is at first sight a collection of more or less disjointed anecdotes, with huge gaps that preclude totalisation into the narrative of a life. Thus, for instance, we eventually realize that he is married, that his wife's name is Katia, and that she is Jewish and lost her parents at Auschwitz, but we never know when and how he met her, what sort of person she is, or what she does in life. And the manner in which we acquire such laconic information is singular. In a passage of *Pomo pero*, he is describing his father's funeral: 'With me came my wife who might well be the *young executive wife* and who, having adopted my parents as her own, has come to be a kind of sister – her own parents she lost sight of during the war, in that open air railway station, on the border between Poland and Czechoslovakia, Oswiecim. She told me that towards the South one could see distant mountains, the Tatra range'.[40] The reader is caught unawares: she must have been deported to Auschwitz herself, and survived, but we shall not know anything about it, and the traumatic separation from parents who must have been taken to the gas chamber is merely hinted at through the ironically banal phrase 'lost sight of'.

The reason for our (well-deserved) disappointment is not the author's understandable reserve, for why should he satisfy our prurient curiosity? Meneghello's autobiography in fact sounds like a Gramscian analysis of culture: he is not interested in narrating an ordinary individual life but in chronicling the historical evolution of a whole culture, during fascism and after. His object is not so much personal events and memories as customs and mores (a potentially comparative study, as Italian mores are compared with English mores), as inscribed in the words and phrases that make up the languages Meneghello successively practised, from the vernacular to the vehicular, the referential and the mythical, from the local dialect he spoke in his childhood, to vehicular Italian, to literary Italian, and eventually to the English language he adopted as a second Mother tongue, without ever relinquishing his first. In short, the object of this very strange autobiography – which we can hardly call such – is what linguists sometimes call a *linguaculture*. Meneghello appears to have adopted Gramsci's thesis that a language is a conception of the world.

[39] Luigi Meneghello, *Opere*, Vol. 2 (Milan: Rizzoli, 1997).
[40] Luigi Meneghello, *Opere*, Vol. 1 (Milan: Rizzoli, 1993), 327 (the words in italics are in English in the Italian text).

It appears, therefore, that the answer to the question, what is Meneghello's Mother tongue, which at first sight was obvious (he was born and bred in Italy, and he is an Italian writer and a teacher of Italian), is rather more complex, and that his works are susceptible of a tetraglossic analysis. The first two of the books mentioned above are indeed devoted to an account of the *vernacular* of his family origins and of his childhood, the dialect spoken in Malo, his native town, the dialect of a community of farmers in a northern province of Italy, in which he was nurtured. The end of *Pomo pero* (which begins with his earliest infancy and evokes his later visits to a town he has left for good) consists of lists of dialect words, without translation, classified according to number of syllables and place of accent: the common and garden reader, who has no idea of the dialect, must read this as a kind of phonic poetry, a paean to the sounds of the dialect, Meneghello's tribute to the *lalangue* of his infancy, his true Mother tongue, the tongue of his mother and of his entry into language.

At this stage there is no Italian, that is, no standard dialect. For the inhabitants of Malo, Meneghello says, Italian is a written language, not a spoken language (this was, of course, in the first three decades of the last century). To him, Italian came later, when he went to secondary school in Vicenza: a *vehicular* dialect, which only became his vernacular over the years, as his life took him further and further away from Malo. We are moving, in Monique De Mattia-Viviès's terms, from *lalangue* and the *interior* language of the family – in both cases, the local dialect – to the *exterior* language of the school, which, in Gobard's terms, is also the language of the city; for Meneghello, it is the language of his social ascension (even if his family were better off than the average peasant). For the young Meneghello was a promising scholar: he even won a prestigious prize in a national school competition, which suggests that standard Italian had complemented and probably partly replaced the initial form of his Mother tongue. And, later in his life, the same could be said of the English language, since he settled permanently in England and only went home during vacations: if anyone can give a positive answer to the initial question Barbara Cassin was asked, it is certainly Meneghello.

But standard Italian was not only for him a vehicular and secondary vernacular; it soon became a *referential* dialect. It was not so much the bombastic Italian of the fascist regime, as exemplified in the now obsolete rhetoric of Mussolini[41] (although the prestigious prize he won was for 'fascist doctrine'), as the language of Italian literature – his career as an academic in a foreign land made him a sort of functionary of that type of language, which he inculcated to generations of English students, lecturing, I suppose, on the great names and marking myriads of prose assignments in which any deviation from

---

[41] Augusto Simonini, *Il linguaggio di Mussolini* (Milan: Bompiani, 1978).

the rules of official grammar was underlined in petulant red (even if such deviations from the standard norm were no more deviant than the productions of his native dialect). To which must be added, again, another field of reference, that is, of values as carried by language – the English language that he now daily inhabited and the English culture with which he had fallen in love.

Lastly, his childhood and youth in a deeply Roman Catholic environment gave him, in the guise of what Gobard calls his *mythical* language, a familiarity with Church Latin (increased by the classical Latin he learnt at school – the very title of *Libera nos a malo* is an instance of such familiarity).[42] The Vicenza province and the foothills of the Alps were traditionally 'white' regions: the people there abhorred the reds, respected the priests, and took part in the requisite religious rituals; they were indifferent Fascists and after the war faithfully voted for the Christian Democrats – in other words, they were prime examples of the cultural hegemony of the Church, which, in Gramsci's terms, not so much dominated as directed their lives, as reflected in their culture and dialect. Thus, although Meneghello himself does not appear to be particularly religious and did not marry his Jewish wife in church, neverthe- less the young couple went to see the local priest for a private blessing.

At this point, an objection is bound to be raised. The tetraglossic analysis of Meneghello's language, or rather languages, does show that what we call his Mother tongue (in the banal statement: Meneghello's Mother tongue is Italian) is the complex synchronic result of a diachronic development. But this con- cerns what we ought to call not his *first* but his *only* Mother tongue, since the various dialects that constitute it are all closely linked to 'Italian', even if this 'Italian' is no longer to be taken as a single entity but, rather, as Deleuze used to say, as a system of variations and displacements. Such complexity excludes the English language, which he learnt much later, even if he became entirely bilingual: a Mother tongue should be, almost by definition, unique. However, I think Meneghello's case does not fit in with the ordinary form of bilingualism the objection implicitly refers to. Indeed, his style has a remarkable character- istic: the frequent use of English words in his Italian sentences, without any typographic mark of difference, neither italics nor inverted commas, which means that, since his published writings are for obvious reasons in standard Italian, English is on the same level as the dialect of his childhood, whose terms and phrases are present in the same form. Sometimes the English words are commented on (e.g., when he gives an idea of their pronunciation, between brackets), and the fact that they express a nuance of meaning Italian fails to express is duly acknowledged – but dialect words receive exactly the same

---

[42] Deliver us from Evil / Deliver us from Malo.

treatment. This, I think, goes beyond code switching: it is a fusion of dialects, whose mixture, which is no juxtaposition but an organic synthesis, defines what we are entitled to call Meneghello's total Mother tongue.

Meneghello is entirely aware of the complexity of his 'Mother tongue'. In 1990, he published a book on the Vicentine dialect, *Maredè maredè*, which starts with a short note on his use of abbreviations:

I have used a number of abbreviations: VIC for the Vicentine dialect (in its northern variety between 1922 and 1947, which is what I am familiar with); IT for the Italian that I take to be standard in Northern Italy (*Alta Italia*): IT-VIC for the Italian commonly spoken by the locals (whom I call VI-phones) in so far as it differs from IT; VIC-RUS for the dialect of the countryside and VIV-ARC for utterances that I judge to be archaic; EN for the English I sometimes quote; NS for *native speaker*; TRAS (as in *Libera nos a malo*) for my transpositions from IT to VIC [. . .][43]

What Meneghello is keenly aware of is that a language is not a single entity but a system of variations, both diachronic (his description of the dialect of his youth is dated) and synchronic (that Mother tongue of his is not merely the clash between local and standard dialects, the vernacular and the vehicular, but a system of differences, from VIC to VIC-RUS, to IT-VIC, and to IT, and even IT, the standard form of a language, is geographically restricted to *Alta Italia*, and therefore only a sort of dialect). What interests me here is that, in what is implicitly an analysis of the complexity of his Mother tongue, Meneghello includes the English of his adult years, which is used liberally and not simply 'quoted' – he provides an example of this in this very text, by using the English phrase 'native speaker' (which he immediately translates into Italian).

My contention, therefore, is double: (1) Meneghello's 'native' language, what I call his Mother tongue, includes the language of his adult life, English – no longer a foreign tongue to him but an external language internalised, even as standard Italian was initially an external language to the young VI-phone and later became an integral part of his Mother tongue; (2) a Mother tongue is not merely a collective system, not even a plurality of systems, but an individual construction, sometimes called an idiolect or a style, through fusion and transposition (this is the role of the TRAS element, which is a form of literary idiolect).[44]

But since this is a little abstract, let us look at a passage from *Il dispatrio*, its opening paragraph:

---

[43] Meneghello, *Opere*, Vol. 1, 433.

[44] On a natural language as a collection of idiolects, see Salikoko Mufwene, *The Ecology of Language Evolution* (Cambridge: Cambridge University Press, 2001); on style as the dialectical opposite of system, see my *De l'interpellation* (Paris: Amsterdam, 2019).

Death qui in Inghilterra non è donna, naturalmente, non porta la veletta coi i lustrini, non va a dire ai giovanotti orfici '*Je suis ta mort*': ma nel complesso non è nemmeno uomo, è un *transvestite*.[45]

(Death here in England is of course not a woman, doesn't wear a sequined veil, doesn't go about telling Orphic young men '*Je suis ta mort*': but on the whole it isn't even a man but a transvestite.)

What this incipit is suggesting is that the text is about not so much the clash as the fusion of languages, which is also, inextricably, a fusion of cultures. The title of the book, to the best of my knowledge, is a coinage. Meneghello could have chosen the more common *espatrio*, except that he wanted to use the two meanings of the prefix – not just a separation (from the fatherland and, consequently, the Mother tongue) but also a redoubling (of said fatherland and Mother tongue): beneath the Latin 'dis-', we may hear the Greek 'di-', as in 'diglossia' or bilingualism. We are told Meneghello was impressed by the statement of a critic who said (erroneously, it seems) that he had found the term in Henry James – his situation would have been the same as that of the characters in *The Europeans*,[46] with the separation of the expat which is also an acquisition, the acquisition of a new fatherland, and an enriched Mother tongue.

But the opening sentence does not do justice to the fusion of dialects: being objects of comparison, they are still separate, even if the choice of 'transvestite' above the common Italian term 'travestito' seems to indicate that English is no longer an external language for Meneghello, but a component of his tetraglossic dialect. The crux will be reached if we decide that for him English is no longer only a vehicular and a referential, but also a vernacular and a mythical dialect. The following passage is a good illustration of this fusion, of the integration of English in Meneghello's Mother tongue:

Curioso: 'sussiego' è una delle parole che non so dire meglio, o almeno altrettanto bene, in inglese. Per rendere l'idea bisogna ricorrere a un rafforzativo, come bloody: anzi direi che per chi usa le due lingue una buona traduzione inglese di 'sussiego' è bloody sussiego.[47]

(Strange: 'sussiego' ('self-importance') is one of the words I cannot say better, or at least as well, in English. In order to express the idea I need a word of emphasis like *bloody*: I can even say that if you speak both languages, a good English translation of 'sussiego' is '*bloody* sussiego'.)

As we can see, the language commonly available to Meneghello in order to express his meaning – what we usually mean under the term 'Mother tongue' –

[45] Luigi Meneghello, *Il Dispatrio* (Milan: Rizzoli, [1993] 2000), 7. English translation by Jean-Jacques Lecercle.
[46] Ernestina Pellegrini, *Luigi Meneghello* (Fiesole: Cadmo, 2002), 117–18.
[47] Meneghello, *Il Dispatrio*, 105.

is a mixture of languages: English has become a second Mother tongue, in a state of fusion with the original one (which is already, as we saw, a fusion of various dialects).

2.7   Conclusion: How to Acquire a Second Mother Tongue

It would be difficult to generalize from Meneghello's case: we can hardly ask all students of English as a second language to become professors of their native Mother tongue in a British university. But, on the other hand, his story can be a source of hope for our students.

In official circles, the explicit object of the acquisition of a second language is the acquisition of a second vehicular. A French secretary of state for education once famously said that English was the French's second Mother tongue. By this he meant not the language of Shakespeare but a form of Globish (if possible, with a servile imitation of the BBC accent). This, of course, has nothing to do with the acquisition of English as a second Mother tongue: in order to acquire it, we must forget both Globish and the BBC accent.

The first step is to get rid of the servility of the accent: the sounds and rhythms of our initial Mother tongue, the tongue of our mother, will never be forgotten, and, as English speakers of foreign extraction, we need not parrot the natives in what is essentially a class dialect. There is room for our very own xenolect, English as it is pronounced by an initial French or Italian speaker, whose productions are no more 'deviant' from the celebrated 'Received Pronunciation' than those of a speaker of Wenglish or the English one may hear in many parts of London. This unashamed practice of a xenolect, however, is not sufficient: it provides no more than a vehicular.

The second step, therefore, is to acquire the second language as a referential, that is, to take seriously the phrase 'the language of Shakespeare' (or of Dickens, or of Faulkner, or whoever – and this will inevitably include authors known as 'postcolonial', as English is not a fixed single entity but a variety of dialects). This requires a process of Marxian *Aneignung*, making one's own a body of sedimented knowledge and beliefs – not only learning the language as a linguaculture (and not merely a grammatical system) but falling in love with the culture, to the point of acquiring a fictitious past in it. The successful learner of a second language is like the God of Philip Gosse, Edmund Gosse's father, who, being a geologist and a Puritan, had sought to accommodate his scientific knowledge and his religious belief by deciding that God had created the world in 4004 BC, complete with fossils of unfathomable antiquity. Our learner will therefore make for herself a fictitious infancy in a Mother tongue that originally was not hers. In doing this, she will already proceed to the third step.

The third step is to make the second language a mythical and above all a vernacular language, in other words, to treat it not merely as a language of communication and knowledge (a vehicular and a referential) but as a language of affect. Here, we may have recourse to Heidegger's metaphor of inhabitation: a true speaker of a language dwells in that language – she does not merely use it as a tool of communication. Like Meneghello, she has made its sounds and rhythms, as well as its nuances of meaning, hers, for a Mother tongue is made up of this: fondly remembered words and phrases, clichés and metaphors, and prosodic sequences, as embodied in nursery rhymes, lullabies, and favourite poems. The speaker of such increased Mother tongue must turn the whole of a language into a fictitious *lessico famigliare*, which involves more than what is usually called acquiring an encyclopaedia. If this process is pursued to the end, the result will be a style, the result of the individual counter-interpellation of the various linguistic interpellations the subject has been subjected to in her learning process.

For this is what a Mother tongue is: the extension of the inalienable language of desire (Arendt's experience is witness to such inalienability), the tongue of the mother, an extension that goes from *lalangue* to the internal language of the family and to a variety of external languages, with a possibility not only of alienation (this is Derrida's experience) but also of extension through fusion (this is essentially Meneghello's experience). What we must strive to teach our students is not a means of communication but ways of acquiring a style.

Bibliography

Althusser, Louis. *On Ideology*. London: Verso, 2008.
Arendt, Hannah. *La langue maternelle*. Paris: Eterotopia, 2015.
Balibar, Renée. *Les Français fictifs*. Paris: Hachette, 1974.
Butler, Judith. *Excitable Speech: A Politics of the Performative*. New York: Routledge, 1997.
Cassin, Barbara. (ed.). *Vocabulaire européen de la philosophie*. Paris: Seuil/ Le Robert, 2004. *Dictionary of Untranslatables: A Philosophical Lexicon*. Translated by Emily Apter, Jacques Lezra, and Michael Wood (eds.). Princeton, NJ: Princeton University Press, 2014.
Plus d'une langue. Paris: Bayard, 2019.
De Mattia-Viviès, Monique. 'Entrer dans la langue ou dans les langues: de la langue maternelle à la langue "mat-rangère"'. *E-rea*, N° 16.1, 2018. https://journals .openedition.org/erea/6502
Derrida, Jacques. *Le monolinguisme de l'autre, ou la prothèse d'origine*. Paris: Galilée, 1996. *The Monolingualism of the Other, or the Prosthesis of Origin*. Translated by Patrick Mensah. Stanford, CA: Stanford University Press, 1998.
Ginzburg, Natalia. *Lessico famigliare*. Milano: Mondadori, [1963] 1974.
Gobard, Henri. *L'aliénation linguistique*. Paris: Flammarion, 1976.

Gramsci, Antonio. *Quaderni del carcere*, Vol. 1. Turin: Einaudi, 2007.

Lecercle, Jean-Jacques. *De l'interpellation*. Paris: Amsterdam, 2019.

Marx, Karl, and Friedrich Engels. *Études philosophiques*. Paris: Éditions Sociales, 1961.

  The German Ideology. London: Lawrence and Wishart, 1965.

Meneghello, Luigi. *Il Dispatrio*. Milan: Rizzoli, [1993] 2000.

  Opere, Vol. 1. Milan: Rizzoli, 1993.

  Opere, Vol. 2. Milan: Rizzoli, 1997.

Mufwene, Salikoko. *The Ecology of Language Evolution*. Cambridge: Cambridge University Press, 2001.

Pellegrini, Ernestina. *Luigi Meneghello*. Fiesole: Cadmo, 2002.

Saffioti, Tito. (ed.). *Le ninne nanne italiane*. Turin: Einaudi, 1994.

Sève, Lucien. *'L'homme'?* Paris: La Dispute, 2008.

Simonini, Augusto. *Il linguaggio di Mussolini*. Milan: Bompiani, 1978.

Wittgenstein, Ludwig. *Tractatus Logico-Philosophicus*. London: Routledge and Kegan Paul, [1921] 1961.

3   Embracing the Bilingual Overlap in Creative Second Language Learning

Sara Greaves

To my sons Paul and Léo, for teaching me so much about the Mother tongue.

> my homeland gifted me
> a language with soft corners
> it feels like sugar in my mouth
> and the language i learned to speak
> is made up of wax; it often melts
> and burns my mouth
> leaving my words
> soundless
> shapeless
> helpless
> and i cannot help but sound like
> someone utterly unknown
> {accent}
>
> Noor Unnahar[1]

The word 'language' derives from the Latin 'lingua', which in turn developed from the Indo-European root 'dnghu', meaning 'tongue' – a body organ. The relation between root and derivation is thus a metonymical shift, a natural step from body to sound, since the tongue provides the muscle power, along with other parts of the human vocal apparatus, necessary for speech. 'Language', the word – in English (but not in French, for instance, which uses the word *langue* for individual languages ('tongue') and *langage* for language in general) – stands apart from the 'tongue' and, as a concept, has long led an independent life in the rarefied atmosphere of philosophy or linguistics or psychoanalysis, coming centre stage in the twentieth century as the star of structuralism, the 'linguistic turn' or French theory. Yet it remembers its bodily origins too, in everyday expressions such as 'tongue-tied', 'tongue-twister', and the biblical phrase 'speaking in tongues'; or in the question asked of overawed children, 'what's the matter, have you lost your tongue?' or, in

---

[1] Noor Unnahar, *Yesterday I Was the Moon*. Reproduced by kind permission of Clarkson Potter, an imprint of Random House, [2017] 2018.

annoyance, 'Has the cat got your tongue?'; as well as in poetry, jokes, and theories of the signifier – and, of course, in the phrase 'Mother tongue'. Just as the etymological evolution from body to sound seems smooth and untrammelled, so we tend to expect the psycho-neuro-physiological language learning process to unfold unperturbed too. In some people, this naturalness and ease carry over into other learning situations, including second language learning; in others, learning a second language is more tortuous and the process from tongue to language, from body to meaningful sound and authentic pronunciation, proves fraught with difficulties.

These difficulties are our starting point in this book, as we saw in Chapter 1. It is noteworthy that the terms 'teaching' and 'healthcare' are both euphemistic, in that both take rose-tinted spectacles to evoke what is their principal challenge: to overcome learning difficulties and treat ill health, although the phrase 'learning difficulties' may raise eyebrows, given that the context I shall be referring to in this chapter is university lecturing (albeit a term barely satisfactory to the approach I wish to present here). Students are adult learners and are generally assumed to have overcome any difficulties they may have run into earlier on (or, in the case of dyslexia or other forms of disorder, to be offered facilities such as extra time in exams), so what 'difficulties' might they encounter? Studying a language is not the same as studying maths or physics or even the humanities (although I would hesitate to proclaim a qualitative difference, and who knows what would transpire from researching mathematics and the Mother tongue?), especially when you are studying it not merely for communicative purposes, but in order to gain the skills and knowledge required to become a modern language teacher, thereby in a sense representing it, becoming its ambassador within another linguistic and cultural context (in the case described here, that of France, in French schools and universities) – in turn embodying abstract language by means of a foreign tongue, a foreign body, raised in a foreign culture.

The demands on French English students, then, are high and paradoxical, not least because while they are busy projecting themselves into a new linguistic identity, their usual, habitual one may manifest itself in unexpected, sometimes unhelpful, ways. With bilingualism, when speaking one of the two languages, the other one is never very far away;[2] it is a special mode of being in which the languages are not divided by a sharp boundary, neatly separating off two distinct territories, but suffused by the other's ghost, as Alain Fleischer puts it in Chapter 6 of this volume, in the form of an accent or beset by

---

[2] 'Fluent bilinguals show some measure of activation of both languages and some interaction between them at all times, even in contexts that are entirely driven by only one of the languages'. Ellen Bialystok, Fergus I. M. Craik, and Gigi Luk, 'Bilingualism: Consequences for Mind and Brain', *Trends in Cognitive Sciences*, 2012, 240–50, www.ncbi.nlm.nih.gov/pmc/articles/PMC3322418/.

unannounced incursions – lexical, syntactical, and phonological – into one another's territory. Indeed, the language student is faced with an aporia: primed to become an authentic representative of the second language and culture, they are in fact becoming bilingual; trained to become, so to speak, monolingual twice over, they are actually inhabiting an in-between space and developing the strategies and reflexive skills of linguistic relativists and cultural comparatists. It is surprising to consider how little these contradictory paths are taken into account, and for many years now, language teaching in schools has been largely carried out in the target language, often rejecting the use of the Mother tongue altogether.[3] And yet, that monolingual ideal is more likely to be achieved, or at least approached – as Monique De Mattia-Viviès argues in Chapter 1 – if what we might call the bilingual overlap were to find its way into our teaching methods.

What, then, might second language didactics look like when it makes room for the Mother tongue? How can the language learning process of infancy be harnessed – or, when an inhibiting force, short-circuited and counteracted – to enhance adult language learning situations? How can this bilingual overlap, whether a help or a hindrance, a source of interest and aesthetic pleasure or of shame and embarrassment, be usefully introduced into a French university course in English studies? These are the questions and this is the context that will be discussed in this chapter, devoted to presenting an approach and practice developed in the English department at Aix-Marseille University, subsequently reinforced by action research in a medical centre in Marseille, involving plurilingual creative writing workshops. Adopting an interdisciplinary approach using diverse frames of reference, including poetics, plurilingualism, psychoanalysis, and translation studies, I will first consider the bilingual overlap in second language learning and then discuss the use of plurilingual creative writing workshops in healthcare, before presenting two English studies courses aimed at exploring and enhancing a 'bilingual' approach to language learning.

3.1   Bilingual Overlap

3.1.1   *Language and the Body*

Unintentionally breaking the rules – whether of grammar, syntax, vocabulary, or phonetics – is the most visible, or audible, form of bilingual overlap. Adding

---

[3] Cf. 'The Natural Approach' of Tracy Terrell and Stephen Krashen, in Jack C. Richards and Theodore S. Rodgers, *Approaches and Methods in Language Teaching* (Cambridge: Cambridge University Press, [1986] 2007), 178–91, in which the natural and traditional approaches 'are defined as "based on the use of language in communicative situations without recourse to the native language"', 178.

an 's' on English adjectives, for instance, because in French adjectives agree with nouns; dropping the 's' on plurals or third-person verbs because in French the consonant is either graphically absent or phonetically silent; or using the relative pronoun 'which' for people, because in French the equivalent pronoun distinguishes between subject and object (*qui* and *que*) but not between extra-linguistic categories such as human and non-human: these are all common instances of French/English overlap. Unfortunately, it is not always sufficient to draw students' attention to their mistakes, and an unbidden force sometimes seems to be at work undermining second language speech. As in Noor Unnahar's poem above, it is as if that language were made of wax and 'often melts / and burns [their] mouth'.

The hypothesis underpinning the research presented in this chapter is that second language learning involves, perhaps exacerbates, questions of exist-ence and identity to a degree that is rarely acknowledged; and that language students are not merely learning new skills and competences, learning to master and apply the codes of a foreign linguistic system, with new rules, new phrasing, and new vocabulary, but they are also having to project them-selves intellectually into a new mindset and a new culture. Ideally, they are also learning to experience their own physicality and sensibility in the new language: they are learning to think from a new perspective, to feel with a new skin. It is this corporeal experience in language learning that tends to be overlooked. Yet without it, second language speakers run the risk – to quote Noor Unnahar once again – of feeling 'like / someone utterly unknown'; or, to quote Julia Kristeva's evocative title, 'strangers to ourselves'.[4]

Linguistic philosophy and anthropology, not to mention translation studies, have long familiarised us with the concepts of linguistic and cultural relativity, according to which structures of thought are dependent on the structures of the language. This theory has recently been forcefully illustrated by *The Dictionary of Untranslatables: A Philosophical Lexicon*, a collective endeav-our directed by Barbara Cassin, which highlights what Georges Steiner called linguistic 'alternity',[5] by inventorying untranslatable philosophical terms from different languages.[6] A more individual, intimate illustration is provided by video artist Yolande Zauberman and Paulina Mikol Spiechowicz, who

---

[4] Julia Kristeva, *Strangers to Ourselves*, translated by Leon S. Roudiez (New York: Columbia University Press, [1988] 1991).

[5] Georges Steiner writes: 'We need a word which will designate the power, the compulsion of language to posit 'otherness', and suggests 'alternity'. *After Babel: Aspects of Language and Translation* (Oxford: Oxford University Press, 1975), 22.

[6] Barbara Cassin (ed.), *Vocabulaire européen des philosophies: Dictionnaire des intraduisibles* (Paris: Seuil / Le Robert, 2004). *Dictionary of Untranslatables: A Philosophical Lexicon,* translated by Emily Apter, Jacques Lezra, and Michael Wood (eds.) (Princeton, NJ: Princton University Press, 2015). See also, for an article questioning the notion of untranslatability, Pascal Engel, 'Le Mythe de l'intraduisible', *En attendant Nadeau: Journal de la littérature, des idées et*

interviewed migrants in Paris and asked them to describe the words they missed most from their language, subsequently gathering the terms in a book, an encyclopedia written on the intimate side of language.[7] The use of video emphasises the way language is anchored in the body, and the result is a poignant testimony to language difference. Comparing international sign languages also provides a striking lesson in how not just culture and concepts but especially bodies differ depending on the language they 'speak'. Ideally, speaking a second language would mean being as much 'at home' physically in that language as signers in theirs – and as in the Mother tongue.

When a language student is invited to express themselves in their new language and makes a syntactical or grammatical error, or chooses the wrong word or a word from another language or of an inappropriate register, they may, when corrected, breezily assimilate the correct phrasing or word and remember to use it next time, but they may in some cases feel strangely embarrassed and ashamed, as if suddenly transparent, or even mortified, as if found guilty of some kind of (self-)betrayal. Awkward self-consciousness such as this is often accompanied by physical manifestations such as blushing, and there is good reason to think of language errors as symptoms – symptoms, perhaps, of a paradoxical reluctance to be 'translated', as Salman Rushdie writes in *Shame*.[8]

This is not to argue that language lecturers should re-train as psychotherapists, but to suggest that an awareness of the social and emotional stakes can prove beneficial to students' well-being – and to their success in mastering their chosen foreign language. Much progress has been made in the field of didactics with respect to assessment of pupils' work (with particular attention paid to marking papers, although providing oral feedback is equally important) and formative evaluation.[9] Given that an essay or any piece of written or oral assignment may be deeply psychologically invested in by the student, it is important to bear this in mind in such a way as to stimulate and encourage without humiliating or inhibiting. In the case of language learning, this phenomenon of psychological investment seems to be exacerbated by the fact that, consciously or unconsciously, studying another language often reflects, to varying degrees, the desire to construct a new identity and reinvent oneself,

---

des arts (2017). www.en-attendant-nadeau.fr/2017/07/18/mythe-intraduisible-cassin/. Another work of interest is Pierre Legendre, *Tour du monde des concepts* (Paris: Fayard, 2014).

[7] Yolande Zauberman and Paulina Mikol Spiechowicz, *Les mots qui nous manquent: Encyclopédie* (Paris: Calmann-Lévy, 2016).

[8] 'I, too, am a translated man. I have been *borne across*'. Salman Rushdie, *Shame* (London: Vintage, 1995), 29, where the homophone 'born' also suggests a rebirth, a new identity.

[9] Cf. *L'évaluation à l'épreuve du contexte: Pratiques et réflexions*. Anne Demeester, Bernard De Giorgi, and Yannick Gouchan (eds.) (Aix-en-Provence: Presses Universitaires de Provence, 2020), including Florent Da Sylva and Sara Greaves, 'Encadrer des projets d'écriture collective en anglais: d'une évaluation pour la forme à une évaluation formative', 53–66.

either due to the force of attraction of the foreign language or as a kind of refuge – or a bit of both.

And what can it mean when we hear students say, as I do fairly frequently in creative writing or creative translation classes, that they love English and feel they can express themselves much more freely in that language than in their Mother tongue?[10] Or, conversely, that however many languages they learn and however proficient they become, they still feel inadequate and inarticulate in all of them?

3.1.2   Linguistic Diversity

Moreover, in connection with 'broken English' or incorrect grammar or syntax, the very notion of language 'errors' in second language speech and learning is an open question: while lending themselves to interpretation as instances of literary creativity – such as in nonsense poetry – when found in the appropriate context,[11] certain 'errors' are also produced and systematised by the effects of languages in contact, as has been shown by research into world Englishes, with the emergence of language varieties such as Punglish, Spanglish, or Chinglish, or by exophonic or plurilingual writing.[12] According to George Steiner, it is the anomaly that keeps language alive:

But it is its great untidiness that makes human speech innovative and expressive of personal intent. It is the anomaly, as it feeds back into the general history of usage, the ambiguity, which give coherence to the system. A coherence, if such a description is allowed, 'in constant motion'.[13]

---

[10] Possibly because in this second language they can lower their guard more easily, as Nancy Huston has observed: 'The *I* which I used so freely in my essays was also, no doubt, one of the effects of my *uprooted knowledge*. A certain shamelessness was made possible by the fact I was writing in a foreign language – partly because, at least in my imagination, my parents did not speak this language, but more importantly because for me, *French has nothing to do with my intimate, inner life*. In French I could say, quite calmly and even with a certain indifference, things it could have been impossible for me to reveal or even think about in my mother tongue'. Nancy Huston, *Longings and Belongings: Essays* (Toronto: McArthur, 2005), 341–2.

[11] In his book *The Violence of Language* (London: Routledge, 1990), Jean-Jacques Lecercle quotes Somerset Maugham's *Cakes and Ale*: 'I'm not so young as I used to was'. He goes on: 'Were I to read this in a student's paper, I would underline the last word in petulant red. As a reader of fiction, I enjoy the sentence', 7.

[12] See Chapter 2 of this volume and, for the study of plurilingual literary manuscripts, Olga Anokhina and Emilio Sciarrino, *Entre les langues. Genesis: manuscrits, recherche, invention*, 46/18, ITEM/CNRS (Paris: Presses Universitaires de Paris Sorbonne, 2018). For world Englishes, see Jennifer Jenkins, *World Englishes: A resource book for students* (New York: Routledge, 2009).

[13] George Steiner, *After Babel: Aspects of Language and Translation* (Oxford: Oxford University Press, 1975), 203.

Added to which, 'standard English' as spoken in Britain today is itself a multifaceted and extremely fast-changing language,[14] with yesterday's grammar mistakes or mispronunciations becoming tomorrow's usage (e.g., 'good' as an adverb, the first-syllable stress in 'weekend', a hard /k/ in schedule, and the regrettable decline of the present perfect tense), with many of these changes being perceived as intralingual overlap due to the hegemony of American English. Given the acceleration of language evolution in recent years, one may wonder whether the concept of distinct languages is outmoded.

Yet despite the rich new field of research into plurilingualism, whether its focus be on orality to reveal the paths and patterns of code switching between languages in contact, or on the written word to disclose the multilingual secrets of would-be monolingual writers,[15] distinct languages of course continue to be taught, and students of English in French universities, for instance, are offered a traditionally polarised approach to their subject, with issues of bi- and plurilingualism mostly left off-syllabus. Literature, linguistics, and 'civilisa-tion'[16] are generally taught within their language boundaries (e.g., Britain, USA, Commonwealth), with phonetics classes seeking to attune students' ears to received pronunciation (RP) phonemes through dialectical comparisons, and any comparatist approaches such as English and French stylistics or intercul-turality are mostly the remit of translation and translation studies classes.[17] Yet the transition from one language to the other, the biographical, psychological, physiological, and sometimes social journey from the Mother tongue to the other tongue, the success of which is necessary for an authentic-sounding command of English, is generally overlooked and left to individuals, when possible, to work out for themselves.

For some students this proves far from easy. What is it like for students from plurilingual backgrounds to study English in France? Is linguistic diversity, such as having a Mother tongue other than French, or socially or regionally distinct from the norm, a help or a hindrance, and how can we take this sociolinguistic or cross-cultural dimension into account in our teaching? Researchers in plurilingualism often emphasise the educational benefits of being raised in two or more languages, but although for some this is true, for others the journey from what could be described as a 'second Mother tongue'[18]

---

[14] For a masterly presentation of the evolution of language and literature through time, see chapter 1 of George Steiner, *After Babel*, 1–48.

[15] Anokhina and Sciarrino, *Entre les langues.*

[16] Modern languages departments in French universities are divided into three, sometimes four, sections: literature, linguistics, civilisation (an umbrella heading for history, the history of ideas, and cultural studies), and translation.

[17] See the seminal work of Jean-Paul Vinay and Jean Darbelnet, *Stylistique comparée du français et de l'anglais* (Paris: Didier, [1977] (re-edited several times)).

[18] See Part II of this volume.

to the academic English required of future language teachers is a rough ride. Monique De Mattia-Viviès deals in depth in Chapter 1 of this volume with the distinction between interior (the family circle) and exterior (school) languages, along with the risks and rewards of the transition between the two; but she makes the point that whatever the family's linguistic environment, whether or not it be socially or ethnically diverse from the norm propounded by the worlds of school and work, the transitional process from one language or language variety to another sometimes confronts children with an unsolvable conflict of loyalty, a conflict that may return and haunt the adult learner's linguistic proficiency later on.

Given this psychological dimension, the opportunity to carry out action research in healthcare with plurilingual adults – the parents of small children with speech impediments or other developmental difficulties or disabilities – was warmly embraced.

3.2   Action Research in a Medical Centre

3.2.1   Plurilingual Creative Writing Workshop

Between 2013 and 2018, I joined forces with a team of clinical psychologists and child psychiatrist and psychoanalyst Dr Jean-Luc Di Stefano, head of the Centre for Early Infancy Socio-Medical Action (CAMSP) at Salvator Hospital in Marseille, to help ease tensions around language issues observed during consultations.[19] Many of the children (all under six) receiving care were suffering from language difficulties, and the clinicians were looking for ways to make it easier for non-Francophone parents to open up to medical staff about their children's symptoms, and to broach certain areas of their home life in a language with which they were often ill at ease. Without the aid of translators, they felt it was often hard to get the full picture and that this was due not only to the parents' insufficient knowledge of French, but also to a reluctance or difficulty to use that language for the intimacy of the home.[20] We decided to offer these parents plurilingual creative writing workshops, first and foremost as a way of indicating that the clinic was not a purely monolingual space but a plurilingual one – a place at least where all languages were

---

[19] My sincere thanks to Dr Jean-Luc Di Stefano and the psychologists from CAMSP Salvator and other medical centres, who met for discussions on psychological or language-related issues at Dr Di Stefano's monthly seminar, 'Handicap et symptôme', especially Julia Maraninchi, Myrto Rapti, Katja Wesselmann, Evelyne Chamla, and Delphine Goetgheluck.

[20] Marie Rose Moro (cf. Chapter 4 of this volume) describes the important role of translators – not only linguistic but also intercultural – in *Parents en exil: Psychopathologie et migrations* (Paris: Presses Universitaires de France, 1994).

welcome.[21] The workshops were presented alongside other therapeutic activities on offer at the medical centre, thus also suggesting to the parents that the medical team supported the idea of them taking self-reflective time for themselves – that doing so was perceived as potentially beneficial for all the family, including for the child being brought to the clinic for therapy.

Present at each workshop were four to eight participants, all women, mostly from the Mediterranean shores and the Middle East (e.g., Algeria, Turkey, Iran, Israel, Lebanon) but also from further afield (Vietnam, Thailand, Mali, Brazil...); a psychologist or psychiatrist from the clinic (many of whom were themselves bilingual: Italian/French, Greek/French, German/French); and me, the workshop leader.[22] The participants did not simply sign up for a workshop but were selected by the medical team; nevertheless, they had received different levels of formal education, and for some the workshop was a real challenge. It was important to make it resemble school as little as possible. The objective was not to have the participants write a monolingual text in their Mother tongue, as some nevertheless chose to do, but to write a plurilingual text using whichever languages they spoke. In other words, they were invited to code-switch, inserting words or phrases from other languages in a basically monolingual text, or to use alternate languages at the sentence or paragraph level.

The original aim of the workshop was modest and experimental. I had already observed the potential of similar workshops with English students at Aix-Marseille University, but here was an opportunity to work outside the institutional constraints proper to a university course, in a healthcare context where nothing was required to be taught – no skills or competences – and no assessment was necessary. The minimum requirement was to extend our hospitality to people's languages[23] and to set up a safe space in which the women who – often with some difficulty – had set aside precious time to take part in a workshop could in some way benefit from it, whether aesthetically (the rewards of writing, of constructing a text), socially (the 'decolonising'

---

[21] Cf. Sybille de Pury: 'France is constitutionally and ideologically monolingual, and France's national education board is a fervent champion of monolingual ideology' (my translation). 'Les Apatrides linguistiques', academic paper given on 31 January 2020 as part of the series 'Language and the Century' (*Le langage et le* siècle), Bibliothèque Publique d'Information, Centre Georges Pompidou, www.ethnopsychiatrie.net/actu/Boburg.htm.

[22] For the complete outline of a plurilingual creative writing workshop, including participants' annotated visual documents and texts, see *Atelier d'écriture plurilingue sur l'exil*, with Jean-Luc Di Stefano, *Non-Lieux de l'exil* (Paris: Fondation Maison des Sciences de l'Homme, 2015), http://nle.hypotheses.org/3711.

[23] Cf. Antonio Prete: 'Hospitality towards the migrant, the observation of their rights – of asylum, to healthcare, education, work and citizenship – also concern their language, which is the visible sign of their identity, memory and belonging'. *À l'ombre de l'autre langue: Pour un art de la traduction*, translated by Danièle Robert (Cadenet: Chemin de Ronde, [2011] 2013). Extract translated by Sara Greaves.

effect of mixing languages and hearing them spoken in an institutional –
culturally dominant – context), or psychologically (the acceptance and
acknowledgement of one's cultural identity, the boost to self-confidence of
using one's Mother tongue). As time went on, however, the potential of the
workshop came more clearly into view.

Two firm principles underpin this work: *indirection* or *distancing* (the one
subject on all the participants' minds, in this case their concern for their child
and their illness or disability, was not broached by the writing tasks), and
decentring (the writing tasks were designed to discourage the participants from
writing 'as themselves' and to jolt them out of their natural, habitual train of
thought). This, in a nutshell, is the stimulating, creative effect of Oulipian
writing constraints.[24] The final piece of writing produced during the workshop,
ideally multilingual, is the culmination of several preliminary tasks, such as
compiling a multilingual list of words relating to a given topic or a personal
memory, noting words or phrases that come to mind by association of ideas or
through rhyme, assonance, or alliteration, or in a semi-collective writing
process, scrutinizing one's neighbour's multilingual list (an example of a
decentring strategy) in search of lookalike or soundalike words, and incorpor-
ating them into one's own piece of writing. The participants are thus invited to
write creatively with other people's words, to copy them, some in foreign
alphabets or calligraphies, to try and divine their meanings and their pronunciation and to find rhymes for them, or to use them to make up new
words altogether.

Each workshop ends with readings, some followed by spontaneous translation, some left untranslated – and all the more powerful for that. Many of these
reading sessions were moments of emotion, sometimes leading to discussion
about the children for whose benefit the women were there, about the languages spoken at home and their relationships with those languages – and the
left-behind worlds they were linked to. As well as enabling the satisfaction of
earning the praise and approval of others, these workshops also acted as a kind
of giant icebreaker, joyously exploding the taboo surrounding languages and
authorising their use within the bounds of the rather intimidating, institutional
context of the clinic, in which so much was at stake for their children,
expanding and reinforcing the participants' sense of self.

3.2.2   Lalangue *and Regression*

However, the nature of the invitation thus extended to the participants is not
simply to use their Mother tongue, but perhaps, more interestingly, to relive

---

[24] Oulipo is derived from OUvroir de LIttérature POtentielle. The Oulipo website has examples of
writing constraints: www.oulipo.net/.

the experience of learning it – to be offered the opportunity of rekindling the embers of that process by rediscovering the reassuring pleasures of *lalangue*: the sensual, prelinguistic baby talk that occurs in the early stages in the development of the Mother tongue.[25] Each workshop, moreover, begins with the reading of a literary extract by the workshop facilitator, either fiction or poetry, in French or in another language followed by its French translation, aimed at transporting the participants into that remote yet intimate world of words, initiating that co-creative space in which the imaginations of facilitator and participants can converge, which is the hallmark of creative writing workshops.[26] A space of reassurance and containment, in which someone gives out a prompt (a word or phrase, a writing task) and someone else takes up the lead and uses it to write, the workshop comes in a way to resemble the babble and prattle of the mother/infant 'sound envelope' or 'sound bath', likewise based on imitation and co-creation. Didier Anzieu writes:

The Skin-ego as a psychic representation emerges out of play between the body of the mother and that of the infant, and out of the vocal and physical responses of the mother to the sensations and emotions of the baby, with the sound envelope reproducing the tactile one. These responses are circular in character in that mother and infant imitate each other's echolalia and echopraxia, thus allowing the baby to gradually begin to feel its own sensations and emotions without feeling overwhelmed.[27]

This regressive function goes further. The plurilingual texts produced in the space of a 90- or 120-minute workshop are suggestive of what could be termed a plurilingual 'Skin-voice' (*Voix-peau* in French), a concept derived from psychoanalyst Didier Anzieu's theory of the psychic envelope or 'Skin ego' (*Moi-peau*), at once protecting and projecting the psyche, just as the physiological skin contains the body and allows it contact with the outside. As with Anzieu's concept, the plurilingual Skin-voice (based on a rhyme between the French words for ego, *moi*, and voice, *voix*)[28] allows exchanges with the Other, embodied here by the fragments of other voices, of other people's writings or words intertwined with one's own, thereby insinuating the construction of self as a self–other hybrid, or as plurilingual and pluricultural. The plurilingual text

[25] Cf. Yoann Loisel on Samuel Beckett's regressive writing in Chapter 8 of this volume.
[26] As taught on the Facilitating Creative Writing course at Aix-Marseille University (Diplôme Universitaire, *Formation à l'Animation d'Ateliers d'Ecriture*), founded by French writer and Honorary Professor Anne Roche. See also André Bellatorre et al., *Devenir animateur d'atelier écriture: (Se) former à l'animation* (Lyon: Chronique sociale, 2014), and Anne Roche et al., *L'atelier d'écriture: Éléments pour la rédaction du texte littéraire* (Paris: Armand Colin, [1989, 2000] 2005).
[27] Didier Anzieu, *Le Moi-peau* (Paris: Dunod, [1985] 1995), 25 (my translation).
[28] The notion of poetry as a 'Voix-peau' is developed in Sara Greaves, *Côté guerre côté jardin, excursions dans la poésie de James Fenton* (Aix-en-Provence: Presses Universitaires de Provence, 2016), 77 passim.

is thus an attempt to reconcile conflicting selves through a transcultural voice, which, like skin, both contains these diverse selves and allows them to interact with the outside. The Skin-voice also recalls a phrase from George Steiner's *After Babel: Aspects of Language and Translation*, 'Words seem to go dead under the weight of sanctified usage.... Instead of acting as a living membrane, grammar and vocabulary become a barrier to new feeling'.[29] Recapturing the energy and sensuality of *lalangue* through plurilingual creative writing can restore life to language and its codes. An aesthetic model for these texts could be the modernist poem, with its juxtaposed fragments of contrasting languages and registers contained within a central overarching consciousness; here, however, we inhabit the realm not only of poetics but also of poethics.

3.2.3   Linguistic Therapy

Plurilingual creative writing workshops offer an experience of linguistic and cultural plurality that can serve as a sort of model for a hybrid identity: a 'way of being' or a 'style', as conceived by literary theorist Marielle Macé, that can be tried out and perhaps adopted. She writes:

[It is] as if every aesthetic experience offered the individual the opportunity to act upon their own modes of being; not exactly on their being, but on their modes of being, which is to say on their style, the possibility they have to shape or fashion themselves.[30]

She specifies in her book *Styles: Critique de nos formes de vie*:

This opportunity is what Ponge calls stepping out of the human 'groove', an opportunity born of assuming responsibility for styles – those that are new to us and those we find ourselves to be.[31]

A co-created or participative aesthetic experience – such as that provided by creative writing workshops – offers a still greater incentive to individual action on the 'subject in process', to borrow a phrase popularised by Julia Kristeva. Moreover, Kristeva's conception of the Greek *chora* is pertinent to an understanding of the psychical potential of the workshop: a signifying space within which the self can set itself in movement and reorient itself towards a new 'destiny'. While for Plato the *chora* is 'a mobile receptacle of mixing, of

---

[29] George Steiner, *After Babel: Aspects of Language and Translation*. (Oxford: Oxford University Press, 1975), 21.

[30] Marielle Macé, 'Styles littéraires et formes de vie – Sartre au balcon'. CÉRÉdI, Centre d'Études et de Recherche Éditer/Interpréter, 2012, http://ceredi.labos.univ-rouen.fr/public/?styles-litter aires-et-formes-de.html.

[31] Marielle Macé, *Styles: Critique de nos formes de vie* (Paris: Gallimard, 2016), 69 (my translation). See also Marielle Macé, *Façons de lire, manières d'être* (Paris: Gallimard, 2011).

contradiction and movement, vital to nature's functioning before the teleological intervention of God, and corresponding to the mother',[32] for Kristeva, the *chora* is not situated in any particular body and becomes a 'semiotic *chora*' representing the subject in process, a chaotic space that 'is and becomes a precondition for creating the first measurable bodies'.[33]

Like the *chora*, then, the workshop functions as a regressive space in which people entrenched within distressing mindsets (as mothers of children with disabilities) or entrenched identities (as exiles) can open up new horizons.[34] Seeing and hearing words or phrases from one's Mother tongue that have been woven into someone else's signifying chain, writing a text that incorporates other people's signifiers that, in the process, have become one's own – these creative acts are a step back from the dark hole of loss (of a homeland, of a language, of an idealised child, of a certain self-image) in the direction of a more fluid, self-confident plural identity. Propounding the idea that both nature and the psyche abhor a vacuum, and the symbolic role of artistic creation in resilient self-construction, Boris Cyrulnik writes:

We feel better once we have constructed a self-directed decoy, a self-narrative, an identity – a representation that one can successfully inhabit because it has removed us from emptiness, from confusion. We perceive this decoy as natural, we adapt to it, organising our life around the creative imagination that gives shape to our needs.[35]

These embryonic decoys – the co-created multilingual texts produced in the safe space of the workshop – can prove a promising starting point for a linguistics-based psychotherapy and a trigger to resilience.

For, although not written as language biographies, such as those recommended by the Council of Europe to enhance mobility within the European Union,[36] the texts produced in these workshops can nevertheless be read as a kind of language map of the mind, providing an insight into the author's

---

[32] Julia Kristeva, 'Le sujet en procès', *Polylogue* (Paris: Seuil, 1977), 57.

[33] Kristeva, 'Le sujet en procès', 57. See also Johanne Prud'homme and Lyne Légar, 'Le sujet en procès', Louis Hébert (dir.), *Signo* (Quebec: Rimouski, 2006) www.signosemio.com/kristeva/subject-in-process.asp. For a cultural translation of this concept, see Stephanos Stephanides and Karna Singh's comparison of Kristeva's semiotic chora with the ritual bath that occurs during the Hindu ritual known as Kali's Feast, in Guyana, during which the devotee enters a space of being and becoming: 'a space or womb which is nourishing and maternal, the place where the subject is both generated and negated'. *Translating Kali's Feast: The Goddess in Indo-Caribbean Ritual and Fiction* (Amsterdam: Rodopi, 2000).

[34] Cf. Alexis Nouss's work on exile, in which the 'economic' migrant is placed on a par with famous literary exiles such as Joyce, Nabokov, or Conrad. *La condition de l'exilé* (Paris: Fondation Maison des Sciences de l'Homme, 2015).

[35] Boris Cyrulnik, *La nuit, j'écrirai des soleils* (Paris: Odile Jacob, 2019), 281–2, translated by Sara Greaves. Boris Cyrulnik is a household name in France, best known for his interdisciplinary work on the psychological concept of resilience.

[36] Cf. www.coe.int/en/web/portfolio/the-language-biography.

relationships with their languages. In this plurilingual hermeneutics, both formal and thematic characteristics are relevant: a person's handwriting, for instance, can in some cases vary in aspect as they change languages, sometimes suggesting a change of personality, or at least be read as an indicator of the value attached to a language. One piece of writing produced during a workshop was neat and studious for the Arabic calligraphy of the participant's Algerian childhood, and scruffy and careless for the Italian and French she had learnt on the hoof in her adult life, spent in Italy and then in France, and mostly used orally.[37] Similarly, poetic images and aesthetic emotion were expressed in Arabic, with factual detail and narrative in French or Italian.

In borrowing this method of analysis from the study of multilingual literary manuscripts,[38] I aim to show how literary and creative writing can converge; yet this plurilingual hermeneutics could, I believe, be of use in therapeutic contexts.[39] The writing produced in plurilingual creative writing workshops could serve as tools in a way similar to children's drawings, or Donald Winnicott's famous 'squiggles', with the therapist continuing the child's drawing and vice versa.[40] The comparison is all the more striking, as these workshop-produced texts are the fruit of co-creation between facilitator and participant.[41] One participant, for instance, had several languages at her disposal and in her text used each one several times; a system emerged, and it was possible to correlate the languages with different modes of writing or themes. However, discussion with the author about the text revealed that none of those languages were the one she had heard in infancy, any more than she used that language – the one used for lullabies and nursery rhymes in her childhood – with her own, silent, child. The workshop, it would seem, had brought to light a significant gap in this mother's linguistic repertory, and this absent, perhaps atrophied, Mother tongue was undoubtedly an important lead to be followed up in therapy.[42]

---

[37] This and the following examples and their analyses can be seen, along with reproductions of the manuscripts, in Sara Greaves and Jean-Luc Di Stefano, 'Écrire en langues pour penser entre les langues: Un atelier d'écriture plurilingue au CAMSP'. In Violaine Houdart-Merot and Anne-Marie Petitjean (eds.), *Écritures contemporaines et processus de création, Cahiers d'Agora: revue en humanités*, n° 1, 2018, www.u-cergy.fr/fr/laboratoires/agora/cahiers-d-agora/numero-1/ecrire-en-langues-pour-penser-entre-les-langues-un-atelier-d-ecriture-plurilingue-au-camsp .html.

[38] Cf. Olga Anokhina and François Rastier (eds.), *Écrire en langues: Littérature et plurilinguisme* (Paris: Édition des archives contemporaines, 2015).

[39] For a discussion of the use of creative writing workshops in psychotherapy, see Nayla Chidiac, *Ateliers d'écriture thérapeutiques* (Paris: Elsevier Masson, [2010] 2013).

[40] Donald Winnicott, *Playing and Reality* (London: Tavistock, 1971).

[41] 'The prompts are the workshop facilitator's creative input and they are a kind of literary writing'. Corine Robet, in André Bellatorre et al., *Devenir animateur*, 13.

[42] Cf. research on the attrition of the Mother tongue, such as Barbara Köpke and Monika Schmid, 'L'attrition de la première langue en tant que phénomène psycholinguistique'. *LIA - Langage,*

Instances of partial or non-transmission of the Mother tongue are not rare in second- or third-generation migrant families; they are also a rich source of poetic inspiration among postcolonial or transcultural poets, and the notions of both bilingual overlap and the absent or beleaguered Mother tongue are possible points of convergence between migrant families and students of a foreign language.[43]

3.3   Transcultural Poets

3.3.1   Lessons for Language Learning

What lessons, then, can be drawn from this action research in a medical context for university teaching? How can the conditions of early language learning that were activated in the plurilingual creative writing workshops be helpfully recreated in the classroom? More broadly, how can language teaching be adapted to make it more meaningful to the young people of today, whose world is more unstable and mobile than before, with frontiers around identity, gender, or language impermanent and fluctuating? Using creative writing, and as a starting point the model of the creative writing workshop as conceived and taught by Anne Roche et al. and André Bellatorre et al.,[44] adapted and transformed in collaboration with Marie-Laure Schultze into a plurilingual creative writing workshop and classes in creative translation,[45] I have further developed this creative plurilingual pedagogy in English literature and translation teaching at Aix-Marseille University, with courses entitled 'Transcreation and Interculturality' and 'Transcultural Poetry: Criticism and Creation', among others. All these courses aim to achieve an effective compromise between the safe, signifying space of the mother–baby sound envelope at work in the healthcare workshop and the higher education requirements of a course in English studies. Such a course could not afford to encourage the regressive approach to writing described above without at the same time opening cultural and intellectual doors onto the English-speaking world. The course I will now focus on is an optional course for third-year undergraduates,

---

Interaction et Acquisition / Language, Interaction and Acquisition, 2.2, 2011, 197–220, https://doi.org/10.1075/lia.2.2.02kop.

[43] See Keltoum Staali's text for an example of non-transmission of the Mother tongue: 'Can I Write in French...?' in the appendix to this chapter.

[44] Cf. André Bellatorre et al., *Devenir animateur*, and Anne Roche et al., *L'atelier d'écriture*.

[45] Cf. Sara Greaves and Marie-Laure Schultze, 'Roll Up, Roll Up for the Language Circus!' in Foued Laroussi and Fabien Liénard (eds.), *Language Policy, Education and Multilingualism in Mayotte* (Limoges: Lambert-Lucas, 2013), and 'Du gravier ou du savon dans la bouche', in Cyril Trimaille and Jean-Michel Eloy (eds.), *Carnets d'Atelier sociolinguistique (CAS), Idéologies linguistiques et discriminations* (Paris: L'Harmattan, 2012), 169–86. My thanks to Marie-Laure Schultze for her originality and creative thinking.

consisting of one two-hour session per week over a twelve-week semester entitled 'Transcultural Poetry: Criticism and Creation'.

The study of transcultural poetry lends itself particularly well to questions of in-betweenness, biculturalism, identity, language loss, hybridity, exile, inter-culturality, nostalgia, and postcolonial 'writing back', as well as linguistic and stylistic experimentation – transcultural emancipation.[46] Poetry is where the public and the private, often the political and the private, meet.[47] It is a language of intimacy and sensual pleasure that transports the reader back to the early experiences of language, while challenging the norms and represen-tations of language and society. Poetry can be the crucible in which language is melted and remoulded: the language closest to *lalangue* with its insistent sound patterning and wordplay, while at the same time pertaining to the epic voice, a kind of collective rallying point. These are the interior and exterior spheres mediated by the Skin-voice.

This public–private duality is inscribed in the structure of this poetry course, with its focus on 'criticism' and 'creation'. By critical discourse, I mean the formal academic exercises taught in French schools and universities, the practical poetry criticism called *explication de texte*, and the notorious French *dissertation*, whereas the creative part involves workshops along similar lines to the healthcare workshop.[48] Here, though, the text that serves as the opening prompt is a transcultural poem on the course syllabus, and the writing tasks borrow formal and/or thematic characteristics from the poems and invite the students to imitate and recreate them, to transpose and relocate them in a different geographical, cultural, and linguistic context. So Scottish poet Tom Leonard's 'Jist ti Let Yi No' in Glaswegian dialect – adapted from William Carlos Williams's 'This is Just to Say' – might find itself relocated in La Réunion and rewritten in English shot through with Creole, or Jamaican

---

[46] I use the term 'transcultural' with reference to Mikhail Epstein's definition: 'Transculture is a different model of cultural development, an alternative to both leveling globalism and isolating pluralism. Among the many freedoms proclaimed as inalienable rights of the individual, there emerges yet another freedom that is probably the most precious one, though so far most neglected – the freedom from one's own culture, in which one was born and educated'. Mikhail Epstein, 'Transculture: A Broad Way between Globalism and Multiculturalism', *American Journal of Economics and Sociology*, 68.1, 2009, 327–52.

[47] Emily Taylor Merriman and Adrian Grafe (eds.), *Intimate Exposure: Essays on the Public-Private Divide in British Poetry since 1950* (London: McFarland, 2010).

[48] A *dissertation* is an academic exercise, considered to be typically French, that plays a major role in university exams but also in secondary education. With a given discussion topic as a starting point, requiring sound knowledge of the subject, the aim is to find a line of enquiry and organise one's arguments, generally in three parts, from the introduction through to the conclusion. Because of its formal and cultural nature, the dissertation is a demanding and often dreaded exercise.

poet Kei Miller's 'The Law Concerning Mermaids', in which a ban on mermaids gives rise to a postcolonial critique combined with an ode to poetry, might be revisited meta-poetically in the context of an imaginary 'Great Academy of Arts' in which a ban on poetry is decreed. The following is an example of a text produced in an online class during the COVID-19 pandemic. Starting with British-Nigerian performance poet Patience Agbabi's 'The Wife of Bafa', a rewriting of Chaucer's *The Wife of Bath*'s prologue set in Lagos – which, during a previous year, had been recycled as a Senegalese poem based on Baudelaire's 'Correspondances' – is here transposed, with Saint-Exupéry's *Le Petit prince* relocated in the world of social media and non-binary gendering:[49]

The Little Monarch – Chapter 2, by Ninon Pau

I lived alone, with nobody to talk to in a meaningful way,
until a breakdown in the middle of the internet,
three years ago.
Something broke down in my heart.
And since I was with neither doctors nor kindred spirits,
I readied myself to succeed, all alone, a difficult repair.
It was, to me, a life-or-death situation.
I only had enough joy left to last for a few days.

The first night, I fell asleep, my phone still unlocked on some LGBT+ web
   page;
so deep in the internet that I could never find the site again.
I was much more isolated than a castaway on a raft in the middle of the
   Ocean.
So, you might imagine my surprise when, early in the morning,
a message on the chat woke me up.
It said:
'Please, draw me a human being.'
'Draw me a human being. . .'

I stood up in my bed as if struck by lightning.
I rubbed my eyes, I looked again.
And saw this little bubble, still connected, waiting for my answer.
[. . .]

Since I had never drawn a human being, I drew for them one of the only drawings I was capable of.

---

49 Tom Leonard, *Nora's Place* (Newcastle-upon-Tyne: Galloping Dog Press, 1990); Kei Miller, *A Light Song of Light* (Manchester: Carcanet, 2010); and Patience Agbabi, *Transformatrix* (Edinburgh: Payback, 2000).

A random man. And I was stupefied to read the bubble answering:
'No! No! I don't want a random man.
A random man is to be found everywhere and that's not what I'm looking for.
I need a human being.
Draw me a human being.'
So I drew.
The bubble looked at the drawing I sent, and answered:
No, this one is still a man.
Draw another.
I drew.

My bubble sent me a smiling emoji:
But, you know that what you sent me is not a human being,
it's a woman, with round shapes...
I drew again.

But I received the same rejection.
This one is too precise, I want one that is a human: not a man, not a woman.
Then, since I was growing impatient, and wanted to start fixing my broken
      heart,
I doodled this.
And said:
This is just the colour and outline.
The human being that you want is inside.

And I was surprised to see a very happy emoji:
That's exactly what I was looking for. Do you think people will understand it?
Why?
Because I want to be understood.
I think it will work out, with some people at least.
I gave you a very vague shape, you can do everything you want with it.

The bubble stayed quiet, looking at my drawing I guess.
Not that vague. Oh, they've fallen asleep...

And this is how I met the little monarch.[50]

This text beautifully illustrates how creative writing offers a space for the
reappropriation of canonical culture and its adaptation to contemporary concerns. A wide range of British multicultural poets are presented (and pillaged)
over the semester, with classes alternating critical discussion and creative
exercises. However, the course also invites the students to pilot their own
studies, and the final assignment is a personal portfolio for which they are

---

[50] Reproduced by kind permission of Ninon Pau, a third-year English undergraduate at Aix-
Marseille University.

required to choose a poet, either among the set poets or from their own reading, and to select poems for poetry criticism, on the one hand, and to inspire their own writing, on the other, elaborating their own tasks along the way.[51] Every year it is striking to see how deeply the students engage with this assignment, the avidity with which many choose transgender or exophonic poets to explore their own experience of existential in-betweenness, split identity, or even medical conditions such as ADHD. Some clearly welcome the opportunity to lower their guard and 'play' with the English language, producing richly alliterative texts and savouring the teeth, lips, and jaw of English phonetics. English is not their Mother tongue: on the contrary, part of its attraction is its promise of a new, as-yet-to-be-invented self; yet for these students, through writing such as this, introspective and playful, which recalls and reverts to the primordial wordplay of *lalangue* – in which the Mother tongue originates its transition from bodily tongue to coded language – English can perhaps become not a usurping second language, in which they 'cannot help but sound like / someone utterly unknown', but a (M)other tongue as defined in Chapter 1: a source of sensual pleasure irrigating the speaker's relationship to language – and to their languages.

3.3.2   Self-Reflexivity

One major distinction between the healthcare workshops and 'creative' teaching at university is the question of self-reflexivity. Context is all, and although both groups, plurilingual parents and students of English, may well take it on trust that the care or teaching offered them is worthwhile and has been properly prepared and planned, the latter group are in effect invited to take a self-reflective, theoretical approach via the portfolio, and to assess the value to them of taking literary transculturality and plurilingual writing as models for their own aspirations to French/English bilingualism. The portfolios, for instance, contain passages such as this:

Noor Unnahar writes about being bilingual and I am also concerned by bilingualism. My dad is half English, it's my second mother language and I really value it, but I always thought I wasn't good enough. Therefore, speaking several languages is difficult for me even though I have always been fascinated about languages and the way they work. Bilingualism represents my being torn between two identities, and the way I was able to reconcile to the different parts of myself.[52]

---

[51] Hopefully, this experience will also serve when – if – they themselves become language teachers.
[52] Reproduced by kind permission of Nina Raoul-Duval, a student at Aix-Marseille University.

Or this, with its focus on the body:

When working on Joshua Jennifer Espinoza, I tried not to focus too much on the transcultural theme but rather on how she approaches poetry and her poetical universe. All her themes, ideas, obviously revolve around the very core transcultural setting of transidentity, with matters and struggles deeply carved in the queer community, but they offer, in their relations, an infinity of visions of poetry. [...] Because Espinoza's poetry revolves a lot around the body, working on this poetess has offered me a new window on poetry I think, another way to feel it, or perhaps rather to process it. I like poetry for the music it offers, which in time can make it difficult to say why I liked a poem, other than 'well, I liked how it sounded', and I think that I learned how to really process it through my body.[53]

Encouraging self-assessment and self-reflexivity is also important from the point of view of our students' professional ambitions: many aim to train as teachers, and their future pupils – probably reflecting still more diversity than their own generation – clearly stand to benefit if they can supplement their cultural and linguistic knowledge of the language with insights into some of the psycho-emotional and environmental factors at stake. A few years ago, I took a slightly different approach to teaching creative writing and creative translation, arguing that it was important not to disclose the teaching objectives (essentially rekindling psycho-affectivity within languages and symbolising the transition between languages through fictional scenarios) in order to enhance spontaneity and pre-empt the ascendancy of fixed, pre-established identities.[54] Self-reflexive learning may indeed seem more appropriate to the time scale of lifelong learning than to the short-term objectives of assessing linguistic competences;[55] yet I would argue now that time is of the essence and that more input is better than less: why not organise one's teaching in such a way as to teach how to teach – to give insights into the theory and research underpinning one's methods and choice of materials?

One way to do this is to initiate undergraduate students to self-reflexive research (e.g., the poetry portfolio); another approach is encapsulated by a new course designed in partnership with Professor Monique De Mattia-Viviès and planned to begin in 2022, entitled 'Vocation bilingue!'.

---

[53] Reproduced by kind permission of Ophélie Vaudé-Vitalis.
[54] Cf. Sara Greaves and Marie-Laure Schultze, 'Dissociating Form and Meaning in Bilingual Creative Writing and Creative Translation Workshops'. In Monique De Mattia-Viviès (ed.), Les Déconnexions forme / sens et la syntaxe dite 'mensongère'. E-rea, N° 9.2, 2012, http://erea .revues.org/2601.
[55] See the European Commission's recommendations for lifelong education, ec.europa.eu/education/ education-in-the-eu/council-recommendation-on-key-competences-for-lifelong-learning_en.

3.3.3   *Vocation Bilingue!*

The title of this course (A Bilingual Vocation!) presents a conception of modern language teaching outside the (monolingual) box.[56] As mentioned above, often it seems that there is in language teaching an unspoken ideal (or myth), which is that students should become not so much bilingual as twice monolingual. Yet more often than not studying a modern language does not lead to a professional life spent within the target language, but rather to a life moving between languages, whether as a teacher, a translator, or a cultural mediator of some kind. What might be the benefits of a pedagogical approach that not only allowed languages to overlap, but also set up an overlap between the codified and body-oriented dimensions within language? The notion of a bilingual overlap is reminiscent of 'subtractive' and 'additive' bilingualism, terms coined by psychologist Wallace E. Lambert as a result of his work with migrant communities and developed in ESL teaching by Jim Cummins.[57] These contrasting terms draw attention to the developmental and academic stakes: additive bilingualism develops the first language and culture along with the second language, while subtractive bilingualism seeks to replace the first language with the second language, often with negative effects. This *Vocation bilingue!'* course will aim to create an additive bilingual environment by creating fluidity between these often separate, polarised linguistic dimensions. The course is intended as action research in which the same group of undergraduates will be followed from first year to third year. They will be involved in the conceptual framework, and appropriate forms of assessment will be elaborated with their lecturers along the way.

Drawing on her long experience of English grammar teaching, and of reflecting on grammar didactics, Monique De Mattia-Viviès sees in this approach a means to counteract the often-observed tendency to transform the living English language into an artificial code, highly inhospitable to language students who are unable to speak fluently, cowed as they are by the fear of making mistakes.[58] The course will comprise two contrasting yet complementary interconnected methods: first, as well as learning grammar via imitation, repetition, and encouragement, students will be invited to explain in

---

[56] This experimental course has been selected for funding by an Aix-Marseille University pedagogical programme entitled Dream-U and is shortly due to be set up in the English department (Département d'Études du Monde Anglophone) of Aix-Marseille University.

[57] Jim Cummins, 'The Acquisition of English as a Second Language'. In Karen Spangenberg-Urbschat and Robert Pritchard (eds.), *Kids Come in All Languages: Reading Instruction for ESL students* (Newark, DE: International Reading Association, 1994), 36–62. See also www.youtube.com/watch?v=H0Ndm8Roe2M. My thanks to Monique De Mattia-Viviès for drawing my attention to this work.

[58] Monique De Mattia-Viviès, *Leçons de grammaire anglaise, Volumes 1, 2 et 3: De la recherche à l'enseignement* (Aix-en-Provence: Presses Universitaires de Provence, 2018–19).

French their own understanding of the grammar point under scrutiny. Rather than painstakingly urging them on with technical (external) explanations, reciprocal reteaching will be set up until students are able to explain grammar points in their own words, proving that they are embedded. This metalinguistic understanding may not immediately improve a student's bilingualism, but it is one of its prerequisites, given that mastering grammatical codes gives self-confidence; and as our teaching and research demonstrate, confidence in the Mother tongue is important for second language fluency. The fact that the metalinguistic explanations are in French does not inhibit access to English; on the contrary, reinforcing subjectivity in the Mother tongue makes it the necessary foundation upon which to build the second language.

The second part of the course is devoted to plurilingual creative writing, in which whichever languages each student has at their disposal are used and mixed. As described above, the plurilingual creative writing workshop is designed to encourage reactivation by second language learning of the early stages of the language learning process in infancy, in which the child is enveloped within the sounds of the language before speaking it, in a containing, reassuring environment. Writing exercises combining English poetry and grammar points may be used, with the aim of facilitating a playful, bodily relationship with the second language, and an enhanced fluidity between it and the Mother tongue. The idea of this course is thus to harness together the two linguistic extremes of grammatical correctness and regressive *lalangue,* so as to obtain a corporeal, interiorised relationship with the second language while attaining a good command of its codes. Students will thereby be helped to inhabit the English language with an enhanced level of fluency – and pleasure – moving seamlessly from one to the other as English becomes a (M)other tongue.[59]

We have all forgotten what it felt like to be an infant entering into language; with the experience of plurilingual pedagogies, students, parents, medical staff, or fellow lecturers can find themselves revisiting that founding moment of the early stages of language learning, plunged into a creative act of imitation and improvisation, copying and (co-)creation.[60] Within the safe space of the workshop, we can try to reconnect language with the body (from 'language' back to 'tongue') and recapture something of the pleasure of *lalangue,* its vibrancy and sensuality, and irrigate our second language speech with the

---

[59] Examples of students' plurilingual creative writing produced during a master's degree course in creative translation are provided in the appendix to this chapter.

[60] I have led numerous workshops with medical staff and, more recently, with colleagues: 'Looking Through a Mousehole in the Edifice of English Studies: A Self-Writing Workshop for University Lecturers', a workshop facilitated for an event organised by Professor Sophie Vallas, Programme D2 'Nouvelles frontiers du récit de soi', LERMA, Aix-Marseille University, 27 January 2021.

affect it often lacks, so that it too can be 'a language with soft corners / [that] feels like sugar in [our] mouth[s]'.[61]

Appendix A

The following is an end-of-semester assignment for a course in creative translation involving three exercises: plurilingual poetry, self-translation, and reflexive commentary. The students whose work is presented below were in the second year of an ECMA master's degree (Cultural Studies in the Anglophone World) at Aix-Marseille University during 2020–21. They were invited to choose one of the two assignments below or to draw on both and combine them into one poem. Only their poems are presented here, not the self-translation or the commentary. In order to appraise writing that makes use of languages unfamiliar to me, in particular for assessment purposes, I rely on the accompanying self-translation and the commentary for insight into the creative processes and translation strategies deployed. Any grammar mistakes have been left as they were written, the objective in creative writing or creative translation classes being not to demand 'proper' English, correctly reproducing the codes, but to use the language creatively to experiment with voice or style.

(1) 'Ars Poetica: Water for Poetry' by Stephanos Stephanides (*Blue Moon in Rajasthan and Other Poems*, Kochlias Publications, 2005). The epigraph to the poem is taken from a poem by a Turkish Cypriot poet, Gür Genç, whose name the speaker in the poem attempts to pronounce. The poem draws on phonetics and Hinduism to create a transcultural bridge across the divide.
   – Make a short list of words that are dear to you and which you would miss if you moved to another country and were no longer able to use and hear them.
   – Imagine you were trying to explain to someone how to pronounce one of them, using phonetic terms and/or phonetic translation from another language.
   – Write a plurilingual poem using English as the main language, along with either foreign languages or intralingual language varieties, working with the attraction of foreign words, the desire to pronounce them, and the difficulty of doing so.
(2) An extract from *Omeros*, Nobel Prize winner Derek Walcott's Caribbean epic poem (Faber and Faber, 1990, 138), beginning 'No man loses his shadow except it is in the night'. The extract concerns an 'aporia' of

---

[61] Noor Unnahar, *Yesterday I Was the Moon* (New York: Clarkson Potter, [2017] 2018).

language transmission.[62] In a dream, a twentieth-century St. Lucian man, Achilles, whose forebears were uprooted and transported to the Caribbean as slaves, meets his African ancestor, who deplores Achilles's inability to relate properly to the language.

– Imagine a character, in a family or a community, who is a sort of guardian of language. What does their language mean to them and what is their relationship with it? Imagine as precisely as you can the speech of your character, their voice, intonation, timbre, possibly basing your 'sound picture' on a relative or family friend. Write down some of their typical words or phrases, in whichever language, dialect, or register is appropriate.

– Write a plurilingual poem using English as the main language and either foreign languages or intralingual language varieties. The poem might take the form of a dialogue, or a monologue, involving a young adult and this guardian of language. It might help to imagine that they are on either side of a border.

The first two poems, 'E-T-S-A-P' and 'Parla pountchu', deal with an aporia of transmission, first of Italian language and culture, then of Provençal. In the first poem, this leads to desire for the unlearnt language, in the second to a conflicted self and feelings of non-belonging, with the granddaughter accused of speaking with a 'pointed' Parisian accent: 'parla pountchu':

E-T-S-A-P, by Manon Ruggieri

A life ago,
with my cousin,
playing in the kitchen.
The walls are French,
the foundations,
Italian.
Abundance of smells and sounds,
in the air,
the sun and warmth of Milan.
Tomatoes and rolled Rs,
then *pesto* and long As.
The papà cooks,
but the *Nonna* rules:
hands as loud as vowels.

---

[62] 'Aporia of transmission' is a phrase used by Marie Rose Moro and Rahmeth Radjack in Chapter 4 of this volume, with reference to families in which the parents' Mother tongue is not transmitted to the children, for a variety of reasons.

I would swallow these words
as I'd eat my *paste*:
with pleasure, love, and greed,
plus extra *parmiggiano*;
although the recipe
remained a mystery.
Could not cook it myself,
for nobody'd taught me.
Unknown ingredients,
mixed up randomly,
although their prosody
worked as spells on me.[63]

Parla pountchu, by Lucie Brillet

The sun's too bright here,
The air's too hot.
C'est le cagnard
What's Kyne-yard?
It's scorching hot.
I'm burning.
L'a oublié le capeou
What's cap-hew?
My face's melting,
My skin's boiling...
Què die?

It's stifling,
I should know,
I should belong.
When I'm talking,
Don't you know,
It's your tongue,
All these new words,
It's a new world,
I bring along.
La compreni pa
Parla pountchu la pitchoun
Fait pas bon se faire viei[64]

The following poem is to be performed with exaggerated stresses, as in slam
poetry. It is a meditation on the pronunciation of words in foreign-yet-familiar

---

[63] Reproduced by kind permission of Manon Ruggieri.
[64] Reproduced by kind permission of Lucie Brillet.

languages (Polish and Japanese) and the difference a simple cedilla can make. It recalls Alain Fleischer's reflection in Chapter 6 of this volume on accent, and how it connotes belonging – and non-belonging.

Untitled, by Julie Verstavel

Foreign is far, foreign is near,
And as I plunge into the fear, of never having to feel,
This too strange of a sensation,
I lose myself in explanation,
But why does it matter so much
That a simple sound complicates it such
As if foreign was far, when it is just here,
I can meet you there, I promess it's near.

Dzióbnąć, dziobac, mais quelle différence?
If the sound of the cedilla is just a pretense
I know it's a letter, and the word is the same
But the word lost its soulmate, now it's all pain

I won't pretend It didn't occur to me
To wipe it all clean and how easy
It would be
Better to not lose yourself in complications
When this clearly is not a representation
Of what you can do, on a better day
When you feel respectful, and you bet (a)way

The sound that does not exist, was never on my list
Natsukashii, or was it 'tsou', I've got the gist
Or maybe I am lost, Would they shame me for it?
Or will they understand, that sometimes that one strand
Of my tangles thoughts is the one that stand
hight up and it bends my will to do better
and at the end of the day, I know it, it's not just a letter[65]

The following poems, 'Lost in madness' and 'The Woman', offer two further meditations on the language barrier. The first focuses on the confining confusion of incomprehension, using Korean to convey a certain eloquent silence that leads to images of artistic creation and a sense of release. The second is a narrative poem using French and Croatian, in which fusional love and fusional language are superseded by misunderstanding and falling apart. It is a love poem, but it could be read as an allegory of the progression from

---

[65] Reproduced by kind permission of Julie Verstavel.

lalangue to articulated language in early childhood – of a traumatic entry into language.[66]

Lost in madness, by Mathilde Cousin

Can you hear me now?
Standing here, reaching out,
The words I speak cannot be heard
Somewhere in between clarity and a blur

외로움이 내게 평화를 가져왔어
In the silence I found relief
To let go of the things I've lost
And forget about grief

I let my thoughts be translated into words
Down the river of my mind to shake the
Earth

더 이상 물은 없고 불만 남았다,
As blood is running through my veins
Geijutsu wa bakuhatsu da
Time to break off these chains

What is creativity if not freedom
To express yourself without reason
May art be turned into explosion
In a fire burning in the middle of the
Ocean

We shall find each other again
In another place in another land
Looking back on everything we said
And then you'll understand[67]

The Woman, by Julie Caillol

I met her
On the first sunrise of my existence
I was born in the restlessness of the sea
She took her first breath
In the hollow of dawn

We grew up
Like sisters, just us two
And the sky watering our feet

---

[66] Cf. Chapter 1 of this volume.   [67] Reproduced by kind permission of Mathilde Cousin.

I knew no other than her
I never wished for somebody else

She sang words only I understood
She spoke of poets and painters
How they sought her beauty
In our Eden

She was Eternity
With pure stars in her eyes
She dissolved them into the sky
Un chef d'orchestre
Guidant nos nuits sombres

One day, I drank life from her veins
She made flowers bloom on my skin

Efflorescence
Fascination
Srce
Srećo

Darkness
Le ciel gronda contre mes flancs
I opened my eyes
She was here

Stars dropped,
Died on the ground
Frightened, she spoke
I could understand her no more
Her words, the poets, the painters
I spoke too
She cried,
In her eyes, I was a stranger
Who could not feel her soul anymore

Silence, a threatening cloud
Seized us

I forgot about her
She forgot about me

The red moon
Damned the flowers
To a painful agony

Eternity was after me

Along the Thames,
Under a faint sun
And the smell of old books

A woman
With pure stars in her eyes
Places a petal on my heart
'Well? Do you remember me?'[68]

Appendix B

The following text has a different genesis: it was written by a French PhD
student and writer, in response to a question about which language she had
used for the interviews conducted for her research with former Algerian
activists.[69]

Can I Write in French...?

Sara Greaves asked me which language I use in my interviews with the
protagonists of the Algerian student movement in the 1970s and 80s. The
answer is: mainly French, that eminently Algerian language, mixed with
Derdja Arabic, the constantly evolving oral language that is mostly a mixing
of Arabic and Berber, but also French, Spanish, Italian, and Turkish, among
others. At the time I replied a little sharply that language was not an issue, as
we mostly spoke in French. She then said that that was not what she had
meant. Now that I am working on the question of language for my PhD
research, and thinking about my desire to write, this question comes back to
me, and I can see its pertinence more clearly.

The interviews take place mostly in French, with words and sometimes
sentences in Arabic dialect. This is firstly because French is the language I am
most fluent in, secondly because it is the language most frequently used in
Algiers by this category of the population (intellectuals, academics, executives,
etc.), and by this generation, who were born shortly before the Algerian War.
What else is there to say? I realise that my initial reluctance to think about this
was perhaps because I wanted to keep these moments of intimacy to myself,
particularly the interview with Ali Hocine, a communist and former leader of
the student movement. When an Algerian speaks Arabic to me, it feels like
I have been recognised – accepted as a member of a family. I feel proud to be
considered so. For a few euphoric moments I (re-)discover that Other that

---

[68] Reproduced by kind permission of Julie Caillol.
[69] An exchange that took place during a PhD progress session organised by Doctoral School
354 in Languages, Literature and the Arts, Aix-Marseille University. Keltoum Staali's PhD in
Practices and Theory in Artistic and Literary Creation is supervised by Professor Michel
Bertrand and French writer and Honorary Professor Anne Roche.

I seek in my literary writing; – she who has not existed, who has not been able to exist, or rather who has not been able to grow up speaking her native language because it had vanished in her parents' exile, but who exists nonetheless, somewhere, and wants very much to *speak*. This mode of communication, mixing French and Algerian Arabic, produces a strong sense of connivence. It means a lot to me. When I learnt French at school at the age of three, and lost my language, it is as if I had lost a thread, a link with my parents, a certain quality of bond – a bond that could only exist by sharing that language with them. My desire to write originates in that severance of the language, in the impossibility for me to be the person I should have been, or could have been, had my parents stayed in their country, or simply been able to transmit their language to me in a less fragmentary, utilitarian way. But can one transmit a language when one no longer lives on the land that bestowed it? Can a sort of *above-ground* language survive strongly enough to be shared and transmitted, especially when in competition with the French language with all its force, its prestige, and its 'weapons'? Yet when – through writing and all that goes with it – I try to be the Other, that imaginary fantasised creature, I find myself in a parody, albeit a jubilatory one, akin to the make-believe scenarios of child play; but can one be anything other than a fictional character when one writes? When one writes in French, one's literary language – my language? In other words, can I write in French how Algerian I am?

Bibliography

Agbabi, Patience. *Transformatrix*. Edinburgh: Payback, 2000.

Anokhina, Olga, and François Rastier. (eds.). *Écrire en langue: Littérature et plurilinguisme*. Paris: Édition des archives contemporaines, 2015.

Anokhina, Olga, and Emilio Sciarrino. *Entre les langues. Genesis: manuscrits, recherche, invention*, n° 46/18, ITEM/ CNRS. Paris: Presses Universitaires de Paris Sorbonne, 2018.

Anzieu, Didier. *Le Moi-peau*. Paris: Dunod, [1985] 1995.

Bellatorre, André, Philippe Cheminée, Annick Maffre, Simone Molina, Corine Robet, and Nicole Voltz. *Devenir animateur d'atelier écriture: (Se) former à l'animation*. Lyon: Chronique sociale, 2014.

Bialystok, Ellen, Fergus I. M. Craik, and Gigi Luk. 'Bilingualism: Consequences for mind and brain'. *Trends in Cognitive Sciences*, April 16, n° 4, 2012, pp. 240–50. www.ncbi.nlm.nih.gov/pmc/articles/PMC3322418/

Cassin, Barbara. (ed.). *Vocabulaire européen des philosophies: Dictionnaire des intraduisibles*. Paris: Seuil / Le Robert, 2004. Translated by Emily Apter, Jacques Lezra, and Michael Wood (eds.). *Dictionary of Untranslatables: A Philosophical Lexicon*. Princeton, NJ: Princeton University Press, 2015.

Chidiac, Nayla. *Ateliers d'écriture thérapeutiques*. Paris: Elsevier Masson, [2010] 2013.

Cummins, Jim. 'The Acquisition of English as a Second Language'. In Karen Spangenberg-Urbschat and Robert Pritchard (eds.), *Kids Come in All Languages: Reading instruction for ESL students*. Newark, DE: International Reading Association, 1994, pp. 36–62. See also www.youtube.com/watch?v= H0Ndm8Roe2M

Cyrulnik, Boris. *La nuit, j'écrirai des soleils*. Paris: Odile Jacob, 2019.

De Mattia-Viviès, Monique. *Leçons de grammaire anglaise, Volumes 1, 2 et 3: De la recherche à l'enseignement*. Aix-en-Provence: Presses Universitaires de Provence, 2018–19.

De Pury, Sybille. 'Les Apatrides linguistiques'. Academic paper given on 31 January 2020 as part of the series 'Language and the Century' (*Le langage et le* siècle), Bibliothèque Publique d'Information, Centre Georges Pompidou. www .ethnopsychiatrie.net/actu/Boburg.htm

Engel, Pascal. 'Le Mythe de l'intraduisible'. *En attendant Nadeau: Journal de la littérature, des idées et des arts*, 2017. www.en-attendant-nadeau.fr/2017/07/18/ mythe-intraduisible-cassin/

Epstein, Mikhail. 'Transculture: A broad way between globalism and multiculturalism'. *American Journal of Economics and Sociology*, Vol. 68, n° 1, 2009, pp. 327–52. *JSTOR*, www.jstor.org/stable/27739771

Greaves, Sara. *Côté guerre côté jardin, excursions dans la poésie de James Fenton*. Aix-en-Provence: Presses Universitaires de Provence, 2016.

Greaves, Sara, and Florent Da Sylva. 'Encadrer des projets d'écriture collective en anglais: D'une évaluation pour la forme à une évaluation formative'. In Anne Demeester, Bernard De Giorgi, and Yannick Gouchan (eds.), *L'évaluation à l'épreuve du context: Pratiques et réflexions*. Aix-en-Provence: Presses Universitaires de Provence, 2020.

Greaves, Sara, and Jean-Luc Di Stefano. Atelier d'écriture plurilingue sur l'exil (Complete outline of a plurilingual creative writing workshop on exil). *Non-Lieux de l'exil*. Paris: Fondation Maison des Sciences de l'Homme, 2015. http://nle .hypotheses.org/3711

Greaves, Sara, and Jean-Luc Di Stefano. 'Écrire en langues pour penser entre les langues: Un atelier d'écriture plurilingue au CAMSP'. In Violaine Houdart-Merot and Anne-Marie Petitjean (eds.), *Écritures contemporaines et processus de création. Cahiers d'Agora: revue en humanités*, n° 1, 2018. cyagora.cyu.fr/ cahiers-dagora-revue-en-humanites

Greaves, Sara, and Marie-Laure Schultze. 'Dissociating Form and Meaning in Bilingual Creative Writing and Creative Translation Workshops'. In Monique De Mattia-Viviès (ed.), *Les Déconnexions forme/sens et la syntaxe dite 'mensongère'. E-rea*, N° 9.2, 2012. erea.revues.org/2601.

'Du gravier ou du savon dans la bouche'. In Cyril Trimaille and Jean-Michel Eloy (eds.), *Carnets d'Atelier sociolinguistique (CAS), Idéologies linguistiques et discriminations*. Paris: L'Harmattan, 2012.

'Roll Up, Roll Up for the Language Circus!' In Foued Laroussi and Fabien Liénard (eds.), *Language Policy, Education and Multilingualism in Mayotte*. Limoges: Lambert-Lucas, 2013.

Jenkins, Jennifer. *World Englishes: A Resource Book for Students*. New York: Routledge, 2009.

Köpke, Barbara, and Monika Schmid. 'L'attrition de la première langue en tant que phénomène psycholinguistique'. *LIA: Langage, Interaction et Acquisition / Language, Interaction and Acquisition*, Vol. 2, n° 2, 2011, pp. 197–220. hal .archives-ouvertes.fr/hal-00923124

Kramsch, Claire, Danielle Levy, and Geneviève Zarate. (eds.). *Précis du plurilinguisme et du pluriculturalisme*. Paris: Éditions des archives contemporaines, 2008.

Kristeva, Julia. *Strangers to Ourselves*. Translated by Leon S. Roudiez. New York: Columbia University Press, [1988] 1991.

'Le sujet en procès'. *Polylogue*. Paris: Seuil, 1977.

Lecercle, Jean-Jacques. *The Violence of Language*. London: Routledge, 1990.

Legendre, Pierre. *Tour du monde des concepts*. Paris: Fayard, 2014.

Macé, Marielle. 'Styles littéraires et formes de vie – Sartre au balcon', 2012. ceredi .labos.univ-rouen.fr/public/?styles-litteraires-et-formes-de.html

Medgyes, Péter. 'Native or Non-Native, Who's Worth More?' *English Language Teaching Journal* Vol. 46, n° 4, 1992. www.researchgate.net/publication/ 249252344_Native_or_non-native_Who's_worth_more

Miller, Kei. 'The Law Concerning Mermaids'. *A Light Song of Light*. Manchester: Carcanet, 2010.

Moro, Marie Rose. *Parents en exil: Psychopathologie et migrations*. Paris: Presses Universitaires de France, 1994.

Nouss, Alexis. *La condition de l'exilé*. Paris: Fondation Maison des Sciences de l'Homme, 2015.

Prete, Antonio. *À l'ombre de l'autre langue: Pour un art de la traduction*. Translated by Danièle Robert. Cadenet: Chemin de Ronde, [2011] 2013.

Prud'homme, Johanne, and Lyne Légaré. 'Le sujet en procès'. In Louis Hébert (ed.), *Signo*. Quebec: Rimouski, 2006. www.signosemio.com/kristeva/subject-in-process.asp

Richards, Jack C., and Theodore S. Rodgers. *Approaches and Methods in Language Teaching*. Cambridge: Cambridge University Press, [1986] 2007.

Robet, Corine 'Écrire. Faire écrire: Atelier d'écriture didactique'. In André Bellatorre et al. (eds.), *Devenir animateur d'atelier écriture: (Se) former à l'animation*. Lyon: Chronique sociale, 2014.

Roche, Anne, Andrée Guiguet, and Nicole Voltz. *L'atelier d'écriture: Éléments pour la rédaction du texte littéraire*. Paris: Armand Colin, [1989, 2000] 2015.

Rushdie, Salman. *Shame*. London: Vintage, 1995.

Simpson, James, and Anne Whiteside. (eds.). *Adult Language, Education and Migration: Challenging Agendas in Policy and Practice*. New York: Routledge, 2015.

Steiner, Georges. *After Babel: Aspects of Language and Translation*. Oxford: Oxford University Press, 1995.

Stephanides, Stephanos, and Karna Singh. *Translating Kali's Feast: The Goddess in Indo-Caribbean Ritual and Fiction*. Amsterdam: Rodopi, 2000.

Taylor Merriman, Emily, and Adrian Grafe. (eds). *Intimate Exposure: Essays on the Public-Private Divide in British Poetry since 1950*. London: McFarland, 2010.

Unnahar, Noor. *Yesterday I Was the Moon*. New York: Clarkson Potter/Publishers, an imprint of Random House, a division of Penguin Random House LLC, [2017] 2018.

Vinay, Jean-Paul, and Jean Darbelnet. *Stylistique comparée du français et de l'anglais*. Paris: Didier, [1977] 2019.
Winnicott, Donald. *Playing and Reality*. London: Tavistock, 1971.
Zauberman, Yolande, and Paulina Mikol Spiechowicz. *Les mots qui nous manquent: Encyclopédie*. Paris: Calmann-Lévy, 2016.

Websites

www.oulipo.net/
www.coe.int/en/web/portfolio/the-language-biography ec.europa.eu/education/
education-in-the-eu/council-recommendation-on-key-competences-for-lifelong-learning_en

Part II

From the Mother Tongue to the Second Mother Tongue

Part II focuses on the high stakes of the second mother tongue for children from plurilingual backgrounds. In some cases, the second mother tongue is grafted onto the first mother tongue – the parents' language, the language spoken in the home when distinct from the national language, or the language of school and the workplace; in others, when there is an 'aporia of transmission' as seen in Chapter 3 in 'Can I write in French...?' by Keltoum Staali, it is superimposed on an absence, a missing link in the linguistic filiation. Chapters 4 and 5 strongly suggest that in either case, the second mother tongue will prove a more efficacious instrument in terms of enabling social and cultural assimilation and educational development if the 'first' mother tongue is not ignored or underrated, but considered worthy of interest, ideally held in high esteem by the parents themselves as well as by the host country's institutions. Chapter 6 celebrates plurilingualism while meditating on that 'ghost in the language' or lingering presence of the mother tongue in second language speech, in this case in the shape of a foreign accent.

4   Language Diversity

Time for a New Paradigm

Marie Rose Moro and Rahmeth Radjack

It is up to society to make the right choices for its children, and to bring those choices to fruition through social and political orientations.[1] It is, therefore, of vital importance to defend the needs of children and their parents if public decision making – based on data from the social sciences, the humanities, and life sciences, among others – is to reflect those needs accurately. When necessary, it is also important to speak out for them, loud and clear.

A case in point is the question we wish to examine here, which can be framed as follows: can it be said that diversity of customs and languages contributes to cohesion and social equality? This question is present in the minds of all those who work with the children of today, children living in the multicultural, multilingual environments found in all our European countries. How can we take responsibility for these children's diversity, their family histories, and their relationships with the world, knowledge, and their languages? How can they be given more language power, more language desire? For this is what is at stake: improved access to knowledge for children – all children – and an expansion of their potential, of their capacity to live together and to interact with each other.

We will answer this question with reference to our day-to-day experience as child psychiatrists in a multicultural Parisian suburb, in which several generations of migrants and their children cohabit in a largely disadvantaged context.[2] Our experience of both counselling and research in this field has led us to work with children in contact with several languages, in particular with children of migrant families who speak a different language at home and at school, but also children who change languages when they travel with their parents, or who have been adopted from abroad, or any other of the numerous situations through which children acquire rich linguistic trajectories. However, this linguistic wealth may appear complex in the eyes of those who deem it the norm to speak one single language – which, in today's world, is a situation

---

[1] This chapter was written for this volume and translated by Sara Greaves.
[2] For a description of this context, see Marie Rose Moro, *Aimer ses enfants ici et ailleurs : Histoires transculturelles* (Paris: Odile Jacob, 2007).

93

destined to become more and more unusual. It is crucial, therefore, not to resort to facility and set up as the norm our intuitive responses, thereby transforming into nature or necessity what in fact pertains to culture and contingency.

Here, we will focus on the children of migrant parents, children who are inevitably forced to master several different registers, several different worlds, and sometimes several different languages.

4.1   A Language Is Also a Genealogy

One winter afternoon, the bell rings. It's the end of the school day, and the children are putting on their coats and mufflers. I (Marie Rose Moro) can't find mine. I say to my friend: 'I've lost my boufande',[3] a word I have just made up using the Spanish word *bufanda*, meaning a scarf – a very useful item in these cold climes of northern France. Let me just say here that my parents left Spanish Castile to come and settle in France, and that Spanish was the language of my first lullabies. ...[4] My friend is taken aback: 'You can't speak French!' and she bursts out laughing. And the teacher who walks past just at that moment says for my benefit, and above all for my friend's: 'Why, that's poetry!' Am I really a poet? Probably not, but I was certainly an ephemeral poet, just like my brothers and sisters and everyone who moves between languages. My invention was an instance of a new poetic semiology in which semioticians have so far taken little interest, despite there being a permanent, daily creativity in all those facing linguistic diversity through their personal history. Everything depends on how we view these occurrences, these every-day utterances – on whether we consider them as creations or, on the contrary, as errors to be corrected or, worse still, as the sign of an inability to inhabit a language, a non-desire for language, as linguistic incompetence or as an excessive attachment to the parents' language: the parents' language whose importance is overlooked.

For the children of migrants, torn between conflicting worlds, the French language is nevertheless the only stable landmark. A young French researcher, intelligent and brilliant, is wracked by doubt when faced with the need to write an article presenting her research. Born to Arabic parents in France, the youngest child, she mostly spoke French with her parents and always with her brothers and sisters. Arabic is like a secret language that is part and parcel of the family relationships. Full of self-doubt, embroiled in the difficulty of writing her article, she asks herself: 'When it comes down to it, what am I sure of in life? What reliable point of reference do I have?' And she can only find

---

[3] This is a phonetic transcription of the word.
[4] For an account of this journey, see Marie Rose Moro et al., *Avicenne l'andalouse : Devenir psychothérapeute en situation transculturelle* (Grenoble: La Pensée sauvage, 2004).

one, the French language – not her Mother tongue, the one spoken by her mother, but the language her mother enabled her to learn, the one her father chose for her.

A language, as is well known, is a genealogy. Having to acquire several languages – choosing in some cases to learn several languages (but that is another situation altogether) – necessarily involves accessing a metalanguage to transcend them. It also means having to mix a genealogy transmitted on the inside with another genealogy, acquired from the outside. This process increases personal freedom – provided one has the means to grasp this opportunity and cultivate the desire to create for oneself a complex, multiple genealogy and allow interactions between languages, between genealogies. Diversity – and there lies its charm and its challenge – leads to complexity.

Beyond words, moreover, there lies a diversity of concepts. The following example is taken from Castilian ontological vocabulary. 'Enduring', 'resisting', or in other words 'being' is expressed by the word *aguantar*. The noun, *aguante,* means 'mastery', but it 'suggests a lot more', as Michel del Castillo writes:

It refers not to an event or misfortune that one endures with entire self-control, but to an action carried out by the subject; resistance if you will, but with a combination of defiance and overreaching disdain. . ... In bullfighting, it refers to the interior force of the *maestro* who endures the bull's charge, not only without flinching and totally immobile, but with a contemptuous pride. It is with the same calm dignity that Don Quixote endures his setbacks and failures, and it is this same pride that I observe in Muslim countries. Wherever you look, you find the influence of Islam.[5]

It follows that this word can only be understood with the appropriate concept; however, when changing languages, the word can be kept and the specificity of the context erased or the opposite process can be adopted and the concept retained, in all its radical distinctness, and the word replaced. When the word 'supporter' is used in French, it does not possess the same nuances of meaning as in Spanish; it does not rely on the same cultural references or conjure up the same images. It is this dissociation of words and concepts that is typically observed in migrant children, and as they do the same with words and concepts in French, it leads to situations of hybridization composed of numerous deviations from the norm, numerous processes producing novelty, fluidity, and even in some cases poetry and new possibilities as new word–concept links are found, setting up interactions and unexpected convergences.

A language is thus a system of signs, images, concepts, figurative inventiveness, cyphers – a world one inhabits and transports from place to place. The question that arises at this point is the following: what can be done when

---

[5] Michel Del Castillo, *Dictionnaire amoureux de l'Espagne* (Paris: Plon, 2005).

history confronts you with several possible languages? Although this situation is extremely common in today's world, it remains to contemporary French speakers, taken as a single indivisible entity, a matter of perplexity.

4.2   The Modernity of Children Who Speak Several Languages

Children of migrant parents – like all children but with still more clarity, given the existence of a very sharp divide between the interior world of the family circle and the exterior environment – generally develop at a crossroads between two processes: a process of filiation ('I am the son or daughter of...') and a process of affiliation, of acquiring membership ('I belong to this group and/or that group'), according to a pattern of multiple belonging that can evolve as time goes by. When the child grows up harmoniously, these two processes – the interior one and the exterior one – uphold each other. In the exterior environment, school plays an important part; in our experience as child psychiatrists in a Parisian suburb, we have had to accept a painful truth: many children and their distraught parents are referred to us because their children can't adapt to school – and, one might wryly add, because school can't adapt to them.[6]

This process of adjusting is constructed around three fundamental questions:[7]

- What does a child need to develop harmoniously and find enrichment at school, and thus in the exterior environment that school is part of, composed of language, images, representations, and so on? The question of learning is crucial for his or her development: a child who *appears* healthy but who is unable to learn will not *feel* healthy.
- What is needed for a child to find enrichment at school?
- How and why is it that certain children cannot find pleasure in learning, in interacting, in building a relationship with adults that enhances the transmission of knowledge and the creation of new possibilities?

It should be pointed out, however, that unlike what is sometimes suggested, these questions are not limited to children who have arrived here from elsewhere. They also concern many other children: those who succeed, sometimes

---

[6] Cf. Marie Rose Moro, 'Penser les savoirs du XXIe siècle', *Le Monde de l'Éducation*, July/August 2006, 77–9.

[7] Bernard Charlot, 'Le rapport au savoir en milieu populaire, apprendre à l'école et apprendre dans la vie'. In Alain Bentolila (ed.), *Les Entretiens Nathan. L'école face à la différence (Actes X)* (Paris: Nathan, 2000), 23–9.

at an excessively high psychical cost,[8] and those who fail, who teach us a lot about the processes that all children are forced to endure, whatever their singularity, creativity, or difficulties.

The children of migrant parents find themselves from the outset in a complex environment. They must negotiate between multiple partial affiliations. For one little girl this is how it went: 'My father took me to school. It was my first year, I was in reception. Before that my mother preferred to keep me at home. I understand her, she doesn't speak French; it's hard to go out shopping when you can't speak French. It was the first hour in the classroom and the teacher stood up and said something I didn't fully understand. All the children rushed towards the same object. I followed my classmates without understanding. She said something else, causing the same surge towards another object. I followed the movement, very slowly. I hadn't understood. The teacher spoke again. . ... This time it was too much for me to bear, I stayed put without moving. She came over towards me and said something obviously unkind, I sat down on the floor and she got angry! She shouted, addressing the other children. . ... I felt humiliated, deeply hurt. I wished I could disappear or, better still, go back home to my mother. I promised myself that never again would anyone treat me like that!' Yet, within a matter of days, this little girl became a star pupil and played the colour game better than anyone in the class. Her excellence, comforting although sometimes excessively exacting, was the price to pay for her father's migration to France, as she was later to understand, twenty years on, lying on a psychoanalyst's couch. Although this little girl managed to transform her violent encounter with school into a life-giving experience, other children, for whom the psychical cost is too high, remain frozen around traumatic events such as this, sometimes only micro-events, which are a constant reminder that for them straightforwardness is not an option, and relations with others are often a source of pain.[9]

School is structured around a certain relationship to knowledge that typically belongs to the Western world, and to a certain social milieu (that of teachers). All these parameters determine the pedagogical methods employed and the relationships entertained with pupils, and with their parents. This is why it is important to attenuate the contrast between school and home, a child's two main places of belonging, in which different languages are spoken. Sometimes two forms of logic are perceived and posited as incompatible, yet both are necessary for the structuring of the child; this is why it is so important to move beyond the conflict and take up a position of negotiation and

---

[8] Christian Lachal, 'Les enfants qui jouent sont des dieux', *L'Autre, cliniques, cultures et sociétés*, 7.2 (2006), 195–213.

[9] Marie Rose Moro, *Aimer ses enfants ici et ailleurs : Histoires transculturelles* (Paris: Odile Jacob, 2007).

hybridization. Facilitating the bilingualism of migrants' children at school and in society would, for instance, be an opportunity for the children *and* for society.

Such bilingualism would enable bonding, bridges, and encounters to arise on an equal linguistic and social footing.[10] As things stand, however, being bilingual when one is the child of so-called economic migrants is considered in France as almost a congenital defect – despite the fact that second language learning is encouraged in primary schools. Does this mean there is an implicit hierarchy between languages? Does English have greater inherent value than Arabic? The importance of early-learner bilingualism for highly valued languages is no secret: it is considered an opportunity for the children and is encouraged. That is all well and good, yet where bilingualism involving the parents' language is concerned, objections are made and theories are brandished to explain the detrimental effects of this kind of bilingualism.

It is important for children to learn English, for in a world in which international exchanges are numerous it is useful to be bilingual. But it is just as important to learn Arabic if it is the language their parents speak, the one used to transmit their family history, the language of intimacy, thus enabling them to benefit from their difference and see themselves in the appropriate context – as the descendants of colonial history, for instance: a history they desire to move on from and not merely keep quiet about out of shame, or scream out loud about, with violence. Speaking Arabic will enable these children to speak French better and even English[11] – on the condition that the teaching in both the first and second languages is of a sufficiently high standard and priority.[12]

Why not, then, encourage parents to share their Mother tongue and facilitate learning a language of such great value to their children? In some cases, when they reach adolescence, children born to North African migrants throw themselves heart and soul into the language of the Koran, driven by ideology and sometimes without the linguistic proficiency to read it, while at the same time having no familiarity with the dialectical Arabic spoken by their parents. This may well explain – if we are to believe what we are told by numerous

---

[10] J. Lenclos, 'Metalinguistic awareness in bilinguals', unpublished M.A. dissertation (Amiens: Picardie-Jules-Verne University, 2002).

[11] Concerning the crucial issue of the difficulty observed in France with facilitating bilingualism in children of migrants, despite the fact that to do so would enhance their acquisition of French, and more generally their emotional, cognitive, and linguistic situation, see Marie Rose Moro, *Enfants d'ici venus d'ailleurs: Naître et grandir en France* (Paris: La Découverte & Hachette Littératures, [2002] 2004).

[12] Ellen Bialystok, Fergus I. M. Craik, Raymond Klein, and Mythili Viswanathan, 'Bilingualism, aging, and cognitive control: Evidence from the Simon task', *Psychology and Aging*, 19.2 (2004), 290–303.

adolescents who come to us for counselling, and who speak of this lack of the language through which they are related to their parents – why it is that they are propelled forwards, while at the same time lack the desire to relate to the world outside. It is this desire to relate that is threatened, the desire for metalanguage, the desire for the desire of the other, because of an aporia of transmission. These secondary appropriations are often violent and inefficient as structuring supports for adolescents, unless they are the fruit of a process of sublimation that can lead to a harmonious appropriation – something that is easier for girls than for boys.[13] Taking responsibility for children's diversity, for the complexity of their psychological, educational, social, and cultural needs, as well as for the heterogeneity of parental demands, is the principal challenge facing schools and clinical medicine in tomorrow's world.

Herein would lie the greatness of a society open to the world, and which does not shirk the responsibility of inspiring the desire to relate – the desire for languages!

This issue requires a change in us too, leading us to question our practices and adapt them to this new situation of linguistic multiplicity. When parents speak to their children in a language different from the host language, they not only enable those children to gain greater proficiency in their second language,[14] but also, crucially, to create a system of plural and symmetrical relationships between the diverse worlds that compose their personal history, thereby opening them up, with sensitivity, to multiplicity, fluidity, and, above all, universality.

By way of conclusion, then, the unspoken presupposition that the world of school and the world of home have unequal status must be discarded. This is a matter of ethics, but it is also scientifically founded since it has long been known that there is no hierarchy between cultures. Even on the cognitive level, the home environment has its own values and its own areas of expertise; it deserves acknowledgement and, of course, respect. Furthermore, it comprises the foundation without which educational attainments cannot be easily acquired, except at the price of excessive pain and effort. The home environment enables the construction of self-esteem through the interiorising of attachment, without which nothing can successfully be learnt. Transmission does not inhibit social mobility; on the contrary, it enhances it. No one would dispute this where the privileged social classes and 'high-profile' languages are concerned; it is too readily forgotten for everyone else.

---

[13] Malika Bensekhar-Bennabi and Geneviève Serre Pradère, 'L'univers du bilingue et la réalité des familles bilingues'. *10e session des entretiens de la petite enfance. La Revue des entretiens de Bichat*, 2005, 15–25.

[14] It might also be their second Mother tongue.

Bibliography

Bensekhar-Bennabi, Malika, and Geneviève Serre-Pradère. 'L'univers du bilingue et la réalité des familles bilingues'. *10e session des entretiens de la petite enfance. La Revue des entretiens de Bichat*, 2005, pp. 15–25.

Bialystok, Ellen. *Language Processing in Bilingual Children*. Cambridge: Cambridge University Press, 1991.

Bialystok, Ellen, Fergus I. M. Craik, Raymond M. Klein, and Mythili Viswanathan. 'Bilingualism, aging, and cognitive control: Evidence from the Simon task'. *Psychology and Aging*, n° 19.2, 2004, pp. 290–303.

Bijeljac-Babic, Ranka. 'Acquisition de la phonologie et bilinguisme précoce'. In Michèle Kail and Michel Fayol (eds.), *L'Acquisition du langage (Tome 1)*. Paris: Presses Universitaires de France, 2000, pp. 161–92.

Charlot, Bernard. 'Le rapport au savoir en milieu populaire, apprendre à l'école et apprendre dans la vie'. In Alain Bentolila (ed.), *Les Entretiens Nathan. L'école face à la différence (Actes X)*. Paris: Nathan, 2000, pp. 23–9.

Del Castillo, Michel. *Dictionnaire amoureux de l'Espagne*. Paris: Plon, 2005.

Lachal, Christian. 'Les enfants qui jouent sont des dieux'. *L'Autre: cliniques, cultures et sociétés*, n° 7.2, 2006, pp. 193–213.

Lenclos, J. 'Metalinguistic awareness in bilinguals'. Unpublished M.A. dissertation. Amiens: Picardie-Jules-Verne University, 2002.

Moro, Marie Rose (ed.), with Didier Bertrand, Claire Mestre, Michèle Fieloux, Jacques Lombard, François Giraud, and Eric Ghozlan. *Dire sa souffrance. L'Autre: clinics, cultures and societies, Revue transculturelle*, n° 1.3, 2000.

Enfants d'ici venus d'ailleurs: Naître et grandir en France. Paris: La Découverte and Hachette Littératures, [2002] 2004.

Penser les savoirs du XXIe siècle, 'D'une rive à l'autre' (interview). *Le Monde de l'Éducation*, July/August 2006, pp. 77–9.

Aimer ses enfants ici et ailleurs: Histoires transculturelles. Paris: Odile Jacob, 2007.

Moro, Marie Rose and Isidoro Moro Gomez (eds.), with Tahar Abbal, Ameziane Abdelhak, Taieb Ferradji, François Giraud, Felicia Heidenreich, Isam Idris, Kouakou Kouassi, Isabelle Réal, and Anne Révah-Lévy. *Avicenne l'andalouse: Devenir psychothérapeute en situation transculturelle*. Grenoble: La Pensée sauvage, 2004.

5   Ohé, the Silent Teenager

Nathalie Enkelaar

'Ohé' is the name I gave to the teenage girl I shall be discussing in this chapter, and whose case set me thinking in new ways about the Mother tongue.[1] She came to me for counselling in early adolescence, at the age of thirteen, not speaking at all. She was the daughter of what is known as a mixed couple: a French father and a Korean mother.

This slightly surprising choice of name will take us – via literal meaning and declinations – straight to the heart of the matter:

- *Ohé*, according to the *Historical Dictionary of the French Language*, is an interjection inherited from Greek and Latin and is used to announce one's presence or hail someone.

It suggests the idea of a demand, an appeal, discernible in the teenager's silence.

- *Oé*, the patient's first name, contains that most French of sounds, the succession of vowels *oé*. It is present in the name of her mother's country, Korea (Corée in French); indeed, the girl's first name and that of the country are very similar.[2]
- *Oé*, finally, is a nod in the direction of the Japanese writer Kenzaburo Oé, and we will be concerned, in connection with this young teenager, with both literature and Japan.

The difficulty I had with this case can be summarized as follows: the Mother tongue was grafted upon a language (Korean) that the mother had ceased to speak by the time her daughter was born, speaking to her only in a language of adoption (French), which I will call a 'host language'.

---

[1] This chapter was originally published in Marika Bergès-Bounes and Jean Marie Forget (eds.), *Vivre le multilinguisme: Difficulté ou richesse pour l'enfant?* (Toulouse: Éditions Érès, 2015), 223–36. Translated by Sara Greaves and reproduced by kind permission of Éditions Érès.
[2] The 'h' is silent in French.

5.1   'Her Sleep Pattern Is Time-Lagged'

What led the parents to seek counselling, in particular the mother, was a symptom their daughter developed that was affecting her performance at school: 'Her sleep pattern is time-lagged' (this is a reference – often observed in adolescence – to a deregulation of the circadian rhythm: they go to sleep later and later at night and have trouble getting up), and this disruption of her circadian rhythm is making her late for school.

Speaking over the phone, the mother – who speaks good French – alludes to more serious difficulties: her daughter goes to bed when she gets home from school, stays in bed all weekend, 'has no zest for life', and 'since she was small, has very rarely spoken'.

During our first meeting, although the mother emphasised this disrupted sleep pattern and its effects on her daughter's schooling, she did not herself mention anything about her being depressed, but this was more than obvious as the girl looked extremely dejected, sitting there motionless, staring at me watery eyed but without letting fall a single tear. No words issued from her lips either, and she remained almost totally silent, whether in her mother's presence or alone with me.

It was her mother who provided me with Ohé's explanation of her problem to her parents: the reason she was time-lagged was that she 'could not do her homework in their presence' and had to wait for them to go to bed to make a start on it, ending up going to bed very late. At first sight this seemed a very unusual and paradoxical explanation. Moreover, when relaying her daughter's words, Ohé's mother adopted a slightly ironic tone and rapidly suggested her hypothesis that through this behaviour their daughter was possibly trying to say something she 'could not put into words'. She included this 'impossibility', along with Ohé's provocative side, within a more general rebelliousness, for Ohé was not the most obedient member of the family when it came to doing her homework, tidying her bedroom, and what she called 'health' (by which she meant dietary habits). Ohé was the youngest of three daughters.

'She won't let me look at her exercise books', says her mother, who adds that her husband had always entrusted her with keeping an eye on her daughters' schooling. The father is an engineer, and the mother describes him as rather distant from household matters: he 'keeps well out of it', she says, adding with a smile that she does not leave him much to do! I get to meet this man later on and realise that through her symptoms, Ohé is succeeding in getting him more involved.

Ohé is described as different from the other two daughters; 'at home she's not a chatterbox', says the mother euphemistically, while her two elder sisters 'talk too much' (especially to their mother; she describes a strong bond, from which Ohé is excluded).

Ohé puts up a resistance – through her actions, at least – whereas her sisters may make a fuss but end up, the mother claims, 'carrying out her orders'. This rather military phrase is surprising and leads me to question the mother on the kind of upbringing she received in Korea.

True enough, the mother goes on to describe the military aspect of this upbringing; she mentions the importance of hierarchy in human relations, particularly among siblings – she is the eldest of four sisters. In comparison with the conflicted interactions Ohé often has with her sisters, she makes the point that 'where she comes from, things are quite different', adding: 'But we were little Korean girls, we were!' This implies that her daughters are not little Korean girls, and she confirms that in their household, the children's upbringing and the lifestyle are 'more after the French fashion'.

Thus, what this mother is saying about her daughter is that in some way she does not play her part. She is, to a certain extent, the one who disrupts the harmony that reigns in the home – a harmony from which the father, it should be remembered, is excluded. So this 'time lag' in her schoolwork is making a crack in the edifice of the household values, of which the mother appears to be the guardian and whose stones, as she sees it, are well adjusted.

The stone metaphor is no coincidence: when I ask Ohé what her mother, who does not work, does with her time, she says: 'You can never be sure where my mother is in the house.' And she mentions the fact that recently her mother put paving stones down in the garden, and that she does not understand why she did so. With these remarks, the daughter seems to be indicating *her difficulty in placing her mother, in perceiving her subjective identity or 'Heim'* (this term used by Freud literally means 'house' and refers to intimacy, an individual's familiar world). I see this difficulty as being connected to a language issue.

5.2   My Meeting with Ohé and the Mother–Daughter Time Lag

When I meet them for the first time, what strikes me immediately is the hiatus between this mother and this daughter, who seem as strangers to each other and to have nothing in common. The mother is attractive, feminine, and exceptionally smiley, whereas her daughter is slightly asexual, not at all coquettish, and profoundly forlorn.

Yet the mother does not mention the young girl's sadness – does not refer to it at all – and I am the one who brings it up, addressing the mother as much as the daughter. The mother agrees, adding that it is 'shocking' that Ohé does not get out of bed when she has always been such a responsible child. Ohé does in fact take school seriously.

I am likewise struck by the absence of any exchange of glances between the two – while the young girl looks at me intently.

The mother's words have a sort of hardness or coldness about them that makes me feel uneasy, and which, I realise subsequently, is due to the peculiarity of the language she speaks: an acquired, highly proficient French, despite pronunciation errors that sometimes cause confusion, and the inappropriate use of certain expressions.

In the home, Madame V. speaks to her daughters in French and always has, telling me (in response to my question) that she has done so since the eldest was born.

She came to France at the age of twenty-one 'out of personal ambition', meaning to study and look for work. She began by studying French at the Sorbonne, with the hope – given she also spoke English – of easily finding a job, but this did not happen (her first disappointment). She then studied Japanese, aiming now for 'linguistic versatility' to open up other professional avenues. Her meeting with Ohé's father is given a passing mention rather than subjectively dwelt upon.

She gave birth to her first daughter a few years later, then to the second, and finally to Ohé. 'Why did you speak French to your daughters?' I ask. She says because she was 'cut off from her familiar environment', and speaking Korean seemed strange to her. I fail to conceal my surprise: it can't have been easy to speak to a baby in a language she herself had just learnt – and at university at that! What about the everyday words, the 'familiar' ones, to use her own term, all those words relating to the body (I was thinking of 'weewee', 'sleepy byes', 'yummy', 'peepo'...)? Did she use her Mother tongue then? Did she use it for singing nursery rhymes? Madame V. invariably replies in the negative and looks taken aback (as if at something *taboo*) at my questions.

What verbal expression was given to her daughter, one of whose principal difficulties is that she does not express herself? How did she enter the world of language? This does not seem to have occurred to her mother. Moreover, she adds: 'It was when she started school that we were told she didn't speak. When she was a baby, we didn't worry about it.'

5.3   Silence Perceived as an Entreaty

What is Ohé saying? She remains very passive by her mother's side, without expressing any disagreement with her (unless it be through her silence...). Concerning these household values and the close surveillance exercised by her mother, Ohé says it is normal, thinks her parents are right. She says she simply does not feel like doing her homework when her parents are present.

When I see her on her own, she remains silent for minutes at a time, looking at me with a strange intensity, with big round eyes that remind me of what Freud called a baby's *Hilflösigkeit* (helplessness).

She explains, in one single sentence (she does no more than offer a few fragments of speech against a backdrop of silence, although an active silence with a provocative dimension) that she cannot concentrate when her parents are in the house – when they are awake, at least – and so postpones the time for starting her homework. That is why she is tired and gets up late, missing the first classes of the day. When I ask if something has happened, if she can link this problem to an event, she simply says that 'things have changed', but that she has 'nothing to say' about all that.

For our second consultation I receive Ohé alone. Her first visit, just before the summer holiday, left me feeling very anxious and I therefore gave her a second appointment later that week, which I rarely do. What worried me most was her sadness, for which she had no words, and her apparent vulnerability; afterwards, I realised that in her very peculiar gaze and that silence of hers I had perceived an appeal for help. And sure enough, she had been willing to come again, as she was every time afterwards, moreover, despite making a show of reluctance.

Ohé seems livelier on this second occasion and smiles slightly when I remark upon her appearance, which she has taken more care over (even adding a touch of originality). But she still says little, answering my questions with no more than one or two words. She says she has trouble tidying her bedroom, that she is not 'very organised'. She has nothing to say about her mother's account of her life story, does not seem interested in it, and, when I allude to her mother's phrase 'We were little Korean girls, we were!' (with reference to her sisters and herself), asking her what that remark means to her, she exclaims: 'But I'm French!' There seems to be no doubt in her mind about that. Later, I will find out that the three girls have been called 'Chinks' at school, and that whereas the elder two would answer, 'I'm not Chinese, I'm Korean!', Ohé would say nothing.

It was only on her third visit, after the holiday break, that I learnt a little more, in Ohé's own words. She explains that she cannot concentrate and does other things instead, such as drawing or listening to music. As she speaks, I gather she draws mangas, and although she does not like reading much, she does like Amélie Nothomb's novels – especially those that take place in Japan. She gives very precise details about them, always in response to my questions, especially mentioning a novel she came across through her sister, *Ni d'Eve ni d'Adam* (*Neither of Eve nor Adam*), which interested her very much, even if some of it, she said, went over her head.[3] I am quite surprised by what she is bringing to the conversation, which seems very important, although I hadn't read the book at that stage and miss the point to a certain extent.

---

[3] Amélie Nothomb, *Ni d'Eve ni d'Adam* (Paris: Albin Michel, 2007).

When I again allude to the sadness I read on her face, she acknowledges that she is 'sometimes' sad, without being able to say why. It then occurs to me to ask whether her mother is sometimes sad, and she says she is. I learn then that her mother's brother died that summer, in Korea, and that it was barely alluded to in the home. I am quite taken aback by this as her mother had presented herself as the eldest of four sisters, without mentioning this deceased brother.

This of course leads me, at Ohé's next visit in the presence of her mother, to mention this death: the sudden death from a motorbike accident of her little brother. Seeing my surprise that she had not mentioned it during our previous meetings, Madame V. explains to me that 'they don't speak to children about illness and death' in their home. She describes her two-week trip to Korea, how she arrived when the ceremony was almost over, how there was 'no room for being sad'. She also says that when she got back, she went on holiday with her husband and children, and she tried to put on a brave face but spent a lot of time on the balcony, in a world of her own. She remains stoical as she recounts this but seems poised on a knife-blade or at the edge of a cliff – it is quite scary. She then uses two phrases that stop me in my tracks: 'There is nothing to be said. [. . .] There are no words for it.'

5.4   Untranslatability in the Mother Tongue

My hypothesis is that the 'breakdown' of the daughter, the time lag that has appeared in her life and that prevents her from doing what is expected of her, has brought out into the open an impossibility for the mother: the impossibility of expressing her bereavement – to construct her loss and her lack in her host language. One might say that for this woman, there is something that resists translation into the language she has adopted for everyday life.

In his article on the Mother tongue and the passage from one language to another (in situations of migration or bilingualism), Jean-Paul Hiltenbrand refers to what gets lost on the way. What gets lost and is not transferable is precisely the untranslatability inherent in each language.[4]

Indeed, he shows how what enables a subject to inscribe themselves in a language and find shelter there (the famous *Heim*, which allows the subject to inhabit that language) is the kind of loss that entering that language requires: a loss that is, of course, linked to the castration complex, to the paternal metaphor, as we learn from Charles Melman.[5]

But Hiltenbrand adds that this operation, which is necessary for a subject to be successfully inscribed in a language, must take place *in that same language*,

[4] Jean-Paul Hiltenbrand, 'L'intraduisible', *La Revue lacanienne*, n° 11, Éditions de l'ALI (Association lacanienne internationale), 2011.
[5] Charles Melman, *Problèmes posés à la psychanalyse* (Toulouse: Éditions Érès, 2009).

and precisely during the first exchanges with the primordial Other – with the mother. From the moment the infant addresses the Other on whom they depend, addressing to that Other his or her first demands during the exchanges of unconscious drives (in which, as Freud puts it, are combined the body, on the one hand, and representations, in other words, language, on the other), from then on something is carved out, something beyond the demands themselves, which can never be filled or even put into words – something that will remain unsayable, untranslatable. It is this empty cavity, this untranslatable lack, that feeds the infinite repetition of the demand and provides mediation for the subject's desire.

This gaping hole, this untranslatable lack inherent in each language necessary for the appropriation of that language by the subject, cannot therefore be easily transposed from one language to another. And Hiltenbrand demonstrates how, for a subject expressing themselves in a language that is not their Mother tongue, there are, precisely, significant moments that cannot be experienced or remembered in the acquired language, such as bereavement – but also certain founding emotional experiences. He cites as an example the experience of a Japanese writer, Akira Mizubayashi, as related in his autobiography. He recounts how, as an adolescent listening to recordings of radio programmes, he made up his mind to learn French.[6] When he came to live in France a few years on, having 'abandoned the Japanese language', as Hiltenbrand puts it, and learnt to speak perfect French, it was only at his father's funeral, much later, that he realised that in the language he had adopted he did not possess the syntactical, grammatical, and especially social nuances sufficiently well for an experience such as that.

It seems that it is these shadowy areas of a lag between the two languages and countries that, little by little, from one consultation to another, the mother becomes able to move towards, thereby expressing, in her daughter's presence, her intimate contradictions and, ultimately, her own divided subject.

Similarly, whereas at first the mother presented herself behind a sort of shuttered-up mode of speech, placing herself far out of reach, she has gradually started to let herself be surprised – which has not failed to surprise her daughter and, finally, to move her.

5.5   Surprise and Ambiguity

Being surprised, letting oneself be surprised – is that not an apt definition of the mother in her relationship with that at first unspeaking being, her baby?

---

[6] Akira Mizubayashi, *Une langue venue d'ailleurs* (Paris: Gallimard, 2011).

It seemed indeed that for this young girl, at that significant moment of early adolescence, those primal exchanges between her mother and baby Ohé were being re-enacted. This girl who looked at me like a baby, made me anxious like a baby... Furthermore, the signifiers summoned by the mother gave one the impression that here was the mother of a baby: 'Her sleep pattern is time-lagged'; 'When she started not going to bed at night, I couldn't go to bed myself, I wasn't easy in my mind. I was solicited as much as I was when she was little, I was just as exhausted!'.

In answer to my questions during our first consultations, Madame V. had mentioned the period after Ohé's birth. She was quite vague; she described herself as 'overwhelmed' and spoke of 're-adapting to the life of a mother' because she had given up her job (which she hadn't done for the first two babies).

Concerning her desire to study French and the projects she had had as a young woman, she explained that after having met her husband fairly early on and quickly having a family, she gradually saw her prospects 'diminish', especially her hopes of finding a job that would enable her to come and go between France and Korea.

It was only after this mother-and-daughter course of treatment had been going on for a long while (for many of the therapy sessions, both were present) that the mother really spoke of her emotional turmoil after the birth of Ohé. And, more surprisingly, she mentioned the fact that Ohé was, of the three girls, the one who had spent the most time in Korea, as a small child. Indeed, on several occasions the mother had taken her youngest daughter with her to her home country, 'the only place where I could relax', to enjoy the support of her family, as in France she no longer had 'all the home helps' (e.g., a nanny, a cleaner) that she had had the benefit of with the first two children. She spoke with great emotion of the time Ohé spent with her relatives on her mother's side, in the arms of her grandmother; she spoke of her love of rice when only a tiny baby, adding that of the three girls, she was to this day the one who liked it most.

For the first time, when her mother was speaking of this, Ohé listened to her and even began to look at her; she seemed literally to be drinking in her words, allowing herself practically to be lulled by them.

5.6   From Lag to Lack

It seems, then, that by means of this 'time lag', this hiatus in relation to the values of the maternal discourse, this young girl has been soliciting her mother as a subject and forcing her to bear witness to her own time lag – a lag with respect to this acquired language within which she moved around freely enough, but without really being affected by it.

Does it not seem that the unbearable aspect of her mother's *presence* ('I cannot do my homework when she is there') precisely suggests this failure of a lack in the Mother tongue, in other words that in this language, for this daughter, the mother – to borrow Charles Melman's phrase[7] – is not sufficiently taboo? It seems more than plausible that this flaw in the Mother tongue can become particularly problematic in early adolescence, when the subject is confronted with the problem of their own desire.

Furthermore, through her symptoms, Ohé had managed to mobilise her father and involve him in her schoolwork, despite his habit of delegating to his wife. By the same token, he had perfectly interpreted what his daughter was expressing as an appeal, acknowledging that her real problem was, and had long been, that she did not speak – something he could identify with as he was not himself a very talkative man.

Similarly, this father had finally come to realise that far from losing interest in her education, his daughter was actually struggling with an unspoken desire to follow in his footsteps and study science, and that she set her sights very high: 'If she carries on like this', he said on one occasion, 'she'll end up at Polytechnique engineering school!' – his own alma mater. Ohé did indeed set herself to work and obtained excellent marks in maths and physics. But she had been careful not to mention this nascent desire in front of her mother.

5.7   A Third Language to Translate the Mother Tongue

The untranslatable aspect inherent in all languages, the place where loss is located (the repressed drives), is specific to each one.

Ohé had, in a sense, forced her mother to speak of this non-transparency between languages. Thus, whereas her mother presented her own crossing over to another language as a smooth, straightforward journey, she was to a certain extent forced to reveal what it cost her: her moments of turmoil, of confrontation with something unsayable. Above all, she was brought to acknowledge that in spite of it all, something of her own Mother tongue had been transmitted to her daughter, whether it was through the voice of her own mother when she was a baby, through the singular intonations that she could not eliminate from her spoken French, or through the taste of rice that Ohé loved so much.

What has translation to do with this? It appeared to me that this young girl had found in the 'Japanese' signifier a point of anchorage for her desire, and that this signifier was there to represent – to translate into her Mother tongue, French – something of the concealed language, her mother's Korean. In other words, she had needed the intermediary of a third language.

---

[7] I am referring to one of the definitions Charles Melman often gives of the Mother tongue: 'The Mother tongue is the language in which the mother is taboo'.

For Ohé was interested – increasingly so – in mangas and all things Japanese. Her mother even came to a consultation one day saying she had found the cause of Ohé's time lag: it was jet lag! This had me splitting my sides with laughter; there was no doubt about it – Ohé was suffering from jet lag with Japan, due to her habit of surfing on Japanese websites. Her mother was also familiar with this time lag since it was the same with Korea, and she herself often made phone calls late at night.

Ohé's mother admitted she herself was not a stranger to Ohé's interest in Japan, having taken her daughter to Japanese fairs (e.g., the famous 'JapanExpo', so popular among adolescents).

When she arrived in France, Ohé's mother had studied Japanese in the hope, probably utopian, of finding a job that would enable her to travel between France and Asia. After Ohé's birth, she had given up on all these prospects. Japan probably also represented the mother's shipwrecked desire, something that had finally been put into words during therapy.

I will end with a few words about the Amélie Nothomb novel mentioned by Ohé, *Ni d'Eve ni d'Adam*. Like much of her writing, it is an autobiographical novel. The narrator, a young Belgian woman of twenty-one, goes to spend a year in the country of her birth, Japan, which she left at the age of five. She puts out an advertisement for private lessons in French with the hope – by transmitting French in this way to a Japanese person – of learning, or rather retrieving, the language spoken by the adored nanny of her early childhood.

The encounter of the young woman with her pupil, a young Japanese man, very quickly becomes a romance – it would be more accurate to say a 'language romance', on the edges of two languages. Naturally enough, this encounter is a fertile source of misunderstanding, along with its surprise, even jubilatory effect, expertly and humorously unravelled by means of countless examples.

The special savour of the Mother tongue, its peculiar 'genius' – all those nuances that cannot be learnt in books that lend it its living, bodily dimension – this is most likely what Ohé's Mother tongue was lacking.

What this therapy with Ohé and her mother finally achieved was to carve out a hole at the heart of this Mother tongue that failed to be a *Heim*, which is to say within the language itself, from the encounter with an impossibility for the mother. From that point on, the signifying game – with its surprises, its ambiguities, and even its jubilatory effects – was made possible. Above all, the signifier 'time lag' was explored in different ways (i.e., the time-lagged sleep pattern, the lag or discrepancy between mother and daughter, jet lag). Ohé's initial silence had triggered the whole operation, making it possible to decipher it, to translate it as a demand addressing the space of the Other.

Bibliography

Bergès-Bounes, Marika, and Jean-Marie Forget (eds.). *Vivre le multilinguisme: Difficulté ou richesse pour l'enfant?* Toulouse: Éditions Érès, 2015.

Authors' collective. *Bilinguisme: Incidences subjectives et épistémogènes. Les cahiers de l'ALI.* Paris: Éditions de l'ALI, 2003.

Hiltenbrand, Jean-Paul. *'L'intraduisible'.* n° 11. Paris: Éditions de l'ALI (Association lacanienne internationale), 2011.

Mizubayashi, Akira. *Une langue venue d'ailleurs.* Paris: Gallimard, 2011.

Melman, Charles. *Problèmes posés à la psychanalyse.* Toulouse: Éditions Érès, 2009.

Nothomb, Amélie. *Ni d'Eve ni d'Adam.* Paris: Albin Michel, 2007.

6   Accent

A Ghost in the Language

Alain Fleischer

6.1   Speaking with an Accent

Two syllables suffice – nay, one syllable, or one single spoken word – to reveal the presence – part hidden, disguised, or repressed, or conversely, part accepted, even flaunted – of another language.[1] The lingering echo of a ghost in the language, detected the moment the speech sounds begin (Should I say a spectre in the language? After all, the phrase 'acoustic spectrum' exists...), whether living or dead it is impossible to tell, floats above the words standing in the foreground and fulfilling the immediate needs of communication. This ghost in the language has been summoned as a witness for the defence, or it is an indelicate, undesirable visitor who has dropped in uninvited, who has slipped in and is skulking at the back of the room and now cannot be thrown out. The ghost modulates sound as a common cold affects the voice, creeping in among the phonetic contours and altering them just enough to produce a shape distinct from the standard patterns, yet without modifying the phono-logical structure. If one were to look for a comparison from genetics or the natural sciences, certain forms of hybridization come to mind, such as the aftertaste of apricot in the peach flavour of a nectarine, or a slight malforma-tion, or possibly some abnormal characteristic, but whether hybridization, malformation, or abnormality, its effect on language would not be strictly unique as it is always recognisable as a particular type of hybridization, a particular malformation or abnormal characteristic. Where speech is con-cerned, this is known as having an accent.

The accent a speaker has in a given language is as much a sign of belonging as an indication of distance, and only very rarely is it an individual signature – only when it can be said of someone that their accent is 'unplaceable'. No one can claim to be the unique owner of their accent in a second language, since no one is ever the sole speaker of the language the accent derives from. Moreover,

---

[1] This chapter was originally published in *L'Accent: Une langue fantôme* (Paris: Éditions du Seuil, Collection La Librairie du XXIe siècle, Maurice Olender (director), 2005), 9–27, 107–8. Translated by Sara Greaves and reproduced by kind permission of Éditions du Seuil.

a person's accent is not a tangible distinguishing feature, like their fingerprint, if only because their potential accent in such and such a foreign language may never become a reality. I do not know what my accent would sound like in Japanese or in Swahili, but I do, virtually speaking, have an accent to be heard in those languages – an accent related to my level of proficiency, the intensity of my relationship with the language I am speaking, and the use I make of it. Each speaker is thus the potential depository of an accent deriving from their first language in whichever second language they might find themselves using. There are numerous accents that can affect a language – not just regional or foreign accents but also social ones, such as the accent of the *Incroyables* after the French Revolution[2] – but one will never be able to identify or designate as an accent the pronunciation peculiar to one individual (except when there is a combination of interferences that have fused together in a unique manner), and each personal deviation from standard pronunciation will therefore be an anomalous effect of phonation or speech, such as is observed in dyslalia. If we share languages, any accent in the spoken language must inevitably be shared too, proportionately to the linguistic community the accent comes from, and to the subgroup that shares the same first and second language, such as in the case of Parisian Russians.

Even as they reveal unlikeness, then, accents also display likeness or, in other words, distance from a given majority and belonging to a given minority. One can always compare a person's accent when speaking a second language with that of another speaker of the same language and then detect either a similar phonetic distortion, produced by the same distance, or a different distortion and thus a different degree of distance. From this can be derived in the case of these two speakers either their closeness or their distance from each other, both in a shared linguistic space and in distinct territories situated behind the upstage scenery of the spoken language: a barely perceptible backdrop, indistinct in the depth of field, behind speech's barely visible stage set.

6.2   Home: A Tower of Babel

From my earliest memories of my father's voice, speaking French in our close family circle, especially to me, right up to his very last words, I could hear in each of his utterances the memory, imprint, or ghostlike presence not only of alanguage other than French, but also of another world, another time. The reason I began this essay with the assertion that two syllables suffice is because I had in mind the memory of my father answering the phone in French, uttering

---

[2] The 'incroyables' ('incredibles') were an aristocratic subculture in Paris during the Directory (1795–9), renowned for their frivolity and decadence.

the simple word 'hello'.[3] These two syllables – to anyone familiar with Hungarian – were sufficient to detect immediately the indelible accent of that language. And it suffices for me today to hear someone say 'hello' over the phone in a certain manner for me to know that my interlocutor is of Hungarian extraction. My father's French syntax was perfectly correct, and he had at his command a fairly wide vocabulary, being a great reader of French literature, poetry, and history, and although there remained some amusing curiosities inherited from Hungarian, such as the phrase 'Have you painted your shoes?' to ask whether I had polished them, the hallmark of his first language (Hungarian) in the language of emigration and adoption (French), which had become his everyday language for work and family, was entirely contained within this accent that was so unique, so distinct from that of other languages from the same central European area, be it German or the Slavic languages. Moreover, I used to hear identical versions of it (by which I mean affecting the French language in an identical manner) on the lips of those of his Hungarian friends who had made the same journey to France, and the French language.

Everything would have remained relatively straightforward if, in my family circle, there had been only the one Hungarian accent and only the one host language, French, spoken in this singular way by one single person, my father. However, there were actually numerous languages diversely affected by each other through their reciprocal imprints, forming a warp and weft within the family group, with my sister and I the first to have spoken French as our native tongue. Although half French on her father's side and speaking remarkably good French (her spelling likewise – she was infallible at it), my mother had in early childhood spoken Spanish, the language of her mother. Then, until the age of twenty, she spoke Catalan in Barcelona, where she lived for part of her youth, until the Spanish civil war broke out and French residents were repatriated. This explains the fact that when my mother speaks English, her accent is not French but rather a mixture of accents in which Catalan probably dominates, possibly because she was using this language and studying in it – with its singular phonetics – when making her first steps in English. As for myself, I learnt French (at school) and Spanish (at home with my maternal grandmother, the person I was closest to). Acquiring two languages at once meant that I did not have to project one (the first one) onto the other (the second one), and I learnt to speak both without the trace of an accent. Strange to say, much later, after moving to Rome for a long stay and improvising in Italian, it was Spanish that surfaced over and above the French, as if it were the more deep-rooted of my two languages. It is this accent that Italians detect when I speak their language, to the extent that sometimes they mistake me for an

[3] 'Allô', in French.

Argentinian – more precisely one of those latter-day Italians who emigrated a long time ago and became immersed in the language of the Spanish-speaking countries of South America, a language substantially different from the Castilian of Castile. Or – another unpredictable result of this barely describable concoction – when I speak English to Americans, they often ask if I'm Irish!

To continue this brief autobiographical tableau, whose sole objective is to explain my sensitivity to multilingual matters and to accents, I must mention my family's only other direct relative, since I knew neither my maternal grandfather (who came from Libourne near Bordeaux and spoke, I believe, very well-bred French) nor my paternal grandparents and uncles. This was my Hungarian aunt, my father's sister. She had emigrated to London and married a Czech of Magyar descent, and behind the English she always spoke to me I could detect the same backdrop as that behind my father's French; her husband, however, spoke good French but with a slightly different accent, that of a Magyar-speaking Czech.[4] This small family circle composed of only five adults (my father and mother, my maternal grandmother, and my aunt and uncle) towering over two children, my sister and me, sufficed for us to hear French spoken with a Hungarian accent (my father), French, English, and Spanish with a mix of Czech and Hungarian accents (my uncle), English with a Hungarian accent (my aunt) or a Catalan one (my mother), and German with a Hungarian accent (my father), as well as all the languages spoken impeccably with no accent at all: French, Spanish, and Catalan (my mother), Castilian from Madrid (my grandmother), Hungarian as spoken in pre-war Budapest (my father and my aunt), and Bratislavan Hungarian and Czech (my uncle).

Along with these languages, diversely practised and pronounced by the five adults of the family circle, there were those spoken by my parents' friends who had also abandoned one language for another. One such person was a second-ary school friend of my father who had emigrated to Brazil and spoke French with an accent mixing Brazilian and Hungarian, while his daughter (who was my age) communicated with me only in English with a Brazilian accent; another had emigrated to Australia and spoke Australian English (distinct from British English) with a Hungarian accent; others, female cousins of my mother, one of whom had emigrated to Uruguay, the other to Argentina, spoke Spanish with South American accents, or French with a South American Spanish accent. There was also the professional acquaintance of my father, a Hungarian from Transylvania who had spent some time in the *Légion étrangère* and settled in Algeria, who spoke the French of the *Pieds-noirs* with the accent of a former Hungarian province that had passed into Romanian

---

[4] A Magyar is a member of the principal ethnic group in Hungary.

hands;[5] there were the friends of my mother's from childhood or adolescence who spoke French with a Catalan accent, or the sons and daughters of my father's friends (survivors of the war who had remained in Hungary), children raised in communist schools and whom I heard speaking to my father in a variety of Hungarian (less melodious to the ear, seemingly slightly uncouth) different from his Hungarian, which belonged to the previous generation; lastly, there were the young women employed by my parents, fresh from Spain and stammering barely a handful of words in French with a strong accent and who spoke Spanish to my grandmother – who would pretend not to understand them very well and never stopped correcting their vocabulary and their Valencian or Andalusian accent.

With our school friends or amongst ourselves, my sister and I spoke Parisian French, with its distinctive accent. But in certain social situations in which French was spoken, we would sometimes speak Spanish so as not to be understood by those around us (however, my sister's Spanish and mine were not strictly identical, for I alone was close to the right sources – my grandmother and my mother – whereas my sister was my father's favourite). My mother and father communicated amongst themselves and with us in French. My grandmother generally spoke to us in Spanish, including in the presence of my father who barely understood a word in that language (despite having used the pretext of private Spanish lessons in his youth to meet and court the young girl who would become my mother), causing certain family tensions, which sometimes erupted. My mother and grandmother only ever spoke Spanish to each other, and in our presence my mother would speak to my sister and me in that language too. That is how it came about that Spanish (also the language of the succession of household help we employed) was the language of the women of the family, a linguistic refuge within the home in which we could seek shelter from the authority and severity of our father, perceived as a sort of foreign lord who had come with his language from a distant, mysterious land, both near and strangely remote, out of our ken, at once the only man and the only Other. When my father, his sister, and my uncle got together, two or three times a year, they conversed exclusively in Hungarian. In such circumstances they too could confine themselves in the high tower of their linguistic complicity and their difference, excluding from their restricted circle the other members of the family. My father and those Hungarian friends who had settled in France would switch from French when in the presence of Francophone outsiders and to Hungarian when amongst themselves (I have known Hungarian communities in Paris and in London savouring the pleasure not

---

[5] The '*Pieds-noirs*' or 'Blackfeet' were the French or European inhabitants of Algeria during the period of French colonial rule from 1830 to 1962 who left France when the country became independent.

merely of their common language, but also of their music, their cookery, and their love of swimming or chess). My mother and grandmother only ever spoke Spanish with their female friends from Spain, and my mother spoke Catalan with her friends from her Barcelona days, who often came to stay or whom we visited in Catalonia. My mother never tried to teach us Catalan: this was her private language, the language of her happy youth. My father never tried to teach us Hungarian: it was the language of a country – a society, a world – which, after being so precious to him, no longer existed, having been plunged in horror. Some words, however, circulated freely in the family and were adopted unanimously by all the languages and all the accents, such as *paella* and *goulash*.

In my family circle, a contamination of sorts – an all-embracing 'impurity' – irradiated outwards from these two languages (Hungarian and Spanish), which were situated off-camera with respect to French and which at times had their own off-camera languages: Czech, German, English, and Catalan. Just as Hungary and Spain were behind-the-scenes linguistically and geographically, given that we lived in France and mostly spoke French, so France and the French language were also perceived as an off-camera force that had us surrounded. Let's not forget this besieging language's Trojan horse that crept into the small family stronghold in the persons of my sister and me: little traitors who were nevertheless praised for our treachery. We were the only members of our family for whom French was, if not our Mother tongue as it is sometimes known, at least our first language. Except for my mother, who was perfectly trilingual (French, Spanish, and Catalan), our accent when speaking French remained an obstacle to be overcome, an 'imperfection" to be corrected and erased. But it struck me very early on that the Hungarian, Spanish, or Czech accents gave a special charm to the French (or, from time to time, the English) spoken by the people closest to me, and I would undoubtedly have found it disconcerting, disappointing even, and would no doubt have been deeply dismayed to hear my father, my grandmother, my aunt, or my uncle speaking French like a cheeky working-class Parisian, without the Hungarian, Spanish, or Czech intonation that made that variety of French their personal idiom, derived as it was from their physiognomy, their attitudes, the timbre of their voice, and their identity. No doubt these accents also, to a small degree, gave a special charm to the French I spoke, although in a flipped learning situation since I had a better command of French than either my father or my grandmother. This also meant that I was favourably disposed towards any newcomer whose French was inflected by a new accent, whether Russian, American, Brazilian, Egyptian, or Hebrew. Yet despite the pleasure of hearing different accents, I take a sort of naïve pride in speaking English with better English pronunciation than my non-Anglophone interlocutors when we use English for communication purposes.

When I started learning English at secondary school, I was sent regularly to stay with English families to improve my English, in Reading or Brighton, which were at a sufficient distance from my uncle and aunt in London for me to avoid too much contact with the English they spoke, since the aim of such trips was to acquire what was reputedly the 'proper accent'. (The French will say that one of their countrymen speaks English with a 'good accent', but the same will say of an Englishman that he speaks French 'without an accent', meaning an accent so close to theirs, in their language, that they cannot detect it.) When a little later I was to be sent on the same kind of trip to improve my German, having very little interest in contemporary Germany, it was to Austria that I asked to go, and I had to make do with the accent of Vienna or Tyrol. Fortunately, however, a good secondary school teacher who had studied at Heidelberg attuned my ear to the German of Hamburg. As I write the word 'ear', I realise that if mine has been so sensitive to the music of languages, it is thanks to music itself, which I played from the age of five on the piano. Every evening when I got back from school, my scales and sight-reading mixed their notes with the outbursts and murmurs of my small family Tower of Babel.

I realise I have almost said it all. Everything concerning my language relationships is exposed here, in this personal experience, reaching back to my early childhood. All that follows[6] thus derives far more from what I was spontaneously given to apprehend and learn from infancy onwards than from the theoretical knowledge acquired much later from my university courses in linguistics and anthropology, now a long way behind me – a distance that frees me from the caution or seriousness of spirit that would undoubtedly have inhibited me and prevented me from tackling the subject in the days when I considered becoming a linguist. From this primeval immersion in the mixed waters of a variety of different languages and accents I have retained an interest in both languages and accents, in knowledge about foreign languages as well as in the way French is modulated by accents from other languages. French spoken with an accent from elsewhere is immediately agreeable to me, for I see in it the effort and willpower that has gone into learning to speak our language, as well as the speaker's inability to abandon all their baggage, all the memories of their country of origin – their success therefore in maintaining the presence of that country's ghost in their new language and identity. While hearing French spoken brilliantly and 'without an accent' by a foreigner is to me an impressive performance, which I always acknowledge and admire, I am more spontaneously touched and moved, charmed even, and attracted by French speech in which notes of a foreign music can be discerned – the stitch of a different colour delicately threaded among the others, or the discreet

---

[6] Alain Fleischer refers here to the essay this chapter is taken from, *L'Accent: Une langue fantôme*.

presence of an unexpected instrument, a stowaway in the orchestra and in the musical score.

Naturally, the perception of the accents of diverse languages in another language as more or less beautiful or ugly is more a matter of personal, subjective taste than the result of improbable aesthetic principles. In spoken French one may prefer the English, Russian, or Italian accents to the Dutch, Portuguese, or Chinese ones, or vice versa, for such judgements are in all cases based on relative criteria, most often linked to personal history. The Hungarian accent in French, which I have been steeped in from the beginning, pleases me more than any other and I love it as much in any other language, for it alone transports me to a place I can never return to – a place and a time – to which I nevertheless belong: this accent is a depth of field that opens instantaneously for me, in any language whatsoever, and whichever language it may be, that ghost world appears, floating above the visible and audible one.

French people hearing the Quebec accent in their language for the first time may make fun of it and find it laughable – some would say 'rustic', 'archaic', 'clodhopping' – but the reverse is equally true, and Quebeckers never fail to find the Parisian accent comical, a caricature of affectation, and neither can claim legitimacy over the other. Similarly, the Belgians and the Swiss speak French as 'properly' as the inhabitants of Toulouse, Provence, Alsace, the Auvergne, or Paris, and in today's world the reputedly 'pure' French spoken in and around Tours is a highly dubious reference. To bring this autobiographical fragment to a close, here is a personal memory. As a lecturer at Quebec University in Montreal, addressing Francophone Canadian students, I had attuned my ear perfectly to their Quebecois accent and within our common, shared language enjoyed savouring this sign of an *attractive distance,* which united us on a daily basis in the appreciation of our difference. One day, however, to my great surprise, one of the most motivated female students began to speak, addressing me in French from France, with no trace of a Quebec accent. I expressed my surprise at this sudden about-turn, this ability that I did not know her capable of to abandon her Belle Province accent in French, as if she were turning her back on what was a sort of identity badge. The laughter that then broke out on all sides revealed that I had been the butt of a well-meaning joke: the student had spoken French in imitation of her lecturer, in other words, counterfeiting my Parisian accent in her Quebecois.

6.3   Border Tax

Depending on what is at stake in the speech and communication situation, one may feel ashamed of one's accent or be proud of it, show embarrassment or self-confidence; one may feel able to rely on the other's understanding – even their enjoyment – or, on the contrary, fear the severity of their judgement.

Consider someone seeking employment who feels handicapped by a language not their own and who fears negative judgement because of their accent; or, conversely, think of a foreign employer with jobs to fill, who is aware of their position of power and free of guilt about their accent, considering even that they ought to be able to express themselves in their own language – that it is up to the other, the hopeful candidate for the job, to speak the language of the person who may turn out to be their boss. In Japan, businessmen or managing directors who speak perfect English will prefer to conduct negotiations with a foreign, English-speaking partner through the services of an interpreter – thereby having translated into Japanese what they themselves can perfectly well understand and having translated into English what they could perfectly well say themselves. This is a power relations strategy that neutralises the drawback of not expressing oneself in one's own language and reducing it to an accent tolerated in a second language.

Accents present themselves as both the trace of a compromise and as a gift: an admission of weakness through the renunciation of the first language, but an offering made by the latter to the second language. For there is really no reason why a first language should retire behind a second language, and the second language would be wrong to feel mistreated or offended by an accent that is first and foremost the sign of desire, an expression of interest. All languages, however diverse, were made to love each other, and the accents projected by the different idioms prove that these amorous exchanges, these crossings-over, are not only possible but fertile. Each language has its phonological economy and its autonomy, and it may seem that each one is self-sufficient; but speech follows a more overarching economy that, without foreseeing or regulating these exchanges, nevertheless makes them possible, on condition of payment of this border tax or importation tariff: accent.

The Second Mother Tongue as a (M)other Tongue and the Return to the Body

Part III brings a return to the body. Chapter 7 focuses on the way Freudian psychoanalysis can be seen to derive from the corporeality permeating the German language; this continuity can be compared with the way the second Mother tongue, construed as a (M)other tongue, retains a link to the presence of the body. In Chapter 8, Samuel Beckett's literary use of a second Mother tongue in his quest for the 'maternal side of language' results in a powerful – excessive – illustration of the (M)other tongue; in other words, there is in all foreign language learning a kind of return, a nostalgic yearning for and potential reactivation of *lalangue*, of the sensory cocoon of mother–infant interaction. And Chapter 9, with its description of the development of symbolisation as observed in animal behaviour, and of the way in which language neural circuitry takes shape in the human brain through neurological, emotional, and sociocultural channels, as well as through relating to others, further argues that for a second language to become truly inhabitable, it must be a (M)other tongue, anchored in the body.

7   The Sea of Language

Georges-Arthur Goldschmidt

> Es nehmet aber
> Und gibt Gedächtnis die See ...
> But the sea
> Takes memory and gives it
>> Friedrich Hölderlin, 'Andenken' ['Remembrance']

Human language is like the sea. Its shores and isles are innumerable, and we voyage endlessly above unknown, impenetrable depths.[1] Although always identical to itself, water never ceases to change, to flow, giving way to all that enters it – the better to mould the contours of things. It changes colour constantly and sparkles yellow-green or deep blue in the sun, depending on the latitude or time of day.

Like the human soul, the sea varies in accordance with the slightest breath. There is nothing that does not affect it; a cloud passes suddenly in front of the great sun and the sea's colours lose their lustre, making it dark and sombre. When the weather is fine, the slightest breath of wind ripples its surface.

There is no change of colour, no change of atmosphere that is not registered by the surface of the sea, and all such changes are reproduced, with infinite variations, from one century to the next, from millennium to millennium. But at the same time there is nothing in the sea that is not the sea; there is no cut-off point, and from the far north to the far south the water moves seamlessly, and the flow is uninterrupted.

So it is with languages. They are the same water seen from different places on the shore; one can go on great voyages around the world and always on the same ship: that is what the voyage from language to language is like. Thus, language is what rises from one idiom to the next, what emerges in between them, without one ever leaving it.

Language is that distant line of clouds at dusk; it is the ridge of an island coming into view one morning – but it is still the sea.

---

[1] Chapter 1 of Georges-Arthur Goldschmidt, *Quand Freud voit la mer: Freud et la langue allemande*, Vol. 1 (Paris: Buchet/Chastel, [1998] 2006), 13–34. Translated by Sara Greaves and reproduced by kind permission of Éditions Buchet/Chastel and the author.

Travellers from the beginning of time and from all around the world have left numerous descriptions of the sea, but the seabed they sailed above was always a closed book. They assumed, so to speak, that there was nothing there while dreaming of depths both mysterious and terrifying; only death could hurl them there.

Only recently, at the very end of the nineteenth century, have we begun to explore the seabed – at the same time psychoanalysis started to disclose the hidden depths of the human soul. Just as it was discovered that the sun's rays do not penetrate farther than 250 or 300 metres beneath the surface, so Freud observed that the conscious mind was only the upper layer of the soul and that our awareness fell far short of being able to embrace the whole of it. Just as it was thought that the depths of the ocean were uninhabited, so the life of the unconscious was completely unknown.

The silence of the sea and the silence of the soul are today 'invested' by the spoken word, yet this speech is pervaded by the depths of silence. For while *die Stille* is the silence of things, there is another word for the silence behind words, *das Schweigen*. To fall or remain silent (*se taire* in French)[2] is exactly what *schweigen* means, but whereas French does not have an equivalent noun (any more than English does, since 'to silence' is a transitive verb),[3] in German there is such a noun, as the language allows any infinitive to function as one.

We may then wonder whether the sea's silence is *das Schweigen der See* or *die Stille des Meers* since here too German expresses itself differently from French. *Die See* means 'the open sea, the elemental sea': *wir fahren an die See*, 'we're going to the sea'. *Das Meer* – more distant, more geographical, and more rooted – is not strictly speaking the fundamental element encountered through individual contact; *das Meer* has a character of generality that *die See* does not possess.

'*Es beginnt nämlich der Reichtum im Meere*', 'For riches begin in the sea', says Hölderlin in the same poem,[4] for on a much greater scale the sea (*la mer* in French) contains the *See*, the palpitating ocean. Although German cannot pun on *mer* / *mère* (neither can English: sea / mother),[5] there are detours that lead there; there are other routes.

It is as if the German language contained within it the primeval sea foam, as if it had conserved its fluctuations, its ebb and flow. Like a walker on the beach

---

[2] Throughout this chapter, Georges-Arthur Goldschmidt compares the French and German languages. When necessary, the French words have been given as well as their English translation.
[3] Translator's addition.
[4] Cf. the epigraph: Friedrich Hölderlin, 'Andenken', in *Dichter 1800–1804: Sämtliche Werke* (Stuttgart: Schmidt, 1953). For the translation: *Friedrich Hölderlin: Selected Poems*, translated by David Constantine (Newcastle-upon-Tyne: Bloodaxe Books, [1990] 1996), 61.
[5] Translator's addition.

who unwittingly breathes in and out in time to the beating of the waves, the German language is traversed by the inhalation and exhalation of the lungs.

The whole German language is constructed around the raising and lowering of the ribcage, on its rise and fall – the spatial movement up and down. The small child's famous *fort-da* in Freud's *Beyond the Pleasure Principle*[6] means nothing else: in German, everything begins with the body, everything returns to the body, and everything traverses the body. The word *der Leib* ('the body', in the sense of life itself) has the same etymology as *das Leben*, 'life'. The body is what is living, life *wie sie leibt und lebt*, 'life in flesh and blood'. *Der Leib* is another body altogether from the *Körper* – the body as it derives from Latin, meaning the functional body while also denoting trade corporations. But *der Leib* is the body as I am a body, the body itself.

The language is anchored in the body and cannot be uprooted. Nothing could be more foolish than to speak of the abstract character of German, for no other language is to the same degree concrete, to the same degree spatial; German is, precisely, incapable of any kind of abstraction. It takes its abstract terms from French or constructs them on the French model. Thus, in Hegel we find *immanent, positive, negative, das Subjekt, die Reflexion, das Princip*, and so on. And through this internalisation of the physical presence of the body, can it not be said of the German language that it retains the indistinct memory of the lost unity of *leben* (*der Leib*) and *Erkenntnis* ('knowledge')? It is the spatial character of German that lends it its concreteness; all Freud had to do was follow its trajectories, its contours, its rising and falling motion.

There is nothing more straightforward and immediate than philosophical vocabulary. Chapter 1 of *Phenomenology of the Mind*, 'Sensitive Certainty'[7] (it is true that German barely distinguishes between 'sensitive', 'sensory', and 'sensuous'), *Die sinnliche Gewissheit*, is written with the vocabulary of a five-year-old child from the first to the last word (with the exception, perhaps, of the words *Vermittlung*, 'mediation,' and *Unmittelbarkeit*, 'immediacy'). The deeper German 'philosophy' gets, the simpler and more concrete its vocabulary – the closer, at least, to this *leibliche Befinden*, the locus of the body itself.

All thought necessarily derives from a certain point in space occupied by 'I'. This *Ich*, moreover, can never be 'me', which remains enclosed within it without being able to name itself, as if there were a self, imprisoned within the language. As Wilhelm von Humboldt (whom we too often overlook)

---

[6] Sigmund Freud, *Jenseits des Lustprinzips* (Leipzig, Vienna, Zürich: Internationaler Psychoanlytischer Verlag, 1921). First English version: *The International Psychoanalytical Library No.4: Beyond the Pleasure Principle,* translated by C.P.M. Hubback (London: International Psycho-analytical Press, 1922).

[7] Georg W. F. Hegel, *The Phenomenology of the Mind,* translated by J. B. Baillie (New York: Dover, [1931] 2003).

pointed out, it is always from this coenesthetic point of departure that the German language is organised or rather, on which it is founded.[8]

The overall language derives from a starting point that is a place or a movement in space. This is perfectly illustrated by the figures used to help young Germans learn prepositions such as 'on', 'above', and 'next to', which govern the choice of the accusative or the dative case, depending on whether there is movement.

The language is constructed around a certain number of root verbs, such as *stehen*, 'to be standing', or *liegen* and *hangen*, to which factitive verbs correspond, which is to say those expressing the corresponding spatial movement: *legen*, 'to lay or lie'; *stellen*, 'to stand upright'. Thus, *der Wein steht im Keller* or *der Wein steht in der Badewanne* ('the wine is in the cellar' or 'the bottles of wine are in the bath'). In both cases, it is the verb *stehen* that stands in for the bottles. These are root verbs, for which there is no French equivalent, and they occur in practically one out of three sentences, especially as each one of these verbs, along with the many others like them, such as *sitzen*, 'to be seated', or *setzen*, 'to sit', can be combined endlessly with a multitude of particles. *Legen*, for instance, can be combined with nearly two dozen particles that all have around a dozen meanings, such as *ablegen*, *anlegen*, and *auslegen*.

The same goes for most of the verbs whose combinatory possibilities, always with a spatial connotation, are unending. It is easy to invent perfectly coherent and grammatically correct verbs, for instance, *umfenstern* and *durchlösen*, which do not yet mean anything.

Stehen, 'verticality', and *liegen*, 'horizontality', characterise the meaning of every German verbal phrase. *Hier stehe ich*:[9] 'Here I stand – I can do no other', *Hier stehe ich – und ich kann nicht anders*. Luther could have added: *darauf bestehe ich*, 'I will not go back on my word'. There he stands, standing up for his truth; he will not confess – *gestehen* – what he does not want to confess. He will prove capable of withstanding everything for his belief, standing straight as a rod, *durchstehen*, standing it to the end – enduring all without confessing. This word *stehen* is one of the swivel pins of the language, one of those high stilts in the sea of meaning upon which language builds its pontoons.

But around these piles, the sea never ceases to fluctuate (*schwappen*), to come and go, to rise and fall. This sea from which the language has issued

---

[8] See Wilhelm von Humboldt, *Über die Verschiedenheiten des menschlichen Sprachbaues* (Cambridge: Cambridge University Press, 2009).

[9] Martin Luther (1483–1546), the German theologian who initiated the Protestant Reformation, allegedly made this statement at the close of his hearing before the Diet of Worms in 1521: "According to a traditional but apocryphal account, he ended his statement with the words, 'Here I stand. I can do no other. God help me. Amen'", *Encylopedia Brittanica*, "The Diet of Worms", www.britannica.com/biography/Martin-Luther/Diet-of-Worms.

forth – to such a degree that in German the soul, which plays such an important part in Freud's thinking, derives from the sea. It has, in a word, a saline taste, and it rolls through the sea as it rolls in lymph or in that liquid that so many adolescents have tasted. It is true that the tongue can discern each individual taste, and the German language provides the wherewithal to maintain the delusion.

In his admirable book on Friedrich Hölderlin, Pierre Bertaux observes that in Swabian (Hölderlin was Swabian), *Geist (der Geist*, 'spirit') is *Geischt*, which is to say *Gischt*, 'spurt or foam'.[10] The sea spray one had to shield oneself from, with the help of a sou'wester, was perhaps the outpouring of adolescent rapture. This is at least how the spirit, *der Geischt*, must have appeared to Hölderlin and his friends from the '*Stift*' seminar in Tübingen: for them, no barrier between soul and body. For more on this subject, the pioneering work by Christian L. Hart-Nibbrig should be mentioned, *The Resurrection of the Body in the Text*, in which he reveals the unceasing presence of the body internalised within speech.[11]

Everything constantly evokes not the 'primitive scene' as it is translated into French, but the *Urszene* that Freud refers to. *Die Urszene* rather suggests the 'original scene': *ur* is a sort of prefix related to *er* (approximately meaning *aus*, 'out of', with the idea of deriving from), which can be used before an infinite number of common nouns. It denotes the origin, the primary state of whatever is being discussed, and the language has derived the adjective *urig*, meaning 'fantastic', 'great', and 'pure, unadulterated'.

In an exceptionally good article dating from 1911 entitled 'About Lewd Words', Sandor Ferenczi, following on from Freud (whose work on the young Hans, it should be recalled, is precisely an analysis of the way the German language takes shape), intuits that the whole language possibly originates in a purely physical and regressive tendency, and that all words were originally erotic, with lewdness offering a return to that infantile stage in the language learning process.[12]

Now if we compare French and German, it becomes clear that German derives, in its very intimacy, from the body's gestures and desires. Punctuation serves to indicate the places where it is necessary to take a new breath, dividing the sentence into clauses – or respiratory groups. The subordinate clause, with its infamous 'verb at the end' (What a lot of nonsense has been written about that! And how many serious translators have railed against it!), quite simply follows the lowering of the rib cage. German is constructed around the voice,

---

[10] Pierre Bertaux, *Hölderlin ou le temps d'un poète* (Paris: Gallimard, 1983).
[11] Christian L. Hart-Nibbrig, *Die Aufstehung des Körpers im Text* (Berlin: Suhrkamp, 1985).
[12] Sandor Ferenczi, *Schriften sur Psychoanalyse: Auswahl in zwei Bänden* (Berlin: Fischer Verlag, 1915).

with speech always originating in a muscular effort that mobilises the deepest reaches of the body. The surface comes into view after traversing its own depths – just as the surface waters are only fleetingly present, being in constant motion, conveyed down to the seabed before being brought back up to the surface. The sea breathes.

It is no coincidence that someone can be described as speaking *mit dem Brustton der Uberzeugung*, 'with the barrel-chested tone of conviction'. There is no text, no narrative in which one does not hold one's breath: *Ich atme ein und aus,* 'I breathe in and out' (*expirer*, the French word for breathing out, also means 'to die'), *einen Atmzug lang war nichts zu hören*, 'the space of an inhalation, of a respiration, and everything fell silent'. That up and down motion, that *hecheln*, the gasping breath that the guilty teenager tries to hide – this respiratory rhythm is itself the point of departure from which the whole German language speaks.

With its constant *auf und ab* (from 'top to bottom') or *hin und her* ('there and back') rhythm, German is in a sense suggestive of the unfolding of the 'primitive scene', l'*Urszene*, as stumbled upon by the small child, hearing it rather than seeing it. That may also be what is present in *fort-da*, which was so well elucidated by Freud, guided as he was by the rhythmic alternation within the German language.

In German, this rhythm is the foundation of poetry. Bertaux, for instance, has shown the degree to which the very distinctive rhythm of Hölderlin's poetry was related to walking. *Ein ständiges hin und her*, says German ('endless comings and goings'), where *hin* and *her* are prepositions, the former indicating a distancing movement in relation to the speaker, the latter the opposite, an approaching movement.

Hin und her and *auf und ab* are present in most verbal compounds. 'Don't look!' adults cry out to the child, who must be prevented from seeing what they want to see. *Du sollst nicht hinsehen*, the German child is told. This advancing and receding, this there and back movement, this binary rhythm of sorts – suggestive of some obscene practice that the German adolescent, a late developer, discovers more slowly than the others and continues much longer than them – is the true foundation of the German language, which constitutionally, therefore, for its native speakers, is brought to think of nothing else. Is it the rhythm of this childhood practice that founds German? Reading certain poets, one is tempted to think so. The third of Rilke's *Duino Elegies* has much to tell us on the subject.[13]

There is, in German, a sort of *Urwüchsigkeit*, a sort of self-propagation in the language that somehow always makes it relive its linguistic childhood.

[13] Rainer Maria Rilke, *Duino Elegies* translated by Martyn Crucefix (Enitharmon Press, [1923] 2013).

This can be observed in the example of compound words, of which the least that can be said is that it is hard to take them seriously: everyone immediately knows what they mean. By contrast, who – unless they are a Hellenist or a botanist – can tell what a halophilic plant is? German simply calls it *eine salzliebende Pflanze*, 'a plant that likes salt'. German builds its compound words from existing German words, and they are immediately understandable to everyone. Psychography is quite simply *Seelenbeschreibung*; an ears, nose, and throat specialist (an *oto-rhino-laryngologiste* in French) is a *Hals-Nasen und Ohrenarzt*. The peritoneum is *das Bauchfell* ('stomach-filler'), red blood cells (*hématies* in French) are *Rotkörperchen*, 'small red bodies'. It is as if scientific research had always endeavoured to remain within the bounds of common understanding. Hydrogen, *der Wasserstoff*, is 'water fabric'; oxygen, *der Sauerstoff*, is 'fabric that acidifies things'. Every German child is thus put in the right direction by the language itself. It would be fastidious to inventory all the French words composed of Latin or Greek roots, in some cases both, for which there always exists a concrete German translation. What is known as geography is *Erdkunde* in German, from *Erde*, 'the earth' – everyone knows straight off what the word means.

Mammals are simply *Säugetieren* in German – a word, moreover, that can be read in two different ways: *saugen*, 'to suck', or *säugen*, 'to suckle', the factitive verb of the first verb. In this case, German – and it happens often if not always – reverses the direction of the gaze. Where the French word *mammifère* (or the English 'mammal') adopts the point of view of the mother looking down on her baby, German looks up from the baby towards its mother. A tapeworm (*ver solitaire* in French, a 'solitary worm') is a 'worm in the shape of a ribbon' (*Bandwurm*), and to be sick with liver cirrhosis is in German to have a 'shrivelled liver' (*Schrumpfleber*). Each bone, each muscle is referred to by an easily recognisable name. The shin bone (*tibia* in French) is the 'rail-bone' (*Schienbein*); the fibula is the 'calf bone' (*Wadenbein*); the orbicular of the lips is the 'muscle of the circular mouth' (*ring-förmiger Mundmuskel*), and the zygomatic is 'the downwards puller' (*der Herabzieher*), just as the pancreas is the 'gland for the stomach's saliva' (*Bauchspeicheldrüse*).

And let us not forget the famous *Stilleben*, that 'silent and peaceful life' that is so unhappily translated by *nature morte* ('dead nature', 'still life' in English). Who was it who introduced into French this strange word, which brushes perhaps too quickly over what is most important? Is language innocent? What is it that it wants not to see, when it eludes certain words and makes up new ones? What does it want to *übersehen* ('overlook'), as Jean-Michel Rey would say in his analysis of the term?[14]

---

[14] Jean-Michel Rey, *Des mots à l'œuvre* (Paris: Aubier-Montaigne, 1979).

When the French language speaks of *danger de mort* ('risk of death'), German says *Lebensgefahr*, "a risk to life". When French says poetically *coucher et lever du soleil* ('the going-to-bed and getting-up of the sun'), German says *Sonnenuntergang* and *Sonnenaufgang*, the setting and rising of the sun.

Everything thus varies from one language to another, and yet we speak of the same things: to the silence of one language correspond, perhaps, the words of another.[15] But beneath the surface, a language depends on everything it says. Its unconscious files past, lightly brushing the words, and it is no coincidence that in German 'memory' and 'thought' are the same word, for all to see. In French, the link between memory (*mémoire*), *mens* (Latin), and mind (*l'esprit*), has long been forgotten.

Denke daran, 'remember it, think of it'; *ich gedenke seiner*, 'I remember him'. The past participle of *Denken* is *gedacht*, from which *das Gedächtnis*, 'memory', is derived. *Das Gedächtnis* is what enables me to put things inside myself. *Ich erinnere mich*, 'I put inside myself'; thus, I remember. 'I bring back inside' is exactly what is said with *sich erinnern*: to remember. Clearly, the language had laboured for Freud; it had, as it were, forged on ahead. For if things are brought back inside, it naturally follows that they were out of the immediate reach of the conscious mind. It is true that French says *se souvenir*, *subvenire*, to come to the mind from below, which is even closer to the unconscious. So languages speak clearly: suffice it to hear what they say. Freud's whole process simply amounted to letting the language speak, to paying attention to what it had to say.

This is because languages all chart their own course, following their own inclination; they move smoothly along themselves, little by little, but are so used to themselves that they no longer hear themselves speak, *sie überhören sich*, behaving as if they do not hear what they are saying.

The origin of *die Einfälle*, of those 'intuitions' or unbidden ideas – *die einem ganz unerwartet einfallen*, which fall 'inside' unexpectedly – lies in what is *überhört*, 'overlooked'. 'It has just come back to me', the French language says very aptly – but where does 'it' come back from? What are these 'ideas that rise within me', *die mie wieder einfallen*, these sudden bubbles at the surface? That is where the *Wiederholungszwang* or repetition compulsion is found, although as a sort of by-product: *es ist mir gerade wieder eingefallen*, 'it has just fallen inside me again', says the German language, and what it is that falls inside me in this way is not far removed from 'what I put inside myself again', *das woran ich mich erinnere* – what it is that I remember. The language – and this is what makes it a language – is seen once again charting

15 Cf. Georges-Arthur Goldschmidt, 'Une forêt et ses lisières', *L'écrit du temps*, n° 2 (Paris: Éditions de Minuit, 1985).

its own course. *Einfall* (*In fall*) is only one of the particularities of the verb *fallen*, which can also – like any other verb – go through many variations, all of which will at the same time be linked to each other by this one verb (*fallen*, to fall), as if any verb derived from it had the same nuance, the same colour. The verb *fallen* can, moreover, be combined with all imaginable particles.

This verb *fallen* reveals the extraordinary scope of Freud's thinking on the German language, and it is noteworthy that the unconscious always reveals itself through sudden eruptions ('eruption' could very well have translated *Einfall*), through things that 'fall inside' or that stand out in the flow of speech. Indeed, Freud's entire *oeuvre* may have been, concomitantly, a perpetual modulation of the verb *fallen*. The Freudian slips, the famous *Fehlleistungen* that occupy Freud so much, draw attention to themselves, ambushing speech midflow – they are what *fällt auf*. German says: *es fällt auf*, 'it jumps out at you', it makes itself noticed – even if it is only due to chance, to *Zufall*, to 'what more falls in front of you': *der Zufall fällt auf*. Chance gets noticed, as does what is added on (*zufallen*) and which should not, by rights, be there: *was auffällt*. This random intervention comes on top of the usual course of events, from which it follows that it looks very much as though Freud's attention – seemingly despite himself – had been attracted by the role of 'chance' in language, which in this case says more than is necessary. Moreover, it is strange to observe that this word *Zufall* ('chance') probably derives from the Latin word *accidens*, which it translates very closely, having entered German through the language of the mystics.

This is to put a finger once again on one of the major differences between the two languages: etymological 'recognisability'. Someone who has not studied Latin will be unable to identify the nature of the word *accidens*, which in any case no longer means 'chance' in French. French, one might say, shies away from its own self-interrogation, from that analytical gaze that is always possible in German.

It is well known that the things of greatest interest are to be found in what is discarded, in the crumbs that fall from the table, or *Abfall*, 'that which falls below', or that which falls off: *Im Herbst fallen die Blätter ab*, 'in autumn the leaves fall'.

In dreams, one is literally assaulted (*überfallen*) by the things one dare not think about when fully conscious; dreams set traps and ambush the dreamer (*Uberfall*), who, upon awakening, may fall prey to a fit of nerves, *ein Anfall*, which is to say something that falls upon and to one side (*an*) of the dreamer. It might, moreover, be a regrettable incident (*ein bedauerlicher Vorfall*): something that falls in front of one.

All these unpleasant happenings can be made to disappear (*Wegfall*); they can be got rid of (*sie fallen weg*). But the emotion may be so intense as to cause fits (*Anfälle*) of *Durchfall* ('diarrhoea' is the exact translation) – the stomach cramps attendant on nearly failing one's exams, which brings us straight back to the part of the body from which Freud's thinking has so often started out. For, ultimately, while constraint neuroses (*Zwangsneurosen*) convey exactly the opposite idea, they nevertheless pertain, as the etymology of *Zwang* will show us, to constipation. As long as the patient does not become *rückfällig*, 'does not relapse', all will be well.

Charting its own course, the language that says *einen Einfall haben* ('to have an idea') also says *sich erinnern* ('to remember'), for these *Einfälle*, these *Erinnerungen*, all come from *Ahnung* – part knowledge, part presentiment – an essential word in the language in which a presentiment becomes a memory, in which something takes shape in the mind that is difficult to trace to the present or the future. Nowhere is this more ostensible than with that most popular of writers, Joseph von Eichendorff, whose novel, *Premonition and Present*,[16] delights in flaunting the intimate landscape of the language before the reader's eyes.

For every language is its own landscape – or 'lang-scape'[17] – and has a certain way of moving within the bounds of a given atmosphere. A German train station is nothing like a French one, but amongst themselves, French or German train stations all resemble each other. There is a smell in the air in Austria or Germany that you do not find in France. In Freud's day, far more even than today, the differences of consistency (nowadays sometimes barely perceptible) expressed by the language pervaded everyday life, which, in return, marked the language.

Not only is everything different from one language to another, but also the two languages concur as often as they disagree: 'All exaggerations are insignificant' is an expression constantly voiced by the French since the days of Talleyrand, whereas in German people say: *übertreiben macht anschaulich*, 'exaggeration makes things visible'. It is true that French also says, 'To exaggerate is not to lie' – there is no solution! Venturing onto terrain such as this is indeed risky, as there is no escaping the fact that language is always, where set phrases and proverbial sayings are concerned, refuted by language. With other language levels, however, there is practically always a possible translation. If French had retained its slang – its *Volksmund*, its 'people's mouth', as German has it – it would have less trouble translating certain parts of the German tongue, certain of its characteristic perceptions.

---

[16] Joseph von Eichendorff, *Ahnung und Gegenwart*. In Christiane Briegleb and Clemens Rauschenberg (eds.), *Sämtliche Werke* (Berlin: De Gruyter, [1815] 1984). See also Joseph von Eichendorff, *A Translation from German into English of Joseph von Eichendorff's Romantic Novel Ahnung und Gegenwart* (1815), translated by Dennis Mahoney and Maria Mahoney (New York: Edwin Mellen, 2015).
[17] Translator's suggestion.

This is because German, it should be recalled, is essentially a 'commoner's' language, which derives its etymologies from itself: any explanation it gives of itself is based upon its own resources. *Deutsch* is an old word meaning 'commoner'. *Tuit*, meaning 'people' in Gothic – itself merely a branch of the Germanic languages (in Gothic, *tiudisko*) – also meant 'pagan'. Now this popular, pagan quality is almost the essence of German, which may go some way to explaining its attention to space and its apparent immediacy, as well as its ability to say whatever it likes, to fashion vocabulary at will, abstract or concrete.

Any root word can be combined with a certain number of suffixes such as -*keit*, which indicates the status of things. Thus, to take but one example, *die Sprache*, 'language', becomes *die Sprachlichkeit*; in French, *langagéité* ('languageness' or 'languagehood' in English) produces an unbearably pedantic and pretentious composition, whereas the German word produces not so much as a smile.

We could go on like this, providing all the possible variations and points of convergence or divergence with French for each and every word.

It is because the unconscious exists – *Sprachlosigkeit*, 'the fact of remaining speechless' – that languages exist, and that there are so many of them. The German language, such as it appears in the way Freud put it to use, reveals the gaps through which less the unconscious itself than something close to it escapes. Something close to it... It is a fact, as Freud himself observed in connection with the word *das Unheimliche*, that German possesses a certain number of words that other languages do not have, and that the silence of these other languages in the presence of the German words is precisely that abyss-like vacuum in which language comes into being.

The visual and auditory elements are far further developed in German than in French. As Fernand Deligny would say, 'doing' is given far more scope than 'making', and thus it follows that German is more firmly anchored in the world of childhood.[18] This characteristic, it should be said, had not escaped Leibniz, who in a famous text from 1680 entitled *Unprompted Thoughts on the Practice and Improvement of the German Language* wrote:

It appears to me that the Germans have already raised their language to a high level as regards everything that can be grasped by the five senses, and which a man of common sense can also apprehend, especially where things of the body, art or craftwork are concerned; for educated people, who are almost exclusively interested in Latin, have

---

[18] Fernand Deligny, *Les détours de l'agir ou le moindre geste* (Paris: Hachette, 1979).

abandoned their Mother tongue to its natural practice, which was not such a bad usage, even by those said to be uneducated, according to the teachings of nature.[19]

Now even if German has become clearer and considerably more straightforward since the days of Leibniz, even if its syntax has become far more transparent, particularly since the beginning of the nineteenth century, Leibniz's description nevertheless remains entirely accurate.

German, I say again, is a language that is almost incapable of abstraction – quite the contrary to what a now ineradicable legend maintains, and which the fad for 'German philosophy' in France reinforces still further. Abstract German words are French words – and it is no coincidence that they meet in Freud. All the other terms, and especially those used by philosophy, are, precisely, never abstract. Terms as philosophical as the famous *Aufhebung*, one of the mainstays of Hegel's thought, are to be found in the most everyday idiom: *Das Stück Schokolade hebe ich mir für morgen auf*, 'I'm keeping this piece of chocolate for tomorrow'.[20] It is precisely its rootedness in common speech that is the defining characteristic of German philosophical language: thought is not in any sense exterior to the language. Thus, essence (Thomas d'Aquinas's *essentia*) – the meaning of which, moreover, is displaced in German because it overlaps with being – is a commonly used term: *Wir sind alle lebendige Wesen*, 'We are all living beings', or *Es liegt im Wesen der Pflanze immer zum Licht zu drängen*, 'The essence of plants is to incline towards the light', or, again, *Die Kinder treiben im Garten ihr Wesen*, 'The children are having a great time in the garden'.

The language is practically always at one's disposition, anticipating thought. This perhaps explains a certain potential for disorientation and excess that was seen in operation a short while ago.

The very scope of Freud's work nevertheless derives from the fact that it is not peculiar to a single language, the German language, and its value resides in putting up a resistance to the flow of language. As has been said of the Greeks, German knows all there is to know about the unconscious. If, so to speak, it did Freud's work for him, it remains nevertheless true to say that it was Freud who showed what German meant as it spoke. Before him, Goethe had already – along with Nietzsche – tried similar undertakings, which is why their works are of universal value and are so frequently translated.

But as is well known, the crime of all crimes took place in German, deviated as the language was towards the ultimate perversity. It bore witness –

---

[19] Gottfried Wilhelm Leibniz, *Unvorgreifliche Gedanken Betreffend die Ausübung und Verbesserung der Teutschen Sprache*, edited by Uwe Pörksen and Jürgen Schiewe (Stuttgart: P. Reclam, [1680] 1983.

[20] The word *Aufhebung*, meaning 'rescind' or, on the contrary, 'conserve', illustrates the possibility for the German language to unite contradictory meanings in one single word.

expressed within itself, in its vocabulary and even its grammar – to the organisation of that crime. Confronted with the legal documents and ordinances published at the time, confronted with the speeches and diverse texts produced by those protagonists of oblivion, one can only wonder what monstrous repressed drives could have worked their way like that into the expressive capacities of the language. (A study of Nazi vocabulary and grammar remains to be undertaken, despite the efforts of Killy, Lämmert, Conrady, Polenz de Lutz Winckler, and Wendula Dahle.)[21]

It behoves someone, therefore, to initiate an enquiry of this kind into the language, and it is tempting to ask whether Freud did not sense what was coming. What needs to be done is to try to grasp how Freud saw the language at work and what he saw emerging within it. At a later stage, it may then prove possible to take this analysis further, in particular along the path formerly pointed out by Bertram Schaffner, and to try to begin a psychoanalytical elucidation of the ultimate crime.[22]

Bibliography

Bertaux, Pierre. *Hölderlin ou le temps d'un poète*. Paris: Gallimard, 1983.

Dahle, Wendula. *Die militärische Terminologie in der Germanistik 1933 bis 1945: Eine sprachliche Analyse*. PhD thesis. Berlin: Freie Universität, 1968.

Deligny, Fernand. *Les détours de l'agir ou le moindre geste*. Paris: Hachette, 1979.

Eichendorff, Joseph von. Ahnung und Gegenwart. In Christiane Briegleb and Clemens Rauschenberg (eds.), *Sämtliche Werke*. Berlin: De Gruyter, [1815] 1984.

A Translation from German into English of Joseph von Eichendorff's Romantic Novel Ahnung und Gegenwart (1815). Translated by Dennis Mahoney and Maria Mahoney. New York: Edwin Mellen, 2015.

Ferenczi, Sandor. *Schriften sur Psychoanalyse: Auswahl in zwei Bänden*. Berlin: Fischer Verlag, 1915.

Freud, Sigmund. *Gesammelte Werke, 13. Band: Jenseits des Lustprinzips/ Massenpsychologie und Ich-Analyse/ Das Ich und das es*. Francfort: Fischer Verlag, 1972.

Goldschmidt, Georges-Arthur. 'Une forêt et ses lisières'. *L'Écrit du temps*, n° 2. Paris: Éditions de Minuit, 1982.

'La langue de Freud'. *Le Coq héron*, n° 88. Paris: Éditions de Minuit, 1983.

'Quand Freud entend l'allemand'. *Nouvelle Revue de Psychanalyse*, n° 34. Paris: Gallimard, 1986.

'Les détours de la mer'. *L'Écrit du temps*, n° 14/15. Paris: Éditions de Minuit, 1987.

---

[21] For an in-depth study of the language of the Nazis by German-language specialists, see Walter Killy, Eberhard Lämmert, Karl Otto Conrady, and Peter von Polenz, *Germanistik, eine deutsche Wissenschaft* (Frankfurt: Suhrkamp, 1967); Lutz Winckler, *Studie zur gesellschaftlichen Funktion faschistischer Sprache* (Frankfurt: Suhrkamp, 1977).

[22] Bertram Schaffner *Father Land: A Study of Authoritarianism in the German Family* (New York: Columbia University Press, 1948).

Hart-Nibbrig, Christian L. *Die Aufstehung des Körpers im Text*. Berlin: Suhrkamp, 1985.

Hegel, Georg W. F. *Phämenologie des Geistes*. Heinrich Clairmont and Hans Friedrich Wessels (eds.). Hamburg: Felix Meiner, [1807] 1987.
The Phenomenology of the Mind. Translated by J. B. Baillie. New York: Dover, [1931] 2003.

Hölderlin, Friedrich. *Dichter 1800–1804: Sämtliche Werke*. Stuttgart: Schmidt, 1953.
Friedrich Hölderlin: Selected Poems. Translated by David Constantine. Newcastle-upon-Tyne: Bloodaxe Books, [1990] 1996.
Friedrich Hölderlin: Selected Poems and Fragments. Translated by Michael Hamburger. London: Penguin, 1998.

Killy, Walter, and Eberhard Lämmert. *Karl Otto Conrady and Peter von Polenz: Germanistik, eine deutsche Wissenschaft*. Frankfurt: Suhrkamp, 1967.

Leibniz, Gottfried Wilhelm. *Unvorgreifliche Gedanken Betreffend die Ausübung und Verbesserung der Teutschen Sprache*. Uwe Pörksen and Jürgen Schiewe (eds.). Stuttgart: Reclam, [1680] 1983.

Rey, Jean-Michel. *Des mots à l'œuvre*. Paris: Aubier-Montaigne, 1979.

Rilke, Rainer Maria. *Duino Elegies*. Translated by Martyn Crucefix. London: Enitharmon Press, [1923] 2013.

Schaffner, Bertram. *Father Land: A Study of Authoritarianism in the German Family*. New York: Columbia University Press, 1948.

Winckler, Lutz. *Studie zur gesellschaftlichen Funktion faschistischer Sprache*. Frankfurt: Suhrkamp, 1977.

8   Samuel Beckett's Change of Literary Language

An Apparent Severing of Links to Continue Writing on the Maternal Side of Language

Yoann Loisel

> Every word becomes a concept as soon as it is supposed to serve not merely as a reminder of the unique, absolutely individualised original experience, to which it owes its origin ...[1]

How can one recapture this 'unique ... original experience' that is 'absolutely individualised', yet dependent on another person?[2]

How, through language, can one reach back to what is enclosed within the mother-of-pearl of the word? This, one might say, is the daily labour of all writers, but it is my contention that Samuel Beckett's plurilingualism enabled him to re-enact the primeval dramaturgy of the word in a very unusual way. Language and its Other are like two pieces of flint he rubs together, following the sparks as they revive the long-extinguished flames of the most archaic fires – those in which subject and object glow undivided. This is the meaning of 'translation' in Beckett's writing – the self-translation that, as is well known, became his creative process after the success of *Waiting for Godot*.

Before this landmark in his career, Beckett's writing had traversed two apparently distinct phases. First, there was the pre-war phase, the search for a style different from that of James Joyce, the dazzling 'mentor' whom Beckett had helped with *Finnegan's Wake*. The texts from this phase seem to express a necessity for disengagement, or even rejection, as is suggested by the titles of some of his poems of the time, or by *Sanies* (1933), or the suicide at the end of *Murphy* (1938). The second phase lasted from the war until *Godot* (1953) and the switch to French in his literary production, which seems to have embodied the possibility of a new style and, thanks to the theatre, brought him fame.

This chapter will focus on the post-war period and the switch to French. We will see that this phase not only reflects the will to counteract the Mother tongue, but also aims to reach back and retrieve it. More precisely, the foreign language is appealing to Beckett in that it offers a framework in which to relive

---

[1] Sander L. Gilman, Carole Blair, and David J. Parent (trans. and eds.), *Friedrich Nietzsche on Rhetoric and Language* (New York: Oxford University Press, 1989), 249.

[2] This chapter was written for this volume by Yoann Loisel and translated by Sara Greaves.

an experience that cannot be entirely accessed in the code of his own language. It is my contention that through this foreign language, the sensation – the capacity for arousal, even – of the 'maternal' dimension of language, that extremity of the language that is closest to the body, the primeval flesh of the word in its physical articulations, is revived.

I shall begin by defining this 'maternal' side before focusing on the fascination of the young Samuel Beckett with foreign languages. This will lead us to reflect on how Beckett's knowledge of French gave rise to a style that prolonged his former passions while reorganising the dynamics of his writing. In keeping with this, it is the analysis of the changing status of the narrator and the first-person pronoun, of the ways in which sensory expression and aggressiveness evolved, that confirms the renewed force of Beckett's *oeuvre*, its ability to reach back to the depths of the narrative being – even as a nostalgic, depressive phase was taking hold.

8.1   The Maternal Side of Language

'Say the lost child.'[3]

As in *The Lost Ones*, with that embodiment of the radical Other that everyone seeks in order to be revealed to themselves, in order to be or be again divested by it of all affectation, the maternal side of language can probably best be experienced through contact with a foreign language. This occurs not through family multilingualism, but as was the case for Beckett, through the discovery of a second language, most often at school.

This foreign language provides a living example of another system of representations. Foreign language teaching – which is traditionally deemed appropriate to begin in early adolescence – can provide an intellectual prop at an age when there is an ambivalent need for distance from childhood, as well as for the continuity of an ongoing sense of self, despite the violence of new outbreaks of unconscious drives that demand a broadening of identity. Before dreaming geographically and culturally of foreignness, of an unknown territory to explore, thereby extending the space and frontiers of one's own personality, learning a foreign language exacerbates distance in the relationship between word and thing – hitherto seemingly irrefutable – whether it be external reality or the object inside oneself. The connections being legitimately twisted together between the linguistic code and the body – the body that feels, that is moved to the quick – the foreign language can embody the power of regeneration of the self, sometimes to magical effect.

---

[3] Samuel Beckett, *Worstward Ho*. In *Nohow On: Company, Ill Seen Ill Said, Worstward Ho: 4 Books in One* (New York: Grove Press, [1983] 1995, p. 56.

However, we should probably note that the use of the term 'mother' for one's native language is something of a misnomer; even if we naturally observe a difference between mother and father, why erase the paternal element? Perhaps because, although legally their rights are equal, the language of the father and that of the mother are not at all the same, and they are absolutely not perceived in the same way by the small child. The voice of the mother, her language, is a continuation of the prenatal acoustic experiences associated with the low-frequency sounds to which the foetus is already attentive, and so is recognised far sooner after birth. The father's voice is heard in the distance, without the echo of anatomic all-inclusiveness having hammered out a kind of speech from – along with the voice – heartbeats, hissing blood, and gastric sounds (perhaps recalled by the 'buzzing'[4] beneath the skull that is heard by some of Beckett's narrators).

So it may be, but language would not amount to much and be limited to thought rooted in body words if it were not structured by a code representing its power of differentiation and precision, its power to hold and contain things – first and foremost the impulses originating in the body. As this code is mastered and internalised, the infant may identify with the 'paternal model' as the father readily presents himself to the infant's psyche as responsible for the gap, standing 'to one side' of things yet the organiser of this gap, separating the mother–*infans* monad and the instinctual understanding of its biological plasticity.[5] The language should therefore more rightly be known as the 'father tongue', to account for the fact that linguistic formulation owes more to the code than to the body.

Nevertheless, however arbitrary the linguistic sign, verbal representation is by no means an *ex nihilo* acquisition; it originates in the essential, recurrent experience of desire and satisfaction that links 'breast milk speech' to the arousal experienced. On this foundation, which is continued as a mothering ground bass, there is no difference between the voice, its message, and the bodily warmth of the experience. And even if the child's gradual acquisition of language separates these elements, embodying the transition from senses to sense, from the body to the linguistic code, from crying out to interaction, there nevertheless remains a carnal residue that inheres in language, between words and things. Due to the mother's physiology and childcare reflexes, she has provided the initial link between emotion and representation, and by translating the infant's sensations into actions and words, she has continued for some time to irrigate the language with an embodied immediacy: it is to the mother that the language pays tribute.

---

[4] Samuel Beckett, *Not I*. In *Collected Shorter Plays* (New York: Grove Weidenfeld, [1972] 1984), 217.

[5] An *infans* is here considered a child who does not yet speak, who is discovering the world and finding pleasure in its vast pool of open signs.

The use of the term 'mother' in 'Mother tongue' thus reveals the defining characteristic of language, which is its origin in the body, in a body initially undifferentiated from the mother's body, an 'inter-corporality' that denotes the hazards of subjectivity itself (based on separation and not impingement) as well as its aspiration to return to a place where nothing is lacking and nothing is left over – to the idealised mother's breast (its obverse being a persecution fantasy, that of being swallowed by an all-powerful mother). The gendering of the qualifier 'mother' denotes not so much a sex as a sum of constituent ambiguities: does language register the separation between individuals or provide a foundation for their possible reunion? The answer is both, at once, thereby articulating the forever insoluble interpretation of the universal myth of Babel. Is language a catalyser in the oppression of its subjects, maintaining the hothouse schooling required by speech and subject separation, or does it allow them to claim an imaginary ideal, that of reassembled bodies? Each interpretation is as good as the other; they intersect with the great paradox of identity according to which the subject is always the subject *of...*, in the passive mode (the subject is spoken), as much as in the active one (they speak).

A few more general remarks are required to try to describe what seems to me to found the vibrant bedrock of Beckett's bilingualism. Concerning teenagers, for instance, to what extent does the transition that occurs in adolescence to the constraints of time and self-determination mirror the childhood transition to articulated language? Sharp outlines come to replace indistinctness, the magical experience of being able to say and do everything. It is a step not taken without the apprehension of a kind of loss, even a kind of mutilation propelled by the temporality of puberty, as the adolescent realises that time is no longer theirs to possess, as previously seemed to be the case. For the small child, growing up was a dream to be accomplished in the distant, indistinct future, and generally speaking their parents knew how to make them feel that time was their own. In adolescence something accelerates, differently, marking the body with largely uncontrollable blemishes (Beckett complained about numerous cysts and suffered from eczema, both psychosomatic externalisations that left little doubt to their victim-author as to his internal ebullition, leading James Knowlson, on the acknowledgements page of his biography of Beckett, to express his thanks first and foremost to a general practitioner for having explained to him these recurrent disorders).

Finally, the feelings of perplexity at these blemishes and the desire to have some leverage over them are transferred onto the language; adolescents are suspicious of the words they share with adults, as if their intimacy could be read there too explicitly or might erupt in them, and they readily invest various 'neo-languages' to conceal themselves while at the same time bonding with each other. Thus, for instance, to return to Samuel Beckett, we may wonder whether the lecture he gave in French at Trinity College on a poet who never existed, Jean du Chas, was anything more than a complete hoax: 'In a play on the title of Descartes' famous treatise, du Chas is said to be the author of a *Discours de la sortie (or a Discourse on Exits)*'.[6]

The different versions of the story contradict each other, and it may be that only some of Beckett's fellow students were in the know. Meanwhile, the name he chose ('du Chas') clearly suggests a hard-to-tame animal ('chat' ('cat' in English) is a homonym of 'chas'), as well as the need to thread one's way through the eye of a needle ('chas'). Adolescence is the age of the first time, of the feeling of 'having to go through with it' that is part and parcel of the experience of adolescent temporality, which gives rise to a concretely renewed perception of time's flow in unprecedented scansions from which nostalgic yearning suddenly surges, along with diverse subversive impulses. The adolescent's frequent mutism in the presence of their parents, especially the mother, reflects the desire to continue understanding each other (in the physical sense of 'standing under', both 'withstanding' and 'standing with'), without having to resort to the befuddlement of words. Thus, there is a powerful desire to recover the lost *infans* at the very age when they most need to distance themselves from the figures with whom they first discovered both meaning and love.

On this 'stage', a theatrically exhibited secretiveness reflects a sort of 'double shot': not a compromise aimed at mixing contradictory desires by slightly giving ground on both sides, but, on the contrary, the determination to fulfil them both to the hilt, irrefrangibly, both staving off the intrusion of sharing while completely retrieving a lost sense of harmony. It was this logic founded on an unquenchable desire to comprehend – in the sense of keeping everything while keeping himself – that motivated Beckett early on and steered him towards the study of languages.

8.2   Samuel Beckett and Foreign Language Learning

Hamm: Yesterday! What does that mean? Yesterday!
Clov (violently): That means that bloody awful day, long ago, before this bloody awful day. I use the words you taught me. If they don't mean anything any more, teach me others. Or let me be silent.[7]

Caliban: You taught me language, and my profit on't
Is, I know how to curse. The red plague rid you
For learning me your language![8]

---

[6] James Knowlson, *Damned to Fame: The Life of Samuel Beckett* (London: Bloomsbury, [1996] 1997), 121.
[7] Samuel Beckett, *Endgame*. In *The Complete Dramatic Works* (London: Faber and Faber, 1986), 113.
[8] William Shakespeare, *The Tempest*, Act I scene II.

In Beckett's works, there are numerous scenes that seem to represent the echo of an experience of language learning between two characters, some fairly reminiscent of school, others bordering on the ludicrous. Among these is Clov's speech recalling the beginning of *The Tempest* when Caliban curses his oppressor, Prospero. This rebellion, which follows the usual pattern of the paradox of the colonised – that of having to use the language of subjection in order to break free of it – seems actually to have been directly inspired by the virulent revolt expressed by the narrator of *The Unnamable*:

> It's a poor trick that consists in ramming a set of words down your gullet on the principle that you can't bring them up without being branded as belonging to their breed. But I'll fix their gibberish for them. I never understood a word of it in any case, not a word of the stories it spews, like gobbets in a vomit.[9]

This solid link between language and oppression invites us to take politics into consideration: given the domination of English, how might the divided linguistic reality of Ireland have affected the author? This issue needs putting into its proper perspective, which is to say relatively insignificant, and Beckett's biographers are probably right to devote so little space to the impact of Irish bilingualism on the author's formative years. By contrast with the numerous occurrences of 'maternal' references in his works, and by contrast likewise with the sensory expressiveness that, all things considered, produces the effect of an accusation in the exchanges between the *infans* and the adult (and it is noteworthy that in French, as well as 'to accuse' in the sense of 'to blame', the word 'accusation' also means 'to accentuate', 'to reinforce'), the social environment peculiar to the linguistic expression of his native land does not at all appear to have played a determining role in Beckett's motivation. At most, I would venture to suggest that the surrounding bilingualism opened up his cognitive capacity to comprehend a double system of representation, but that it had little further influence in terms of sociolinguistic subjection or political demands for increased freedom because in the context of the beginning of the twentieth century, the opposition between England and Ireland was not as violent as it had been or would later become.[10] Another, more important reason for this is that Beckett's family, Protestant and middle class, was perfectly well assimilated to English-speaking society. Nevertheless, it is probably worth bearing in mind that his Mother tongue, English, was a

---

[9] Samuel Beckett, *Trilogy: Molloy, Malone Dies, The Unnamable* (London: John Calder, [1959] 2003), 327.

[10] Beckett was born in 1906, and the political party *Sinn Fein* ('ourselves' in Gaelic) was founded the previous year. They won the general election in 1918 by proclaiming Irish independence, and it was this fairly rapid push forward that led to the division of the island in 1921, when dominion status was obtained. Despite this relative victory for the cause of independence, Gaelic remained a marginal language, mostly surviving in rural areas and considered outmoded.

singularly politically connoted language, and that Gaelic, which he would go on to speak, provided him with the image of a language that although dwindling, nevertheless held its own.

However, before turning to the unavoidable question of Beckett's anger directed at English and the quest for a 'pared away' language or, more precisely perhaps, for a language that rejects its own associative and/or pugnacious vigour, I would like to focus on Beckett's taste for languages – in itself rather remarkable. He was aided in his choice of studies by a highly efficient intellectual capacity generally, and by abilities including a propensity for learning foreign languages that would be confirmed to an exceptional degree, which he exercised throughout his life. When he left school he spoke French, German, and Italian fluently; much later, while on holiday on the Madera archipelago, his plurilingual capacities would again prove excellent when he undertook to learn Portuguese: his correspondence shows that it took him about a month to be able to read novels and poetry in a new language, delighting, for instance, in Portuguese's compound pluperfect and future subjunctive.[11]

This fascination undoubtedly began at the private primary school Samuel attended, where he received what practically amounted to individual tutoring from the Elsner sisters: Ida, for the rudiments of French, and Pauline, who gave him piano lessons (he later described them with gentle irony: 'They made a little too much music, that was the only fault I could find with them').[12] The biographers point out that his primary school teachers were of German extraction, and that Ida had a highly eccentric personality that excited the curiosity of the inhabitants of Foxrock, the village where the Becketts lived. There are no other remaining sensory descriptions of this early knowledge crucible, but I can easily imagine the child's curiosity about the fantastical adult interlacing with his school lessons against a backdrop of piano playing and even a particular foreign accent. The music of the language and music through language would seem to have paved the way for Beckett's appetite for what lies beyond the word, especially when we remember that among his precociously manifest character traits was a finely discriminating sense of hearing – certainly a highly refined musical ear, keenly enhanced by his family's love of opera. So it seems fair to say that originally, the magnetic attraction of foreign languages for Beckett may have been inspired less by an interest in cultural differences than by his avid savouring of the sonorous plasticity of the word, that malleability of the concept that makes it revert to thingness – thus reviving

---

[11] George Craig, Martha Dow Fehsenfeld, Dan Gunn, and Lois More Overbeck (eds.), *Lettres, IV (1966–1989)*, translated by Gérard Kahn (Paris: Gallimard, 2018), 52, 234.
[12] Beckett, *Molloy*. In *Trilogy*, 105–6.

the poly-sensory learning process of his own language: its most maternal foundation.

After continuing his school education at Earlsford House, then as a boarder at Portora Royal School, he registered at Trinity College to study English literature, rapidly showing a preference for languages. This orientation seems to have been influenced by the personality of certain lecturers, the most prominent of whom was the Romance languages professor, Thomas Rudmose-Brown, who had already published a major work entitled *Étude comparée de la versification française et de la versification anglaise* (A Comparative Study of French and English Versification) and a bilingual collection of poems.

Deirdre Bair seems right to ascribe Beckett's firm preference for modern languages to the new, attractive – and paternal – influence of Rudmose-Brown:

> Gradually Beckett found himself attracted to the study of modern languages. It was an unusual choice. Modern languages were usually the special province of women, while men were expected to follow the classics, mathematics, or engineering. [...] Men seldom enrolled in modern language courses and almost never were degree candidates. [...] In Rudmose-Brown he found a mentor to whom he could give unqualified admiration, respect and, ultimately, affection.[13]

This was also the age of first love – all the more fruitful in weaving an intellectualised web, for at Trinity College the barrier between the sexes was scrupulously maintained. Later immortalised by the portrayal of Alba ('dawn') and probably the original on whom the girl in the boat recalled by old Krapp was modelled, Ethna MacCarthy enchanted Samuel as she did a number of young men (Georges Pelorson, one of the French *lecteurs* at Trinity, described her as follows: 'Extraordinarily intelligent, extraordinarily witty and with a command of French that was absolutely wonderful').[14] She too was studying modern languages, also specialising in French, and her year ahead of Beckett was perhaps a stimulation to follow in her footsteps and shine. Their age difference was slight yet where social skills were concerned, these two young people were light years away from each other, imposing on the future writer – out of caution but without causing him too much suffering – a Platonic dimension to the relationship.

While the rigid rules and regulations of the institution maintained the need for restraint, allowing the dawn to glow without erupting on a volcanic scale, Rudmose-Brown seemed to be of all the lecturers the one who demonstrated an iconoclasm likely to satisfy certain desires of his students, and to deter the intellectualising tendencies of the more retiring ones. He enjoyed playing the role of matchmaker and organised evenings at the theatre or the pub, even

---

[13] Deirdre Bair, *Samuel Beckett: A Biography* (New York: Simon & Schuster, [1978] 1990), 38–9.
[14] Interview with Georges Belmont, 3 August 1991. In Knowlson, *Damned to Fame*, 60.

sometimes at his flat, and was savvy enough to turn out the lights at the appropriate moments. Like Samuel, Ethna was one of his favourites and they therefore shared in these festive gatherings – even though Beckett seems to have restricted himself to a position of reserved observer. He was the better able to recount the dishevelled ambience of these occasions, with his Alba sufficiently sure of her charms to deign to lend them to whoever desired them excessively, and Rudmose-Brown as an uncouth guide renamed 'the Polar Bear' ('a big old brilliant lecher').[15]

As regards what was expected of him in terms of teaching, this was the professor who introduced Beckett to contemporary French poetry. In particular, he encouraged him to write his doctoral dissertation on Pierre Jean Jouve, a choice that revealed to him the possible inspiration for literary writing to be found in psychoanalytical theory. It was also under Rudmose-Brown's influence that he rapidly translated several French surrealists. His role as librarian of the Modern Languages Society of the university led him to become more sociable, with the added advantage of working in a place much visited by Ethna. Against the backdrop of his mentor's beguiling ways and his ensuing identification, Beckett likewise took on the role of matchmaker – of books, of words – his job at the library (a foretaste of his later employment as (partial) secretary for James Joyce) bringing together intellectual interest and emotional effervescence in an almost ideal combination. Added to this, the loam of his creativity seems to have been definitively enriched by an encounter that would go on to influence him profoundly: his meeting with Bianca Esposito, the Italian teacher he approached at a private language school in town.

Was the decision to supplement his studies in this way linked to the presence on the staff of this small school of the third Elsner sister, who taught music there? It seems to me highly likely that the atmosphere in this school revived the extremely sensitive one of the lessons given by his first primary school teachers, while refining the learning and discussions towards ever more specialised knowledge. It is noteworthy that we have here, at this early stage, one of Beckett's recurrent dualities: to leave – the better to retrieve; his intellect was more completely nourished if it could tune in to a certain melodic line, in other words to a certain sensuality. On this musical stave, the private tutoring would reinforce the teaching received at Trinity by setting up its own rhythm and taking a step back from the institution, thus opening up the possibility so crucial to him of moving back and forth – and probably also of distance from Rudmose-Brown, who elicited some suspicion in his student, as would later be revealed in the portrait of the 'lecher'.

An enchanting little lady, getting on in years, Signora Esposito inspired in him a remarkably caring relationship. It was with her that Beckett fell under

---

[15] Samuel Beckett, *More Pricks than Kicks* (London: Faber and Faber, [1934] 2010), 50.

the spell of Dante's *Divina Comedia*, a spell that would remain unbroken throughout his life, introducing his first collection of short stories with the theory of the spots on the moon as expatiated by Beatrice to the poet. Along with Rudmose-Brown, she was undoubtedly a powerful instigator, and it seems to me no exaggeration to assert that Bianca was Beatrice, a woman Samuel was able to love with a wholly tender affection – a love immediately directed towards shared literary interests (throughout his life Beckett kept an edition of Dante annotated with Bianca's help and enclosing within its pages an affectionate postcard from his former teacher). And, at a remote distance from these two modes of teaching, with his two points of emotional involvement kept always separate so as to prevent – or so it would seem – his being excessively entangled in one or the other of them, this division of arousal and of its hazards is suggestive of the recurrence in his works of a figure of duality, also operative in the choice of living in two alternate homes, the Parisian apartment and the small house in Ussy-sur-Marne, as well as, of course, the generic organisation of his writing between theatre and fiction, and the bilingual tension that underpins it. This confirms how deep-rooted Beckett's linguistic duplication was – and how eminently subjective and singular.

Nevertheless, this kind of circularity, maintained because it corresponds to a deep-seated need, can easily give rise to a sense of enclosure – especially when adolescence brings an explosive, usually repressed ardour that tries to find a way in. Something must open up, if not give, and Rudmose-Brown revealed what seems to have been an excellent understanding of his student when he encouraged him to go on his first visit to France before taking his double degree in French and Italian. The bicycle trip during the summer of 1926 in the Loire Valley added the welcome rewards of the physical exercise he was in need of to the linguistic and cultural benefits of the visit.[16]

Beckett was delighted with the trip, and it had a calming effect on certain mood swings that had become increasingly conspicuous. For his parents, this wholesome experience away from home no doubt helped promote the idea of his removal to the *École Normale* in Paris two years later. The job of *lecteur* there was presented as the first step in obtaining a post as lecturer at Trinity College. However, rather than going on to pursue an academic career, Samuel would set his sights on settling permanently in the French capital, where he had met James Joyce. His friends and family were outraged when he rapidly took the decision to resign from the university soon after securing the post, even if – flouting university rules – the fact that he never gave back his keys is highly suggestive of the ambivalence he was struggling with (the yoke he bore

---

[16] Deirdre Bair writes: 'This brief visit to France marked the beginning of Beckett's serious fascination with that country [...] France had opened the floodgates of Beckett's speech and imagination'. *Samuel Beckett: A Biography*, 49.

comprised his guilt regarding his father, who had accompanied him to Trinity on his first day, and his shame with respect to his mother in seemingly proving to her that he was a layabout).

The intensity of this conflict seems to have given rise to a dramatic event, the car accident he had with Ethna one night when – as was his wont – he was driving too fast and crashed into the parapet of a Dublin bridge. He himself got away with a few bruises, but the young woman had to be admitted to hospital. Later, Beckett referred to this misadventure as a terrible nightmare, which strengthened his intention to leave Ireland and the judgement of his family circle. The abrupt disengagement from Trinity only days after the crash, and the missing keys (the university had to replace all the locks!); this sequence indeed suggests the problematic issue of an escape route, when the constraint is far more deep-seated than if it were simply related to external demands. As he would write to his friend Tom MacGreevy, criticising his aptitude for teaching as if foreseeing what lay ahead of him in the early thirties:

When I cannot answer for myself, and do not dispose of myself, how can I serve? Will the demon – *pretiosa margarita* [precious pearl]! – disable me any the less with sweats and shudders and panics and rages and rigors and heart burstings because my motives are unselfish and the welfare of others my concern? Macché! Or is there some way of devoting pain and monstrosity and incapacitation to the service of a deserving cause? Is one to insist on a crucifixion for which there is no demand?[17]

Beckett cites the theory of alchemy to help decide what to do with his life, using Latin to describe how he sees himself as at once a raging madman and a precious gem awaiting transmutation. The other language does not for the time being provide him with a method, but it does at least circumscribe things. It would soon be of a more substantial help to him when it moved towards French and provided a frame within which to organise his ambivalent impulses.

8.3   Towards the French Language and Settling in France

Tire la chevillette, la bobinette cherra.[18]
Pardon these French expressions, but the creature dreams in French.[19]

Having examined the foundations of Samuel Beckett's investment in the French language, I shall now deal more succinctly with the period that took him from Trinity College to the Second World War.

---

[17] Letter to Tom MacGreevy, 10 March 1935. Trinity College Dublin Library. In Knowlson, *Damned to Fame*, 181. The extract alludes to the alchemical doctor Petrus Bonus.
[18] Compare the well-known fairy tale, 'Little Red Riding Hood': 'Pull the bobbin, and the latch will lift up'.
[19] Beckett, *More Pricks than Kicks*, 73.

Three important – and related – observations can be made concerning this period: the young Beckett's emotional instability, the strengthening of his interest in France, and the attraction of literary writing. It was a time of prolonged adolescence during which he had difficulty determining what would be a safe distance from his family circle, in particular from his mother (his father died in 1933). France became a chosen land because it structured that distance (he used the small stipend inherited from his father to finance longer and longer visits to Paris) and, in so doing, protected him – himself and his mother – from the increasingly violent intensity of their conflictual relationship. France also provided the active Parisian publishing scene, standing in stark contrast to his home country with its arid Puritan politics, which it is tempting to see as a duplication of his mother's 'ferocious love'.

He had met James Joyce during his first long visit to Paris, when he was a *lecteur* at the *École Normale*, from 1928 to 1930; this meeting had a powerful influence on Beckett's decision to turn his mind to literary creation. The two men fell victim to each other's charms: as well as his intellectual aura, Beckett was of course captivated by Joyce as a proclaimed exile, an Irishman who had become a stranger to his own homeland. Except that, whereas in Joyce the categories of the foreign and the familiar had become strangely intertwined, producing a familiarity whose warp and woof was seemingly dependent on being tried within a foreign container, for Beckett – as his ensuing comings and goings between Paris and Dublin would lead him to understand – exile alone would not suffice. A tighter form of bond was necessary, that of an exile within exile.

Another influential encounter, of course, was the psychoanalytical therapy he undertook with Wilfred Bion, testifying to the fact that Beckett was in search of a rational explanation for his internal turmoil. Having moved to London for a while (from 1934 to 1935), he stopped his treatment fairly abruptly by 'acting out' (i.e., returning to his mother's house), while Bion – who was as yet an inexperienced therapist – behaved in a rather informal manner (e.g., inviting him to a lecture given by Jung). Constructing his fantasy of an incomplete birth, directing his arousal towards a mysterious prenatal state, Beckett's therapy ended up incomplete too. It seems likely that Bion lacked the necessary distance for treating this young man, whose fear of reliving the anxiety of intrusion was precisely proportionate to his readiness to go and look for it, to induce it. This seems to me to correspond to a stereotype: Beckett sought that which caused him anxiety; he set up what upset him and would soon create out of foreignness what remained foreign within himself, and which threatened him.

The author-to-be undoubtedly felt the need for a 'site of the foreign', as defined by Pierre Fédida in relation to the psychoanalytical experience: it is because the therapist has become detached from their family interactions that the analysand can freely project their speech – which is no longer at risk of alienation in parental desire – onto this 'negation that installs neutrality'.[20] The primary site of the foreign seems to me nevertheless more internal, and more general than this: it is the instinctual excitement that erupts from within and threatens to spoil things, or destroy them, and it seems to me that Beckett directed his intellectual capacities towards studying languages in order to find – as with a pearl – an intelligible circumscription for them, the means to contain those capacities while at the same time making the most of them.

Philosophy and psychoanalysis both interested him, but he set his sights on writing and on the French language, which is to say on interpersonal relations and sensuality – but with certain adjustments. The doggedness with which he followed this path must not be underestimated: it was a quest for new, constantly reinvented mediations, designed to keep him vigilant, like Ulysses faced with the Sirens, squarely facing what it was that threatened to destroy him. This modulation of his bonds – on the deck of a ship that he felt to be rocking wildly back and forth – would be achieved first by familiarising himself with languages other than his Mother tongue and then by moving permanently to France and changing the language he wrote in. This continued later with his switching from fiction to drama, and finally to stage directing for radio and television, as the drive to play representational 'chords' in his native idiom became increasingly pressing.

And if Samuel Beckett confirmed his choice of settling definitively in Paris on 4 September 1939, on the very day after France's declaration of war on Germany, he did so because neutrality was of no interest to him personally if it amounted to an easing of tension, and he continued to crave a life of tumult that would echo the tumult he felt within himself. This choice forced him, moreover, to keep his mother at a resolute distance and deprived him of the possibility of moving back and forth, which was how he had always managed things so far. This was the nature of Beckett's bargain with himself: in a climate of a kind of danger that was new to him, his capacity to return to his inner self, towards where he originated, would henceforth be solely dependent on his intellect, and on his own abilities, if he were to fulfil his aspirations.

8.4   Exile within Exile

'How could the mess be admitted, because it appears to be the very opposite of form and therefore destructive of the very thing that art holds itself to be?' But now we can keep it out no longer, because we have come into a time

---

[20] Pierre Fédida, *Le site de l'étranger* (Paris: Presses Universitaires de France, 1995), 56.

when 'it invades our experience at every moment. It is there and it must be allowed in.' [...] 'To find a form that accommodates the mess, that is the task of the artist now'.[21]

My contention, then, is that this 'mess' is the indistinct sensation of a sort of island that escapes the familiar capacity of representation; that it is a zone of arousal, leaning towards excess, that must be 'allowed in' or given access, or in some way channelled, so as to prevent Beckett from being enflamed by it to the point of disintegration. This 'mess' neither amounts to meaninglessness, which is to say a kind of madness situated at the far end of the autistic vacuum or at the far end of a descent into delirious suturing (e.g., hypochondria or diverse persecution complexes), nor does it pertain to the absurd, which is a cynical judgement that Beckett never accepted (he is more concerned to resist than to pass judgement). Rather, its nature is to be deprived of meaning while being – inevitably – sensorially present, existing on the inside and demanding some form of representation, as common sense would require. It is not so much an autistic 'black hole' as a 'white hole' – that internal site of the foreign urging for translation, for a change of coding system, the better to be included within it, a coding system that is that other language but not solely: it is also a quality of action on language that activates its sensitive determiners.[22] This means that Beckett's writing is not aimed at 'de-mining', to borrow a term from psycho-analyst Didier Anzieu, who adopts the hypothesis of the 'black hole' in his reading of Beckett's works, but rather that it seeks to stimulate the revital-isation of what generates thought from its earliest moments.[23]

External excess can sometimes soothe the internal 'beast', providing a sort of lid as well as a medium for new ways to reach the enigma. James Knowlson rightly stresses how much the war brought Beckett to a deeper appreciation of human nature's inherent contradictions, such as '[an] acute awareness of the

---

[21] Lawrence Graver and Raymond Federman (eds.), 'Tom Driver in Columbia University Forum', *Samuel Beckett: The Critical Heritage* (London: Routledge, [1979] 2005), 243.

[22] Didier Anzieu, 'I see in him one single black hole that, from *Molloy* to *How it is*, he has never ceased to locate and sew together with words as stitching'. *Beckett* (Paris: Gallimard, 1998), 149. Translated by Sara Greaves.

[23] Anzieu is referencing Frances Tustin's theory in 'The black hole – a significant element in autism', *Free Associations*, n° 11 (1988). Tustin uses the image of a 'black hole' to describe a catastrophic turning point in certain kinds of autism in which, stimulated by the process of separation from the mother, a child's normal psychic reactions go off course. She also maintains that certain neuroses include this autistic element, which resists psychoanalytical treatment, describing an evolutive spectrum, a developmental continuum between autism and certain types of neurosis. However, Anzieu overemphasises this 'black hole' in his discussion of Beckett, confining the writer within a pathological diagnosis and a process of self-healing that allegedly prevented him – constitutionally, as it were – from benefitting from psychoanalysis. In my view, the jubilatory elation produced by the exploration of languages (the incandescent 'white hole' of instinctual arousal), as well as Beckett's legitimate critique of what is lacking in the psychoana-lytical approach, are thus not properly accounted for.

ambivalence that is part of charity'.[24] I also think – strengthened as he was by the precious support of his future wife, Suzanne, and by the idea of a just cause to defend – that the fact of being physically confronted with the extreme violence of his century revealed to Beckett a senseless reality that was convergent with his own.[25] He came across this senselessness concretely in various guises, without the force of the primeval 'mess' seeming to get the upper hand in activating the traumatism rather than literary creation. Nevertheless, recognising on the outside what is happening on the inside may be a terrible surprise, a shock brought on by the collapsed boundary. It is easy to imagine that this state of extreme nervous tension put Beckett at risk, and indeed the depression he fell into first became tenacious and a cause for concern when he was forced to cross over to the free zone and lie low for a while after action in which he risked his life. Yet – akin to the way some people touch the bottom the better to rise back up to the surface – the frantic writing of *Watt* would seem to transport him to a new horizon of creativity.

These two objectives – confrontation with an inner peril that he felt he had to domesticate, and preservation of the risks by revitalising the psychic envelope – were indeed to be found embroiled in the war experience of the as yet unknown author. He quickly joined the Resistance, playing the role of 'letter-box' and translating English intelligence, and was soon to witness the unleashing of the most violent instincts and the possibility of human collapse. The worst of these instincts were at large, so close they seemed on the inside, and at the end of 1942 Beckett's network was dismantled and most of its members arrested or on the run. After some time spent fleeing from one hiding place to another, he and Suzanne were forced to leave Paris. Their covert route led them to the red sands of Roussillon in Vaucluse, to join up with two fairly distant acquaintances: Roger Deleutre, a pianist who had joined his family there, and Marcel Lob, a grammar professor who had been removed from office because he was Jewish.

To begin with the couple took a room at the village's only hotel, whose restaurant was the rallying point for regular card players as well as people avid for the BBC news bulletins, hidden in the scullery. The principal, unrelenting concern was of course to find food without depending on the goodwill of others or on the single resource of the black market. Beckett found casual work for farmers in exchange for food and was extremely proud to learn how to

---

[24] Knowlson, *Damned to Fame*, 351.
[25] Suzanne, often presented as a placid, wifely figure of stability for the writer, was a concert pianist who sacrificed her career to support her partner's. To my mind, however, as well as making herself available for him in this way, her significance lies in Beckett's interest in music, in the musical backdrop he seeks in language, that sensuality that he looks for and which cradles him – and which he found as a child in the Elsner sisters' classes.

harvest crops; how to clip, prune, and dig up trees; and how to plant and pick produce.

These were down-to-earth physical needs – I have, of course, no intention of painting a naïve picture of farm labouring in terms of simple, restorative pleasures; what seems significant above all is that Beckett encountered a humble world and experienced it physically, a world situated within the wider one that constantly weighs down upon it and at regular intervals makes it quake. The uncertainty concerning his own fate, the sadness of having no news of his family, the boredom, and the fear for his friends were the raw feelings that all exiles must inevitably keep in check. However, in this region that was new to him, with its scattered ochre quarries, the combination of nature's exuberance and austerity, as well as the hard labour, impressed upon Beckett other powerful sensations. Many of these were new, but some, such as the barking of dogs at night, would take him back to intimate memories, to that strangeness in childhood and his curiosity about the noises breaking the silence. One can easily imagine that the fright underlying these sudden alarms was no longer experienced in anything like the same way, and that when his sleep was disturbed now what was rather opened up by them was a channel of revivification transporting him back via flushes of nostalgia to the vibrant pleasures of his early years. The apprehension of those years could be replenished by these alarms – to the benefit not of terror, which was never far away, but of vitality, especially physical vitality, the energy he needed to be able to rely upon, and whose living source was always infancy. To put it differently, while constantly at risk of reactivating that psychic collapse, with a body so easily fragmented by sensory excess and a primeval 'ear-body' straining with all its might towards the sensation it craved, this 'body' expanded more harmoniously and regularly till it fit the dimensions of the actual body of the writer, who probably stood to gain – mentally too– a new sense of existence poised upon its very precariousness.

After a break, he went back to his writing in Roussillon upon moving into a detached house with Suzanne. *Watt*, which Beckett had started at the beginning of the war, developed from a mere sketch into a full narrative interlaced with highly 'embodied' reminiscences of places he had known in his youth. Less philosophically serious than *Murphy*, it comprises a new comic attack against the rationality and synthetic aspiration of the mind. Here was a way to both enter that internal site and allow it entry, to avoid being reduced to striving against it or driving it out, as was the case in his more juvenile writing such as *Murphy*, which ends down the lavatory. To be sure, Beckett had his fears, shared in large part by his contemporaries at the time of his exile in Roussillon, but it seems likely that the array of sensations deployed there enabled him to be less beset by inhibitions and muted anguish when examining the depths that were his major concern. (Even if the 'mess' referred to by

Beckett very legitimately includes knowledge of the Shoah, of an unprecedented destructiveness unleashed on the era and discrediting forever the ideal of culture in opposition to the instinctual urge, to my mind this interpretation better accounts for the reception and success of Beckett's *oeuvre* than it does for his deep-seated incentives.)

A prescription can be read at the end of *Watt*: 'the only cure is diet'. I read this as the decision taken or envisaged by Beckett to aim for a resolutely lean style, stripped bare of Joycean pyrotechnics, and more broadly to continue using a language radically different from his language of origin, whose associative ease was too spontaneous and abundant and ultimately illusory. Less would be more, on condition that the body of the language were to change too. Thus, although *Watt* was written in English, the ensuing texts would be written in French, right up to *From an Abandoned Work* in 1955.

Apart from ostensibly making publication easier – although in the immediate post-war context it was as hard to get published in France as in England or Ireland – this very determined choice of French seems not only to derive from a logic of purgation but also from the new powers it gave him to approach his target, which in Roussillon had become clearer to him, although still in the shadows:

For Watt's concern, deep as it appeared, was not after all with what the figure was, in reality, but with what the figure appeared to be, in reality. [...] he was for ever falling into this old error, this error of the old days when, lacerated with curiosity, in the midst of substance shadowy he stumbled.[26]

Yes, indeed: how to go further, deeper, how to rid oneself of the 'old error' and capture the self, the self as other? *Watt*, grounded in Beckett's war, marks the beginning of the true 'fold' in his writing career, a turning point initiated by the title that voices a very open question – right from the very first letter, even, which reverses Beckett's favourite, frequently used M.

In my view, there is nothing coincidental about this title to a linguistic precipitate that launches the debate about possible language universals – the most archaic structures – supporting and organising the speaking being. Indeed, it is easy to imagine the passionate conversations on the subject between, on the one hand, the musicians, Suzanne and Roger Deleutre, and, on the other, Marcel Lob, the grammarian, and Samuel, fairly proficient in both music and language. What, for example, explains the recurrence at the beginning of surprisingly similar words: *maman, mother, mutti, mama*? In Beckett's writing we find Murphy and his asylum, the Magdgalen Mental Mercyseat – later to become Maison Madeleine de Miséricorde Mentale, with a further *M* added in the other language – and then, after 'leapfrogging' over *Watt*, Beckett

[26] Samuel Beckett, *Watt* (London: Faber and Faber, [1953] 2009), 196.

takes a deep-water dive that brings him to see things from underneath: Mercier, Molloy, Malone. . ..

One answer to the question is the observation that this repetition prolongs the most simple sound that can be made with a shut mouth. Due to this physiological convenience, the *Mmm* sound allegedly becomes the baby's – and later likewise the gourmet's – favourite way of reviving the voluptuous satisfaction of milk in the mouth, especially as the mouth moulds itself around the breast or the baby's dummy, in exactly the same way as when they subsequently produce the sound and take pleasure in doing so. It is thus that moment of bliss, of fusion with what feeds it, that a baby would seem to reproduce with this early babble, leading like an echo to the pleasure of the adult who likewise craves returning there and translates the sound into their own language: *Mmm . . . maman, mother, mutti, mama.* The arousal is recognised by the parent and made to deviate imperceptibly towards them and their code, and then it is in turn recognised by the child, who delights in delighting the other and finally adopts the word. With this spiralling attraction, the consensual dimension – which I take in the primary sense of the word as the union of sensory pleasures – fortunately allows us to overlook the violence of the spokesperson: the natural, necessary influence of the adult over the babbling representational capacities of the child. This violence is nevertheless sometimes relived in adolescence when the language shared within the family circle is experienced as a constraint, as the fortified sound wall of an intolerable imprisonment – a terrifying machine for exerting influence or, conversely, a mindless cackling incapable of fulfilling a vital need for meaning.

Later, with the image of 'dead dogs' ('gobbets in a vomit' in the English version of *The Unnamable*)[27] encapsulating this inexorable maw now geared to pitiful devitalisation, we infer an adolescent-like Samuel Beckett who has projected his distress onto his family, in particular his mother (who perhaps lent herself to it through her mood swings). The mental excitement that threatened to overwhelm him was attributed either to her tyrannical disposition or to her outrageous shortcomings, and out of the desire to break free Beckett seems to have dreamt of cutting himself off from his own language, or at least to have set about 'rearranging' it. By forcing the language to another turn of the screw – an exile within exile – his living dogs and other snapping jaws[28] were a means of re-establishing a resource to be used against absolute negativity: the cruel impossibility of sufficient inner security, especially as – I insist on this to the extent that his writing insists – the psychical experience was supported by a bodily one with which he seems to have come to terms.

---

[27] Beckett, *Trilogy*, 327.
[28] The author is working with Beckett's French version, 'chiens morts' ('dead dogs') and not his English version ('gobbets in a vomit'; *The Unnamable*. In Beckett, *Trilogy*, 327).

Thus, the *W* of *Watt* does not so much represent a new distance that the author had established as, more convincingly, the game of toing and froing that he allowed himself to play or that he promised himself to play with his private terrors, towards which he returned with the help of the creative potential of nostalgia. In connection with this potential, which the letter *W* began to reinforce in a similar way to the letter *M* in the linguistic digression mentioned above, the success of the letter *W* is above all to have inscribed a direct incision in the archaic bonds between body and word, between arousal and representation.

Rather than imaging forth a forced exile (a premature birth) or critiquing a closed philosophical or psychological system (an implacable womb), rather than a self-therapeutic quest for an inner void (how could such a thing exist in prelinguistic infancy?), from now on Beckett's major project entailed capturing these essential harmonisations. And *Watt* was its scalding hot wellspring.

8.5   The Fold in Language Thought

> [. . .] tie the bottom of the sack fill it with mud tie the top it will make a good pillow.[29]

The fold conveys the idea of a return to the past, a reuniting of what had become disunited; I use this dressmaking image to further my contention that although Beckett's use of French is generally seen in connection with the necessity to counteract his Mother tongue, it also contains a regressive tendency geared towards reunion, opening up a kind of pocket of nostalgia for the writer to rummage around in. This intention was already apparent in Beckett's first serious attempts in French, Knowlson maintains, in 1938–9, when he wrote a poetry sequence featuring a character known as 'Little Fool':

> There are two very long ones that do not belong at all to the series, being quite straightforward descriptive poems (in French) of episodes in the life of a child. I do not know what they are worth.[30]

A few friends were called upon to give their opinion, with Beckett asking for his text back rapidly because, he wrote, 'I can't wait to take it to pieces',[31]

---

[29] Samuel Beckett, *How It Is* (London: John Calder, [1964] 1996), 52.

[30] Samuel Beckett, Letter to Thomas MacGreevy, 18 April 1939. Trinity College Dublin Library. In Knowlson, *Damned to Fame*, 294. These texts remain unpublished. Avigdor Arikha possessed a manuscript that he found inside a complete edition of Kant's works that Beckett had given him. This anecdote was related by Anne Atik in *Comment c'était: Souvenirs sur Samuel Beckett* (Paris: Éditions de l'Olivier, 2003), 14.

[31] Samuel Beckett, Letter to George Reavey, 16 June 1939. Harry Ransome Humanities Research Center, University of Texas, Austin. In Knowlson, *Damned to Fame*, 295. This rather aggressive phrase stands out from the short letter because it alone is in French.

an inclination that sheds a clearer light on the fragmented narratives that would follow, in that they seem to me to come straight from that period in early infancy when children build, take apart, and rebuild.

If we turn now to his books' editorial career, the 'official' turning point at which he changed languages for literary creation stands out because of an anecdote whose surface comedy barely conceals its underlying pain (although this editorial landmark probably only holds for the works of fiction since his essay on the Van Velde brothers, *The World and the Trousers*, may have been written a few months earlier in French). After returning to Paris in October 1945, Beckett began a new short story in English and then, beneath a line vigorously drawn across the manuscript a third of the way through, he continued in French. His correspondence reveals that he believed he could write faster in French, and this text did indeed lead to what he himself would call a real 'writing frenzy', including in particular *Waiting for Godot*, which at last confirmed him as a writer and brought him the material security that had hitherto been such a problem.

The bilingual narrative is entitled *Suite*. Simone de Beauvoir took the first part, translated by the author, for her review *Les Temps modernes*, but taking it as a joke or finding it in rather bad taste, she refused what he subsequently submitted. The high-flown style is admittedly interrupted by random lavatorial interpolations concerning wanting to urinate or break wind, or the importance of knowing how to scratch one's most private parts discreetly in public (there is nothing surprising in this lavatorial register: the arse is what props up the subject). This uncouthness, presented without the slightest note of pedantic counterpoint, seems to have been accepted naturally by Beckett when writing in French; similarly, in the private correspondence of his youth, he would use foreign languages to give vent to aggressive thoughts, and – out of a sort of modesty, or the wish to keep them confidential – certain scabrous quotations only remained on his desk long enough to be immediately transposed into French.

He found it extremely distressing not to be published because of what he had himself succeeded in accepting in his writing, which he believed in. He reacted in a proud, injured letter to Simone de Beauvoir, to which she did not reply:

> You grant me speech only to withdraw it from me before it has had time to produce meaning. You freeze an existence on the threshold of solving its own enigma. There is something nightmarish about that.[32]

---

[32] Samuel Beckett, Letter to Simone de Beauvoir, 25 September 1946. In *Lettres II: Les années Godot (1941–1956)*. In George Craig, Martha Dow Fehsenfeld, Dan Gunn, and Lois More Overbeck (eds.), translated by André Topia (Paris: Gallimard, 2015), 136. Extract translated by Sara Greaves; James Knowlson quotes the same passage, translated as follows: 'You allow me

Beckett is referring to his protagonist, whose destiny is destroyed by the publication refusal, but of course he makes a full confession here. His speech can only produce meaning – solve its own enigma – if it joins forces with his literary elaboration and the self-imposed restrictions that he goes on to explore (the earlier eruptive *Sanies*, as if the writing were placed over an abscess). This nightmare converged with the deep frustration of not being able to do anything with his episodes of mental excitement – by nature aggressive and immodest. This frustration was aggravated by the fact that no one was prepared to tolerate them, to allow them admittance so that he could perhaps process them, rather than disqualifying them. Beckett recognised the solitary despair of his adolescence, and probably of his childhood, when adults ignored his impulses and he failed to join in the game of letting himself be attacked, the better to demonstrate a survivor's adaptability.

He finally swallowed this disappointment, which did not get in the way of his determination – his conviction – that he had found his way forwards. While writing other short stories he began a novel, *Mercier and Camier*, which he finished in four months; it then took him half that time to write his first play, *Eleutheria* ('freedom' in Greek), although he deemed it unfinished and never sought to have it staged. *Molloy*, *Malone Dies*, and *The Unnamable* then follow in quick succession, again written in French, during the two years in which he began and rapidly finished *Waiting for Godot* (from October 1948 to January 1949).

Concerning the idea of 'freez[ing] an existence on the threshold of solving its own enigma', the view repeatedly voiced (at least in France) that contends that Beckett was only able to say 'I' when he chose to write in French is undoubtedly a romantic one. Those who have bought into this legend are oversimplifying the issue and overlooking numerous passages in the texts. Witness, for instance, the way the theme introduced by the French homophones *Je/jeu* (they get lost in translation: 'I'/'game')[33] is prepared within the English text, which tends to register the separation between the narrator and the action ('I stopped and climbed the bank to see the game').[34] Some ironic turns of phrase are even associated with the personalisation of the narrative, such as when words are used that are likely to be very unfamiliar to the reader and the latter is invited to salute the author: 'and a Kleinmeister's Leidenschaftsucherei (thank you Mr Beckett)'.[35]

---

to speak only to cut me off before my voice has time to mean something. You halt an existence before it can have the least achievement. This is the stuff of nightmares'. *Damned to Fame*, 360.

[33] Translator's note.

[34] Samuel Beckett, *Enueg I*. In *Selected Poems 1930–1938* (London: Faber and Faber, 2009), 13.

[35] Beckett, *More Pricks than Kicks*, 168.

The pronoun also appears in *Watt*, where the nostalgic construction begins, supported by the experience of exile where the sense of lack meets a surplus of sensations, some of which link up with and endow with meaning earlier sensations, thereby lending greater consistency to the 'subject':

[H]ow I feel it all again, after so long, here and here [...] all the old soil and fear and weakness offered, to be sponged away and forgiven! Haw! Or did I never feel it till now? Now when there is no warrant?[36]

Nostalgia is being able to feel sensations when there is no trigger. Excess, prolonged in the writing, meant feeling to the point of insensitivity; nostalgia, by giving access only to the spirit of place, encapsulated the excess, the possible 'mess', thereby liberating the author. That was the hard lesson learnt in Roussillon, but the allegation that he used 'I' 'only in French' does have some justification, is in fact justly confirmed, since Beckett apprehended himself differently, revealing a new mastery over his narrative powers. And his use of the personal pronoun does denote himself, even if it remains insufficient to observe the fold in his *oeuvre* (see *supra*) through the use of 'I' alone. French, as *Watt* leads us to intuit, is not so much responsible for the use of 'I' (*Je*) as for the emergence of a necessary new game (*jeu*) for the author to play, and of what could be compared with a musical score, stretched irresistibly between arousal and language. Admittedly, this tension does give rise to the possibility of another 'I', but not more so than to a new style of writing in terms of sensory perception as well as aggressive impulses (including obscenity). Like three musical staves, the emergence of 'I', sensory perception, and aggressive impulses form the three parts of a structural, structuring trio, in which each melodic line rises distinctly while at the same time reinforcing the two others so as to carry – both supporting and projecting it – the voice of Beckett.

If we take the incipits of the novels, we are immediately struck by the regeneration of the personal pronoun, by the firm hold it now has – while standing on the verge of destruction.

The journey of Mercier and Camier is one I can tell, if I will, for I was with them all the time. (*Mercier and Camier*)[37]
I am in my mother's room. It's I who live there now. (*Molloy*)[38]
I shall soon be quite dead at last in spite of all. Perhaps next month. Then it will be the month of April or of May. (*Malone Dies*)[39]
Where now? Who now? When now? Unquestioning. I, say I. (*The Unnamable*)[40]

---

[36] Beckett, *Watt*, 32.
[37] Samuel Beckett, *Mercier and Camier* (New York: Grove Press, [1970] 1975), 7.
[38] Beckett, *Trilogy*, 7.   [39] Beckett, *Trilogy*, 179.   [40] Beckett, *Trilogy*, 293.

Before *Mercier and Camier*, Beckett's writing style seemed aimed at objectivity while being placed over a sort of ill-adjusted subjective mask. By contrast, his first novel in French shows that 'I' has the upper hand ('if I will'), even if the narrator is not so much part of the action as a witness to it, whereas the ensuing texts place the narrator resolutely in their centre as the subject of the narrative and the narrating subject: a subject in the hands of the author.

Such unveiling is perilous; it is like acclimatising to too bright a light, especially when it involves this textual kneading and the inevitable face-to-face confrontation with the familiar ordeals consisting of violent outbursts or even fragmentation, followed logically enough by the theme of death, that of the mother and the narrator, as if thrown undiscerningly into the mix. But *Malone Dies* opens with a reference to the month of April, which is an allusion to Beckett's death that also evokes his birth in connection with the Resurrection (Samuel Beckett was born on Good Friday, 13 April 1906). This novel is also – given its proximity to what is ultimately another kind of death ('la petite mort') and the attempt to transcribe a kind of bliss – the one that most ostensibly foregrounds the possibilities of game playing:

This time I know where I am going, it is no longer the ancient night, the recent night. Now it is a game, I am going to play. I never knew how to play, till now.[41]

This clarifies his chosen path: to play the high stakes of the epicentre of being, the part that lies closest to primary arousal and which continues to provide the tenuous possibility of a link to words, at risk of it being radiated outwards. This desire to 'pant on to the Transfiguration'[42] is suggestive of a conception of writing as 'trance-figuration' – a 'frenzy' in which the writer falls, plunges towards the depths, and resurfaces, clinging to language. Yet there is no obvious way back up, for within this private geology reversals are no longer opposed; diving headlong is simultaneously an ascension, with the vocabulary of the French language as the leaves and branches of the fall/rise of the subject: Samuel Beckett. Bringing the trilogy to an end, *The Unnamable* testifies to the fact that the ultimate stage of disintegration has been reached, with 'I' only existing in order to reassemble tenuous perceptions and radical aggressiveness (although in fact there is far more than that to this crucible), while also confirming the possibility of running aground ('Where now?'), which we observe in the period of deceleration in his production that was to ensue.

Never leaving the trajectory of the 'I' that continues textually as an arena of play and, naturally, as a history and a geography in which – as with the hoped-for relaxation in the relationship with his mother – an equilibrium is negotiated

---

[41] Beckett, *Malone Dies*. In *Trilogy*, 180.   [42] Beckett, *Malone Dies*. In *Trilogy*, 179.

between engagement (clinging) and release (being torn apart), it was apparently out of discretion and jokingly that Beckett most often answered the question about why he took to writing in French. In a letter to one of his translators, for instance, he wrote, '[here is] a lead, nevertheless: the need to be ill-equipped', and another letter dated 1954 lists diverse reasons for breaking away. First, he mentions the relationship with Joyce: 'I think I felt very early on that the thing urging me on and also the means at my disposal were practically the opposite of the thing urging him on and the means that he had at his disposal'; second, the choice of French, his essay on Proust; and, finally, the possible influence of Kafka: 'I felt myself at home [in English], too much so, maybe that was what prevented me from carrying on. It was an immediately understood cause'.[43]

The infamous remark 'because it is easier to write without style in French' was allegedly confided to a student;[44] but to his friend John Fletcher he gave a different reason: 'to get noticed myself' (*sic*)[45]. Irresistibly, the joke reads on several levels, especially because the *tour de force* of the 'trance-figuration' supported by the language is concealed and revealed in an allusion to symbolist poet Stéphane Mallarmé, who raised himself above the burden of circumstance, including depression and numerous bereavements (the first being that of his mother, who died when he was four years old), and aspired to a sort of oneiric purification. He observed: 'With us, the conscious mind lacks what explodes above. What is it for? A game'.[46]

And this need to play games, such as patience or hide-and-seek, mischievously infiltrates the other alleged reasons. Although it is pertinent to consider Beckett's search for 'no style' in connection with the need to distance himself from Joyce's mentoring, it is more legitimate still to see it in light of his craving, since adolescence at least, to shake off the influence of that familiar linguistic spokesperson, which claimed to regulate his sense of self while overlooking a vast, untranslatable inner barbarousness. Logically enough, a strategy of 're-marking me' is set up in the foreign tongue. This was a new means of figuration that would allow him to grasp 'more truly' his own site of the foreign, obsessively circling round a pared-down style that had been claimed back by an Ego situated as close as possible to the primary enigmas

[43] George Craig, Martha Dow Fehsenfeld, Dan Gunn, and Lois More Overbeck (eds.), *Lettres II: Les années Godot (1941–1956)*. Translated by André Topia (Paris: Gallimard, 2015), 461. Translated by Sara Greaves.

[44] Bair, *Samuel Beckett: A Biography*, 149.

[45] John Fletcher, 'Écrivain bilingue'. In Tom Bishop and Raymond Federman (eds.), *Cahiers de l'Herne: Samuel Beckett* (Paris: Éditions de l'Herne, 1976), 202. Translator's note: I have imitated Beckett's non-standard French grammar: 'pour faire remarquer moi'.

[46] Stéphane Mallarmé, *La musique et les lettres* (Paris: Gallimard, Bibliothèque de la Pléiade, 1945), 647. Translated by Sara Greaves.

that he had experienced, but thus far without establishing any form of representation for them.

Of course, this sense of 'truth' is felt by the reader and is founded not so much on the 'I' as on the expression of what is generally submitted to much more control: obscenity, instinctual aggressiveness, and an unveiled sensitivity pushed right back onto sensory perception. My hypothesis is that this sense of truth corresponds to the Lacanian order of the 'real', approached differently through the use of French; for Samuel Beckett's language switch does indeed seem liberating, enabling him to press further and reach for his so-called 'no style' – the most primeval sounding of subjectivity as it breaks free of language. After *Mercier and Camier*, shutting oneself up in one's bedroom provides an exemplary illustration of the paradoxically regressive nature of the journey, and, directed more towards the body than the word, towards language's most carnal underpinning, his writing makes it possible to represent a corporeality with its senses on the alert – all agog as in infancy (although this aspect is more ostensible in the theatrical writing, with its 'bedroom-stage' and its 'sensory' technique, which places the audience themselves in a waiting position).

In other words, in French, sensory utterance sets up a form of synthesis. It rests on the subjective 'I' or moves towards it, allowing it entry where hitherto it rejected it – or was itself rejected to the benefit of an overly assiduous intellectualism far removed from the flesh. This expressiveness thereby feeds into two descriptive axes, through reciprocal hybridisation: outside and inside, the narrator's immediate environment and the ever more finely sounded inner self. Thus, while each of his works from the outset features a container (a lobster shell in the first short story of *More Pricks than Kicks* – also therefore foregrounding the shedding of the skin – pots, jars, dustbins, the mother's bedroom, the rocking chair, etc.), the presence of the character only fills that container completely in the narratives in which 'I' is the subject of the game being played, which is to say the texts written directly in French, except for the first one in which the 'I' is a witness, and *Texts for Nothing*, probably the last, in which the 'I' is dissolved or rather absolved in the female presence – that presence necessary to the emerging 'I' to envelop it with gestures, coverings, words... at risk of (s)mothering it.

The environment in which 'I' finds itself evolves, therefore, from a stylised Dublin in *Mercier and Camier* to the bedroom in *Molloy* and *Mallone Dies*, a jar in *The Unnamable,* and, finally, an almost complete loss of reference in *Texts for Nothing*. Concomitantly, the role of sensory perception in the texts is above all constantly enriched, to the extent that they seem to rely on it entirely, on those basic perceptive stimulations, in which now and again Irish memories are also inserted, corresponding to an increasing 'Irishness' that replaces the would-be objective naturalism of the novels in English.

There is an increasingly hallucinatory quality in the writing style, as we see, for instance, in the more and more frequent descriptions of Beckett's childhood landscapes that are inserted into the trancelike narrative present. Rather like the palette-knife strokes of a painter and gradually resembling stage directions for the theatre, the thing surges up within the word, seemingly calmly – but with that ecstatic calm that succeeds dazzlement:

> They turned east off the road from Dublin to Malahide short of the Castle woods and soon it came into view, not much more than a burrow, the ruin of a mill on the top, choked lairs of furze and brambles passim on its gentle slopes. It was a landmark for miles around on account of the high ruin. (*More Pricks than Kicks*)[47]

> Even as a spoke he saw a little window opening on an empty place, a moor unbroken save for a single track, where no shade ever falls, winding out of sight its gentle alternate curves. Not a breath stirs the pale grey air. In the far distance here and there the seam of earth and sky exudes a sunflooded beyond. (*Mercier and Camier*)[48]

> His back is turned to the river, but perhaps it appears to him in the dreadful cries of the gulls that evening assembles, in paroxysms of hunger, round the outflow of the sewers, opposite the Bellevue Hotel. Yes, they too, in a last frenzy before night and its high crags, swoop ravening about the offal. (*Malone Dies*)[49]

> The top, very flat, of a mountain, no, a hill, but so wild, so wild, enough. Quag, heath up to the knees, faint sheep-tracks, though scooped deep by the rains. (*Texts for Nothing*) [50]

Even in *The Unnamable* and *Texts for Nothing*, however, where the writing continues doggedly aiming for the depths, what predominates is the atomic explosion of the container, with the odd vague Parisian and Irish toponyms inscribing a 'full' nostalgic quality beside the fragmented descriptions of the primeval-seeming sensory experiences (the most prehistoric sentient subject is Worm in *The Unnamable:* a larva-cum-subject with its single ear and single eye constantly on the alert).

What, then, can explain the fact that French seems able to harbour this nostalgia, even to promulgate it? The consolation it brought seemed unattainable for Beckett before his war experience, and his biographers are right to insist on the personality change that was observed in him after this difficult time, when the weak-willed, sarcastic youth turned into a man so calm and discreet that he was more often remembered as an embodiment of serenity.

I have discussed at some length the reconnection of the past with the present during the writing of *Watt*, but many critics date this evolution at the death of Beckett's mother, as if that previously stimulating, even disruptive being, from

---

[47] Beckett, *More Pricks than Kicks*, 17.   [48] Beckett, *Mercier and Camier*, 41.
[49] Beckett, *Trilogy*, 230.
[50] Samuel Beckett, *Texts for Nothing*. In *The Complete Short Prose* (New York: Grove Press [1958 French version, 1959 English version] 1995), 100.

whom he protected himself through distance, only existed externally and that when she died was then transmuted into a more positively depressive object within him. Appearances can be misleading, however, and although May Beckett's death occurred just before the publication of his new works, in 1950, Samuel had in fact already written his trilogy as well as *Godot*. In fact, the exile within exile was perpetuated by his writing in French. It reinforced his conviction that he was on the right track, and he felt more self-contained and showed it, especially regarding the possibility of a far more peaceable relationship with his mother. But it is nonetheless undeniable that her attitude had greatly changed, probably causing her son – after severing relations with her for almost six years – to start anticipating her death. Upon returning to Ireland in 1945, he noticed the first symptoms of Parkinson's disease and found her surprisingly vulnerable; he would go back to see her in all serenity, without Suzanne, every spring until the end.

The turning point in the life of the man and in his writing is also, legitimately enough, connected to what he disclosed concerning his 'revelation': 'I was able to turn my mind to Molloy and the others from the day I became aware of my madness. From that time only did I start writing things as I felt them'.[51]

Beckett varied in the specifics of place and time of the vision preceding that great urge to write, finally asserting that it took place after the war, during his first stay at his mother's. If such a vision existed, I think it corresponds to his acknowledgement of the inevitable mortality of his mother, followed by a kind of exaltation: life goes on, deep down something at least resists, interpenetrating and transmuting itself (hence the liquid identities of Molloy and the other protagonists), something related to the sensation, the arousal, and the adhesive viscosity of the relationship that life calls for; along with a beyond-the-word 'madness' that must no longer be ignored.

In fact, James Knowlson plays down the impact of the revelation by emphasising that '[t]he ground had been well prepared'[52] for this moment of truth. On the other hand, Didier Anzieu's interpretation seems an exaggeration: in the aftermath of Beckett's course of treatment with Bion, he views it as the conscious crystallising of a process in which Beckett allegedly decided to pursue his therapy via the characters replicated in his literary works. Beckett only alluded to the epiphany long after it took place, so it is impossible to decide whether it was a response to a sudden irruption that was more or less part and parcel of his psychoanalytical experience of ten years earlier, with the war in between and his urgent questioning about limits and death, or whether it was enriched by fictional invention flowing back towards it. Either way, what

---

[51] Interview with Gabriel d'Aubarède, *Les Nouvelles littéraires* (Paris: Larousse, 1961), 7.
[52] Knowlson, *Damned to Fame*, 353.

remains undeniable is its resolution in the highly condensed phrase 'I became aware of my madness', denoting both the accepting – and exceeding – of a part of himself by the writer, as if the arousal of the unrepresentable had become his motivation and his objective. Not the void, I insist, but excitement; not death, but that small death of sexual climax ('la petite mort').

Enveloping his creation in a mythological aura as was his wont, the revival of the fertile lightning flash in *Krapp's Last Tape* ('that memorable night in March, at the end of the pier')[53] is excessively suggestive in its imagery of an existential paroxysm akin to Münch's (anguished, psychotic) painting *The Scream*, especially since Krapp's tape is cut off in the middle and we are prevented from discerning anything else there – no jubilatory climax. But the deafening tumult of the sea may have played a bridging role: there was perhaps a moment when the liquid nature of the Ego, destined to keep on overflowing till death, appeared to Beckett definitively as a force, the force of water passing relentlessly over wood and rocks, tirelessly eroding them. Traversed by that oceanic feeling, he may then have recognised the possibility of flooding the breakwaters, of transgressing boundaries, including that of his mother's death. We can at least make this claim: that what resists is not the solid matter but the water that seeps through, on condition that one feels with – consents to – the liquid solidity of a nostalgia capable of keeping the mourning process alive.

There is a substantial link between mourning and translation, in that the principle of equivalence-but-not-identity in translation is nevertheless able to support the need to register absence; however, the security afforded by translation in allowing Beckett to pursue his liquid fantasy of smoothing over differences will not be discussed here, as the link between mourning and translation more aptly accounts for the bilingual organisation of his creative processes after *Waiting for Godot*. It comes into play in the context of the ensuing play, *Endgame* (1957), which metabolises the death of his brother in 1954 (from that date on, he had no close family in Dublin), at a time when certain solicitations were encouraging a return to his Mother tongue, and from then on his writer's 'workshop' would be geared towards both languages. Regarding liquidation and subversion, what I would add are a few words on the way aggressivity was released by the use of the non-Mother tongue, given how much this particular vigour contributed to the renewal of creative potential in Beckett's writing.

Replying, 'it's easier to write without style' to a French speaker – inevitably convinced that more than any other (and certainly more than English?), their language contains the entire history of literature – was slightly provocative. But to me this remark confirms Beckett's desire for game playing, as well as

---

[53] Samuel Beckett, *Krapp's Last Tape and Embers* (London: Faber and Faber, [1958] 1959).

the fact that the non-Mother tongue was used as a transitional medium aimed at differentiating himself from the primary object (the mother) by providing a supporting medium for the depressive affects, as well as for the aggressive impulses that the inevitable separation elicits; for it is the transitional object that is sullied in order to retain a sufficiently pure relationship with the object he has moved on from. And while this overflow of hostile feelings into literature is observable in Beckett's early productions, in English, the foreign tongue magnificently amplifies the means of expression to the extent that Simone de Beauvoir felt offended by it when she read the second part of *Suite*.

The acme of violence seemed, however, to have been reached at the end of *Murphy*, when the 'hero' commits suicide and his parcel of ashes is used as a football or rugby ball, depending on the aptitudes of the bar's patrons. But, like the complex installation for the removal of fetid air from the lavatory, this scandal was shrouded in farce and smacked of a practical joke. Following hot on the heels of blasphemy but still in a jocular tone, the conclusion of *Watt* seems more radically brutal, suddenly discrediting its protagonist by alluding to him as an orgasm ('a wet dream'), an ejection that is more categorical in translation: 'cette rigole de foutre à la manque'.[54] Nevertheless, it is in the following narratives, in French, that a further step is taken, this time permanently. *Molloy*, especially, exhibits fury of staggering intensity throughout the novel – a degree of rage more or less unprecedented in the history of literature so far (not even Louis-Ferdinand Céline surpassed it – except, of course, when he abused the very value of literary creation by stooping to write racist tracts. Beckett's approach was quite different; to be more precise, he played out his destructiveness differently – in fact, it was not so much that Céline went one step further, but that he went about it with less intelligence).

This aggressive drive can be studied in its various transmutations, whereas, close to Beckett's depressive adolescent soul-searching, what was deposited in *Murphy* was the dead end of suicide, only slightly softened in *Watt*. The new style enables the narrator to stay alive and on edge, as it deflects the lust for murder onto another character who is afflicted with its relentless pressure: the assassination of the policeman by Camier, that of a fellow who could admittedly be Molloy,[55] or indeed himself, by Moran, the crime that regulates relationships in *Malone Dies*.[56] Similarly, it is noteworthy that while the

---

[54] In English: 'that stream of dribbling spunk'. While the two versions contain the same blasphemous attack on Puritan values, the original text, written in English, gushes on, testing the protagonist in slightly less disparaging terms: 'And they say there is no God, said Mr Case. All three laughed heartily at this extravagance. [...] And our friend? [...] the long wet dream with the hat and bags?' Beckett, *Watt*, 214.

[55] '[...] his head in a pulp. [...] He no longer resembled me'. Beckett, *Molloy*. In *Trilogy*, 152.

[56] 'I killed them, or took their place, or fled. I feel within me the glow of that old frenzy'. Beckett, *Malone Dies*. In *Trilogy*, 194.

sadomasochistic associations are common, in the French prose they become archetypes: the father–son relationship in *Molloy* is a model of parental tyranny, and the rope that Pozzo uses to lead Lucky in *Godot* revives the dialectics of master and slave.

The contrast is thus striking between the man Beckett had become and the 'materials' deposited in his writing, and to my mind this is the crux of the fold, its energy. It was not only a matter of being authorised to say 'shit' in the non-Mother tongue even though a certain pre-emptive reticence remained, but rather that his writing catered for a new circulation of internal violence acknowledged as a source of creative power, such as we see garnered up by Malone, and that his ey as man and writer was channelled differently owing to the possibilities projecting it onto a new medium opened up. Meanwhile, off the page the aggressive outbursts did indeed become rare, being practically limited to his famously exacting theatrical directing.

As to the 'frenzy' that had to be marshalled as a principle of continuity, as tenacity, with the illumination of 1945 featuring only as a thrust forwards in search of confirmation of his choice of French, some light is shed by the following programmatic observation in his first book, the essay on Proust (1930):

The only fertile quest is excavation, immersion, a concentration of the mind, a plunging of the depths. The artist may indeed be active, but in a negative manner: he withdraws from the vanity of phenomena situated at the peripheral circumference, he allows himself to be drawn to the eye of the cyclone.[57]

Written before the psychoanalysis with Bion, this text shows Beckett conceptualising negativity and constraint well before meeting the man who would go on to theorise those things (the writer may have inspired the analyst rather than the other way round, as Bion's publications date from the early 1960s). Either way, this passage announces and consecrates the kind of exile Beckett was aiming for, far more an internal exile than a political or geographical one, even though it took the war for him to achieve it. It also sheds light, once again, on how illusory his serenity was, how subordinate to the overriding ambition to reach for 'the eye of the cyclone' and immerse himself in the site of maximum arousal it contained. This path inevitably required audacity – as none can approach the extreme edge of the storms and hurricanes that compose the depths of narrative being with impunity and safety (behind the latch, the wolf's teeth...). Hence the necessity for a certain masochism – some

---

[57] Samuel Beckett, *Proust* (Paris: Éditions de Minuit, 1930), 77. Extract translated by Sara Greaves.

self-directed violence – to provide a boundary and a form of restraint: a rope such as the one controlling Lucky in *Waiting for Godot*. Beckett's self-restraint entailed writing in a less immediate language than his native English, and then contending with self-translation: an impossible task since – as both author and translator – the limitlessness of the imagination is curtailed by a real limit.

Moreover, the death of his mother does not at all reinforce his 'serenity'; on the contrary, it seems, chronologically at least, to give rise to a depressive period of unproductiveness. I have selected here the acme of aggressivity, to be found in the final text of the trilogy ('I'll fix their jargon for them''),[58] that *Unnamable* circumscribed by words gathered during May's final illness, yet one may readily suppose that her death reactivated guilt feelings and inhibited his ability to continue in the same direction. The beginning of the following narrative attests to this very clearly, with the return of a prohibiting force: 'Suddenly, no, at last, long last, I couldn't any more, I couldn't go on.'[59]

In the same way as a state of paralysis can be produced by the encounter of internal enigmas with external absurdity, and this duplication of meaninglessness can lead to a *stuporous collapse*, so Beckett experienced going too far, exceeding his own powers. Viewing the 'I' from underneath, in its earliest determinants, led him face-to-face with the possibility of its annihilation at his mother's death. *Texts for Nothing* took shape very slowly and seems to have been undertaken in the aftermath of *The Unnamable* in order to stay on course as he began to feel stifled. His resolve remained intact, however, fed as it was by the state of arousal motivating him and whose pressure valve or emergency exit he had discovered. Despite that, to continue he would have to embrace a new container – a new exile – the medium of another 'excavation': that medium would be theatre. 'I began to write *Godot* as a relaxation, to get away from the awful prose I was writing at the time', and 'from the wildness and rulelessness of the novels'.[60]

8.6   Conclusion

> 'To get away' – the better to stand guard . . . and to stand guard over himself.

Placed within a more consistent narrative than it may appear, linked to his early, sensual love of languages, Beckett's capacity to change languages not

---

[58] Samuel Beckett, *Trilogy: Molloy, Malone Dies, The Unnamable* (London: Calder, [1959] 2003), 328. But see also 'I walk the streets, I lash into them one after the other, it's the town of my youth, I'm looking for my mother to kill her, I should have thought of that a bit earlier, before being born, it's raining, I'm all right'. Samuel Beckett, *The Unnamable*. In *Three Novels: Molloy, Malone Dies, The Unnamable* (New York: Grove Press), 395.

[59] Samuel Beckett, *Stories and Texts for Nothing* (New York: Grove Press, 1967), 75.

[60] Beckett. In Bair, *Samuel Beckett: A Biography*, 381.

only opened an essential phase in his writing, enabling his 'I', his sensory perceptions, and his vigorous aggressive capacities to mature, but it also, naturally and very pragmatically, provided the scaffolding for his remarkable ability to vary his system of representation throughout his career.

To pursue the paradoxes of language, the great paradox here is that of Beckett's having passed through the feigned coldness of the foreign language, the better to return to the sensory powers of his own, the better to inhabit it, the better no doubt to inhabit himself by voicing the lost *infans*. Based on this, Beckett gradually unveiled the remarkable connection between translation (*traducere*, 'to lead beyond'), death throes (on condition that this is taken to mean a threshold experience in which it is not so much death that is encountered as life exacerbated by close contact with it), and the hypnotic trance. He located his creativity within the death throes of language, the amplification of its vivacity within its finiteness, finding confirmation therein of his 'trance-figuration' method.

His impetus was thus to delve deep, continuing both to bury and nurture his excitement, partly transformed as nostalgia, and to remain deeply covert, not raising himself to the heights of the intellectual as embodied by Joyce. The companionship of Joyce and, more briefly, the psychoanalysis with Bion probably left him with the fear of adhering too closely to them, with the imperious necessity – once again – to detach himself. He was an unrelenting force – akin to the actor Buster Keaton who so dazzled him as a child and whom he repaid in his last true phase (*Film*, 1965), by revealing their common destiny: that irresistible or refractory energy, the very source of that energy for which I have coined the phrase 'beyond the word', to mean *infans* energy, a form of bliss that will not be satisfied merely with words and which requires a wider screen.

Naturally, this beyond-the-word trance turns out to be asymptotic since the quest for a 'pure' language is doomed to fail, as whenever one touches the bottom of the pit it immediately reassembles and recedes farther out of reach. While the experience of lack seems central, it is nevertheless nothing more than the solid margin supporting the writer's straight path. Translation affords salutary collisions with the untranslatable, failure is fortuitous when it keeps arousal alive, and Beckettian exile is a kind of waiting conducive to maximum desire of the other.

Under cover of the void, or rather beyond the void around which he circles, Samuel Beckett's phenomenal power keeps itself warm – *ostinato* right to the very end.

Bibliography

Anzieu, Didier. *Beckett*. Paris: Gallimard, 1998.

Atik, Anne. *Comment c'était: Souvenirs sur Samuel Beckett*. Paris: Éditions de l'Olivier, 2003.

Bair, Deirdre. *Samuel Beckett: A Biography*. New York: Simon & Schuster, [1978] 1990.

Beckett, Samuel. *Proust*. Paris: Éditions de Minuit, 1930.

    Krapp's Last Tape and Embers. London: Faber and Faber, [1958] 1959.

    Not I: Collected Shorter Plays. New York: Grove Weidenfeld, 1984.

    Endgame: The Complete Dramatic Works. London: Faber and Faber, 1986.

    Nohow On: Company, Ill Seen Ill Said, Worstward Ho: 4 Books in One. New York: Grove Press, [1983] 1995.

    How It Is. London: John Calder, [1964] 1996.

    Letter to Tom MacGreevy, 10 March 1935. Trinity College Dublin Library. In James Knowlson. *Damned to Fame: The Life of Samuel Beckett*. London: Bloomsbury, [1996] 1997.

    Letter to Thomas MacGreevy, 18 April 1939. Trinity College Dublin Library. In James Knowlson. *Damned to Fame: The Life of Samuel Beckett*. London: Bloomsbury, [1996] 1997.

    Letter to George Reavey, 16 June 1939. Harry Ransome Humanities Research Center, University of Texas, Austin. In James Knowlson, *Damned to Fame: The Life of Samuel Beckett*. London: Bloomsbury, [1996] 1997.

    Trilogy: Molloy, Malone Dies, The Unnamable. London: Calder, [1959] 2003.

    'Enueg I'. *Selected Poems 1930–1988*. London: Faber and Faber, 2009.

    Watt. London: Faber and Faber, [1953] 2009.

    More Pricks than Kicks. London: Faber and Faber, [1934] 2010.

    Mercier and Camier. New York: Grove Press, [1970] 1975, and London: Faber and Faber, 2010.

    Letter to Simone de Beauvoir, 25 September 1946. In George Craig, Martha Dow Fehsenfeld, Dan Gunn, and Lois More Overbeck (eds.), *Lettres II. Les années Godot (1941–1956)*. Translated by André Topia. Paris: Gallimard, 2015.

    Lettres II. Les années Godot (1941–1956). George Craig, Martha Dow Fehsenfeld, Dan Gunn, and Lois More Overbeck (eds.). Translated by André Topia. Paris: Gallimard, 2015.

    Lettres, IV (1966–1989). George Craig, Martha Dow Fehsenfeld, Dan Gunn, and Lois More Overbeck (eds.). Translated by Gérard Kahn. Paris: Gallimard, 2018.

D'Aubarède, Gabriel. 'Interview'. *Les Nouvelles littéraires*. Paris: Larousse, 1961.

Driver, Tom. 'Columbia University Forum'. In Lawrence Graver and Raymond Federman (eds.), *Samuel Beckett: The Critical Heritage*. London: Routledge, [1979] 2005.

Fédida, Pierre. *Le site de l'étranger*. Paris: Presses Universitaires de France, 1995.

Fletcher, John. 'Écrivain bilingue'. In Tom Bishop and Raymond Federman (eds.), *Cahiers de l'Herne: Samuel Beckett*. Paris: Éditions de l'Herne, 1976.

Gilman, Sander L., Carole Blair, and David J. Parent (trans. and eds.). *Friedrich Nietzsche on Rhetoric and Language*. New York: Oxford University Press, 1989.

Knowlson, James. *Damned to Fame: The Life of Samuel Beckett*. London: Bloomsbury, [1996] 1997.

Mallarmé, Stéphane. *La musique et les lettres*. Paris: Gallimard, Bibliothèque de la Pléiade, [1895] 1945.

Shakespeare, William. *The Tempest, Act I scene II*. In Alfred Harbage (ed.), *William Shakespeare: The Complete Works*. The Pelican Text. London: Penguin, 1969.

Tustin, Frances. 'The black hole – A significant element in autism', *Free Associations*, n° 11, 1988, pp. 35–50.

9   Language, the Brain, and Relating

Boris Cyrulnik

Why is it that no baby speaks on the day it is born?[1] Only Pantagruel, barely out of the womb, cried out, 'Drink! Drink! Bring me some good wine!', and wine was brought from all over the cantons of Beusse and Bibarais.

To discover which natural language the brain would produce, Pharaoh Psametik 1 (664–610 BC), as well as Frederic II of Prussia in the sixteenth century, purchased children from poor parents and had them raised in material comfort by servants who had been instructed not to speak to them. These children died or grew up with severe mental disabilities. James IV of Scotland had a child raised by a mute nurse, which led him to assert that the child had naturally spoken Hebrew. And even in India, Akbar the Great (sixteenth century) carried out the same experiment and obtained the same catastrophic results.[2] These experiments are founded on the following postulate: which language can the brain produce – Hebrew, Greek, or Latin?

> To explain how language develops in the living world, I will proceed with the following:
>
> – A phylogenetic survey of the animal world,
> – A few ontogenetic experimental observations in human children,
> – How the Mother tongue has an enduring effect, with a forceful comeback among the elderly, and
> – A modification of the world-perceiving apparatus through speech.

9.1   Phylogenesis: Steps towards Speech[3]

Sea slugs, with a ganglion containing 20,000 neurons, principally process data relating to heat, hygrometry. and light.[4] A bat organises its existence around

---

[1] This chapter was written for this volume by Boris Cyrulnik and translated by Sara Greaves.
[2] Gabriel Bergounioux, 'L'origine du langage: Mythes et théories'. In Jean-Marie Hombert (ed.), *Aux origines des langues et du langage* (Paris: Fayard, 2005), 23.
[3] Phylogenesis is the study of evolutionary relatedness within groups of organisms.
[4] Hygrometry is a branch of physics concerned with the measurement of humidity, especially of the atmosphere.

echolocation.[5] Birds achieve stupendous visual performances, and higher mammals are governed by the sense of smell. Comparing brains rapidly gives rise to a problem: the gradual development of an assemblage of neurons that is increasingly capable of decontextualising information. A prefrontal lobe, the neurological base of anticipation, connects with the limbic circuit, the neuro-logical base of memory. This neural organisation processes data that is not situated within the present context but belongs to the past and has been committed to memory, or is yet to occur. Birds possess a few prefrontal lamellae above the olfactory bulb. In higher mammals such as cats and dogs, 15 per cent of the total weight of the brain is devoted to this assemblage. In non-human primates, the proportion is judged to be 20 per cent, and in human beings 30 per cent of the weight of the brain means they have a powerful aptitude for responding to information that is not within the present context, but which can be mediated through a sensorial substitute, such as a cry or a pheromone, whose perceived structure signals an unperceived danger.[6] In the living world, a gradual retreat from immediacy can be observed, but we are a long way off from speech.

If you put a baby in an environment in which people speak to each other – without school, without books – they will learn to speak. A dog, in the same environment, will not learn to speak, but it will learn to recognise about 200 words. Does this dog hear meaningful words, or sound structures? I have a friend who has two Irish setters. When he says, 'Let's go out', the dogs run to the door. A child would have heard a triple articulation: 'Let's', all of us together, 'out', outside, 'go', we all go outside together. The dogs probably heard a prosodic figure, 'letsgowout', that signals a future outing. They will have heard a snatch of verbal music that refers to something that is not to be found in the present context, but which is to come. Such information as this is far superior to a reflex, which would be an immediate, non-corticalised response;[7] rather, it is a sensory process on the way to becoming a symbol since this verbal sound comes in lieu of something that does not exist in the immediate context, but which is signalled by a sensory organisation. It is an unconscious cognitive process that allows the living organism to understand the world it lives in and to designate objects or events absent from the context. However, this sensory, signalling process is still a far cry from speech.

---

[5] Echolocation is a process in which animals such as bats can find their way in the dark by producing sound waves that echo when they are reflected off an object.

[6] A pheromone is a chemical substance released by an animal that influences the behaviour of another animal of the same species or group, for example, by attracting it sexually.

[7] A non-corticalised response is a response unrelated to cortex. Cortex is the outer or superficial part of an organ or a bodily structure (e.g., the kidney, an adrenal gland, the cerebellum, or a bone).

Among vervet monkeys, the lookout sends out a cry whose structure indicates the direction of the danger.[8] One cry expresses the emotion triggered by a hovering eagle, another points out a leopard on a branch, and a third signals the presence of a snake on the ground. The monkeys of the group adapt their behavioural responses to the cry, without having seen the predator.[9] The sensory object, the cry, has replaced the predator it designates.

The case of the large apes is frequently cited. Washoe, for instance, a female chimpanzee taught Ameslan (American Sign Language) by the Gardner couple, allegedly learnt a lexigram of 250 signs. Kanzi, a bonobo, could type 348 symbols on a keyboard and invent a sort of pidgin: 'Open orange ... bird water...'.[10]

This brief phylogenetic survey leads to one single assertion: The more encephalised a living organism is, the better able it is to respond to information that is not perceived in reality but which can be mediated by an intermediary sensory organisation that refers to it. In other words, before speech emerges, the perceived world can be analysed, be understood, and elicit behavioural responses adapted to data situated further and further away.[11] A non-corticalised sea slug can only respond to simple, immediate, and non-mediated stimuli (dryness, acidity, heat, and light), whereas a higher mammal can put sounds together that replace an unperceived object.

9.2   Crafting the Word-Producing Apparatus

Cerebral ontogenesis[12] is in preparation from the moment the gametes fuse together. When Laius's spermatozoid enters Jocasta's ovule, the only possible outcome is a human brain. These combined cells, now engaged in cell division, start out immersed in a chemical environment, but the stress hormones (i.e., cortisol and catecholamines) have a very early impact on these cells, and the sexual hormones induce the differentiation of the sexual organs as early as day fourteen.[13] Genetic determinism is undoubtedly a major factor, but it is highly

---

[8] The vervet monkey is a small, black-faced monkey, common in East Africa.

[9] Michel Soulé and Boris Cyrulnik, *L'intelligence avant la parole* (Paris: Éditions sociales françaises, ÉSF éditeur, 1998).

[10] Brian Duignan, "The Language of Apes", *Saving Earth / Encyclopedia Britannica*, www .britannica.com/explore/savingearth/the-language-of-apes.

[11] Jacques Vauclair, *La cognition animale* (Paris: Presses Universitaires de France/Que sais-je?, 1996).

[12] Ontogenesis pertains to the development of an individual organism.

[13] Cortisol is a steroid hormone involved in the body's stress management. At times of stress, it allows a release of sugar to meet the increased demand for energy, particularly in the muscles, heart, and brain. Catecholamines are hormones released into the blood at times of physical or psychical stress.

insufficient as an explanation of the construction of a brain able to understand and produce words.

The genetic mutation that took place 200,000 years ago with the FoxP2 gene may explain motor speech disorders,[14] when there is a malfunction of the neural circuitry of the striatum and cerebellum,[15] but it cannot explain the crafting of a brain able to use language since crocodiles – which possess the same FoxP2 gene – speak less well than humans.

The word-making machine receives constant pressure from the environment. A developing brain performs transactions with the sensory structures that surround it, so that throughout its development it is constantly moulded by an environment that never ceases to change.

The first environment is

– The mother's womb, then
– The mother's or father's arms, which replace it far sooner than was previously thought, then
– The family sensory cocoon, and then
– The family, neighbourhood, and cultural narratives.

This assemblage forms an ecology in which the forces that sculpt the brain originate farther and farther from the body.

9.3   Forging Forces in Uterine Ecology

When a pregnant woman undergoes prolonged stress, her cortisol ends up crossing the placental membrane. The baby she carries sleeps from eighteen to twenty hours a day, but when stimulated, the baby swallows four to five litres per day of amniotic liquid ... full of 'Cortancyl'.[16] If the stress is acute, the rush of cortisol will quickly be neutralised by the effervescence of the foetus's neurons, which branch out into 300,000 synapses per minute.[17] But if the stress is chronic, the cells of the limbic system will swell and burst.[18] The baby will be born with an alteration of the fronto-limbic system, leading to difficulty in memorising things and controlling their emotions. They will have trouble

---

[14] The FoxP2 gene is linked to the capacity for human speech and language.

[15] The corpus striatum or striatum is a cluster of neurons present in the forebrain, which controls cognition, reward systems, and coordination. The cerebellum is a structure of the central nervous system. Located at the back of the brain, it controls the coordination of muscles and the maintenance of bodily equilibrium.

[16] Cortancyl is medication derived from blood cortisol.

[17] A synapse is the point at which a nervous impulse passes from one neuron to another.

[18] The limbic system is a group of neural formations situated deep within the brain and is notably involved in emotional responses and motivation. It includes subcortical structures such as the hypothalamus, the hippocampus, and the amygdala.

learning the words of the family environment. Their emotional disorder will make it hard for them to relate, which will worsen the speech impediment. The baby will be born with a cognitive disability caused by the mother's distress (and not by the mother). This maternal distress may be due to her background, to domestic violence, to social insecurity, to war, or to one of life's accidents.[19] This heterogeneity of causes, mediatised by toxic substances, alters the development of the word-making machine.

In the uterus, touch is a highly effective communication channel. When the mother speaks, the high frequencies of her voice are filtered by her body, but the low frequencies are efficiently transmitted by both her body and the amniotic fluid. In the liquid element, these vibrations are transformed into tactile stimuli of the frontal bone, which transmits the information to the inner ear. The foetus hears a sound just as an adult hears a sound when a vibrating tuning fork is placed on their forehead, which amounts to saying that when the mother speaks, she caresses the mouth and the hands of the baby in her womb.[20]

9.4   Forces Forging the Brain in Early Interaction

This channel of communication (using hearing and touch) explains why, within an hour of being born, the newborn baby recognises the voice of its mother.[21] When the mother's voice is recorded and the higher frequencies filtered out, the baby responds and turns their head and eyes towards the source of the sound. But when the lower frequencies are filtered out, they do not respond to a sound object that means nothing to them. The singular memory of the newborn enables them to establish a continuity between the information perceived in the womb and after birth, thereby creating a reassuring bond of familiarity.

Hardly has the baby been born than they can suckle without being taught, provided they can catch the eye of the woman nursing them.[22] The brightness of the eyes and the saccadic eye movements at about 30 centimetres form a sensory object that attracts the baby and organises their sucking reflex. But a breastfeeding diagnostic device reveals that if the woman watches television,

---

[19] Pierre Bustany, Mélanie Laurent, Boris Cyrulnik, and Claude de Tichey, 'Les déterminants neurologiques de la résilience'. In Claude de Tichey (ed.), *Violence subie et résilience* (Toulouse: Érès, 2015, 17–47).

[20] Carolyn Granier-Deferre and Benoist Schaal, 'Aux sources fœtales des réponses sensorielles et émotionnelles du nouveau-né'. *Spirale*, n° 33, 2005/1. Toulouse: Érès, 2005, 21–40.

[21] Eliane Noirot, 'Réflexion sur la stratégie de recherche du développement humain précoce', *Enfance: La première année de la vie*, n° 36, 1983, 169–97. www.persee.fr/doc/enfan_0013-7545_1983_num_36_1_2810.

[22] Pierre Rousseau, Florence Matton, Renaud Lécuyer, and Willie Lahaye, 'Étude éthologique des premières interactions enfants-parents lors de la naissance', *Devenir*, 31.1 (2019), 5–54.

talks to someone else, or ignores the baby, the sucking action slows down and the newborn baby releases the nipple. The mother's voice is an early sensory object that ties one of the first knots in a reassuring and stimulating attachment bond.[23]

This maternal sensory object also possesses a sculpting action on the left temporal lobe of the baby to whom the mother speaks. This sculpting effect is more powerful than that of any other voice since the baby has been accustomed to this auditory object since the uterine stage. If the baby is surrounded by people talking, the effect is of a hubbub of barely distinguished vocal objects. But if the baby is addressed multisensorially (i.e., eyes, smell, handling, and sucking), the maternal sensory speech stands out and stimulates the auditory cortex, the left temporal lobe, during a highly sensitive period for the development of the neurons and synapses. This maternal auditory object imprints a neural circuit, a cluster that only human beings possess, situated at the upper and posterior sector of the temporal gyrus, the planum temporale.[24] From the age of three months, the baby shows a lively interest in sentences spoken by their mother, as shown by neuroimaging of the baby's left temporal area, which works and burns energy when their mother reads a sentence. But three months later, when the mother is asked to read the same sentence backwards, the cerebral lobe of the child no longer responds. With brain maturation and the repetition of the mother's sentences, the six-month-old baby has learnt to recognise the prosody of the Mother tongue. The auditory object that has imprinted a neural circuit in the planum temporale started out as a sound, a piece of vocal architecture, before rapidly becoming prosody. The baby perceives this object better than any other because 'exposition to a stimulus structured like a language has progressively specialised the cerebral regions'.[25]

The steps towards the Mother tongue result from an ongoing transaction between a certain kind of cerebral development and a certain kind of language with which the mother envelops her baby. If she is constantly angry or depressed, her language envelope will imprint different forms on the child's brain. It is at this early stage that the role of the father comes into play – earlier than was formerly believed. Directed observation on the model of the 'mother-baby-father' triangle has been standardised:[26] when the parents set up a

---

[23] Anthony J. Decasper, Jean-Pierre Lecanuet, Marie-Claire Busnel, Carolyn Granier-Deferre, and Roselyne Maugeais, 'Fetal reactions to recurrent maternal speech', *Infant Behavior and Development*, 17.2 (1994), 159–64.

[24] The planum temporale is an area of the cerebral cortex that is involved in speech.

[25] Ghislaine Dehaene-Lambertz, 'Bases cérébrales de l'acquisition du langage: Apport de la neuro-imagerie', *Neuropsychiatrie de l'enfance et de l'adolescence*, 52 (2004), 455–457.

[26] Elisabeth Fivaz-Depeursinge and Antoinette Corboz-Warnery, *The Primary Triangle: A Developmental Systems View of Mothers, Fathers and Infants* (New York: Basic Books, 1999).

harmonious sensory cocoon characterised by speaking in turn, smiling faces, and interactive gestures, the baby is interested in every sentence and directs their attention to one parent and then the other. But when difficulties interfere with parenting (e.g., conflict, depression, or some kind of accident), the affected parent becomes avoidant and less inclined to share the pleasure of engaging verbally or behaviourally with their partner and with the child. When structured in this way, the sensory cocoon takes another shape and imprints itself differently in the biological memory of the infant. This non-reassuring discord tutors language acquisition less satisfactorily than usual, and the child may manifest relational disorders with the non-reassuring parent and not manifest such disorders with the reassuring one.[27]

At about the tenth to twelfth month, finger-pointing gestures begin.[28] This behaviour reveals that the infant is beginning to escape from the proximity of sensory stimuli. By pointing, they indicate a distant object and direct the mental world of the other person. At the age of about four, if the sensory cocoon has tutored their development successfully, the child becomes able to decentre themselves in order to picture someone else's representations. Their capacity for empathy is developing well. First, they will have picked up the non-verbal communication and sounds of the other person (e.g., smile, verbal caresses), then their intentions (e.g., an invitation to play or the offer of affection or pre-verbal interdictions), right up to finally being able to represent to themselves the other's mental world. The child has become capable of understanding that an agreed sensory object (e.g., a word, a warning finger) has been put there to represent an object or an event that cannot be perceived by the senses in the immediate environment, but which can designate an absent object or an entity totally beyond sensory perception, such as God, history, death, or others' beliefs. At this point, the theory of mind becomes operative: 'I believe that he believes', and the child responds to an invisible object.

This also means that speech has the power to lead to delusion. My black cat clearly perceives the expression of my listless or enervated emotions. He perceives my intention to caress or attack him. But he cannot think that I want to attack him because his fur is black, which to me means that he has visited the fires of hell as was believed in the Middle Ages. By creating virtual worlds for us to inhabit, speech leads to the works of art of wordsmiths, such as novels, films, or essays. It can also lead to non-psychotic delusion, when a

---

[27] Tuula Tamminent and Kaija Puura, 'Infant/early years mental health'. In Anita Thapar, Daniel S. Pine, et al. (eds.), *Rutter's Child and Adolescent Psychiatry* (Oxford: Wiley-Blackwell, [2015] 2018), 85–86.

[28] Anne Robichez-Dispa and Boris Cyrulnik, 'Observation éthologique du pointer du doigt chez des enfants normaux et des enfants psychotiques', *Neuropsychiatrie de l'enfance et de l'adolescence*, 5–6 (1992), 292–9.

coherent narrative that one believes in is severed from the palpable world, as with rumours, prejudice, or persecutory fantasies.

The development of language is the result of constant interaction between the maturing brain and the structure of the Mother tongue enveloping the infant, which they are gradually adapting to. The determining factors of this process are first neurological, then emotional, and finally sociocultural. When the environment lacks words because the mother has not had the benefits of education or because some unhappiness prevents her from expressing herself, the child will only be able to acquire a small stock of words. Some children start nursery school at the age of three with a vocabulary of 200 words, whereas others, from privileged backgrounds, have 1,000 words at their disposal. Guess which ones will fill the ranks of the high achievers! 'The disparity in vocabulary acquisition in relation to the family's socio-economic circumstances is attenuated if the kind of childcare is considered', whether a kindergarten or a licensed childminder.[29]

It is therefore possible to compensate for this verbal handicap by implementing certain political and educational measures.[30]

9.5   Impairment of the Word-Making Machine

The language area of the brain can be impaired by a genetic anomaly or by disease, whether infectious, vascular, or traumatic. Sometimes, as is the case in children with autism, the fast rate of development prevents the brain from being shaped by the environment. The child perceives a blurred world that goes by too fast for them to decipher its non-verbal facial expressions and verbal sounds.[31] Terrified by this sensory tornado, the child concentrates more on self-centred activities that have a calming effect but impede any kind of relationship.

In most cases, what deforms brain ontogenesis is an impoverishment of the sensory cocoon enveloping the baby. This notion was first proved by a Nobel Prize winner in 1981: kittens wear a patch over their left eye, and when they die an atrophied right occiput is observed.[32] When the patch is on the right eye, the atrophied occiput is on the left. Since the recent proliferation of

---

[29] Sebastien Grobon, Lidia Panico, and Anne Solaz, 'Inégalités socio-économiques dans le développement langagier et moteur des enfants à deux ans', *Bulletin Épidémiologique Hebdomadaire*, 1/2–9 (2019), invs.santepubliquefrance.fr/beh/2019/1/2019_1_1.html. Marine Joras, 'CrossDoc: La solution de téléexpertise labellisée adaptée à vos questions en hépatologie, gastroentérologie et nutrition pédiatriques', *Medecine et Enfance*, 4 (2020), 102,.

[30] 'The First Thousand Days Report on Families and Children', a governmental commission chaired by Boris Cyrulnik in 2019. The report was submitted on 8 September 2020.

[31] Carole Tardif and Bruno Gepner, *L'Autisme* (Paris: Armand Colin, 2007).

[32] David H. Hubel and Torstel N. Wiesel, *Brain and Visual Perception: The Story of a 25-Year Collaboration* (Oxford: Oxford University Press, 2004).

neuroimaging, these data have been used in humans to observe how in the early months, during the sensitive period when the development of the synapses is extremely rapid (300,000 synapses per minute), an impoverishment of the sensory cocoon – by failing to stimulate the receptor areas of the brain such as the planum temporale – causes a functional anomaly that, if prolonged, becomes a structural anomaly. Neuroimaging carried out on children who have endured severe sensory deprivation in Romanian 'orphanages' shows that the rhinencephalon amygdala is very swollen[33] because the prefrontal lobes have been atrophied by the lack of stimulation and have lost their power to inhibit the amygdala.[34] Moreover, as there has been no human relationship, there is nothing to memorise, so the limbic system is also atrophied. A brain such as this, shaped by an impoverished early environment, produces a child incapable of controlling their emotions and who has difficulty learning the words of their surroundings because their memory circuitry is atrophied, and the planum temporale has not had any practice in discriminating phonemes.[35] The child hears approximations of words they have difficulty understanding, which provokes emotional reactions in the form of panic attacks or uncontrollable violence. These children are difficult to love, to raise, and to provide with a school education, which leads to socialisation challenges.

When such children are invited to explain themselves, they rationalise with reference to an intensely felt emotion whose cause they cannot locate. They put what they feel into words, thereby giving shape to a world bereft of meaning because their impaired memory prevents them from narrating their own past. They cannot associate it with dreams for the future either since their atrophied prefrontal lobes make it impossible for them to anticipate. They experience a succession of angry or bitter outbursts that for them are self-evidently justified, when actually they are giving verbal expression to sensations caused by a dysfunction of the brain.

Lobotomy can explain the expression of verbalised emotional reactions (car accidents cause a thousand per year). A wounded person who has suffered a lobotomy can no longer connect what they have stocked in their memory with what they anticipate. When asked a question, they can reply properly and there is no speech impediment, but they can no longer relate a narrative. Because

---

[33] The rhinencephalon is the chiefly olfactory part of the forebrain. The rhinencephalon amygdala is activated by all types of novel sensory experience but is inhibited by environmental stimuli that are recognized as familiar (and therefore already stored in some component of the memory).

[34] Mitul A. Mehta, Nicole I. Golembo, et al., 'Amygdale, hippocampal and corpus cellosum size following severe early institutional deprivation: The English and Romanian adopted study pilot', *Journal of Child Psychology and Psychiatry*, 50.8 (2009), 943–51.

[35] David Cohen, 'The Developmental Being'. In M. Elena Garralda and Jean-Philippe Raynaud (eds.), *Brain, Mind and Developmental Psychopathology in Childhood* (New York: Jason Aronson, 2012).

temporal representation has become impossible, they can only produce short sentences without relative pronouns. They cannot tell the story of Little Red Riding Hood, for instance. If the story is related to them, deliberately reversing the time sequence – 'once she had been eaten by the wolf, Little Red Riding Hood took a cake and a jar of butter. . .' – the lobotomised person will correct it. Their memory of the story is therefore intact, but they can no longer retrieve it at will. The intentional force of memory has been destroyed by the lobotomy; the wounded person can no longer anticipate their past.

This means that for human language to develop, for the convention of the linguistic sign to function, each individual must be interested in the mental world of others; in other words, they must have access to a pre-verbal theory of the mind. My grandson was about five years old when my daughter said: 'Before you sit down to eat go and wash your hands'. The washbasin is at the end of a long corridor. The child ran off, and before reaching the basin he turned round to go back. I was standing at the other end of the corridor; I smiled and dropped my arms. He saw that I had seen him, turned round, and went and washed his hands. When he saw that I had seen him, he understood that I had understood his intention to pretend to us that he had washed his hands. When one has access to pre-verbal inter-mentality, one has the capacity to agree to the convention of the sign and not merely to emit signals; all that remains is to learn the words of the Mother tongue. There must be an agreement between two brains for a sign emitted by one of them to be able to form circuitry in the planum temporale of the brain of the other.

This is the reason why I have refrained from using the expression 'language area', as if a particular neurological zone contained an aptitude for speech. The circuitry of this area derives from the converging of multiple sources of sensory pressure. The best metaphor to convey this idea is that of a marshalling yard with numerous railway tracks converging on it to produce a word.

A case in point is optical aphasia. A small vascular accident in the left temporal lobe prevents the patient from naming the object in front of them. 'What is it for?' 'Writing'. 'What is it called?' Silence. The patient is incapable of providing a name. 'What if you touch this object?' 'Oh, it's a pen.' Tactile information is parietal; it converges with the visual data – which is occipital – to associate these railway tracks that transport heterogenous data and stimulate the left ascending frontal F3, making it possible to enunciate the word 'pen'.[36]

The notion of rationalisation recurs with Anton-Babinski syndrome.[37] A scanner in a private clinic shows a small lesion in the right parieto-occipital region. The patient has hemiplegia on the left side of the body but does not

---

[36] The frontal F3 is one of the three frontal lobe convolutions of the cortex.

[37] Anton-Babinski syndrome corresponds to a loss of consciousness in one half of the body, which has become paralysed and insensitive.

realise it. 'Can you lift your left arm?' Yes. 'Please raise it'. No movement. The patient is paralysed and as the lesion has caused anosognosia, he is convinced he is not paralysed.[38] 'Look at your left arm. You can see it hasn't moved.' The patient is outraged: 'Who put that arm in my bed?' Another patient suffering from a similar lesion likewise maintains that he is not paralysed. His arms are under the bedsheets, the doctor touches his left arm, and the patient cries out, indignant: 'Who put that pile of rags in my bed!' He has seen the arm, he has felt it under the bedcovers, but as the marshalling yard is impaired by the vascular accident, he provides an apparently logical reason for disunited points of sensory convergence. The same process is observed in Korsakoff syndrome, in which the mammillary tubers of the memory circuitry have been destroyed by alcohol and the patient suffers from anterograde amnesia.[39] When asked a question concerning their recent past, everything goes blank, and to fill the void they make up a story: 'I didn't say hello to you yesterday because I am snowed under with work. I have other things to do.' A lie would be intentional and serve as self-defence, whereas fabulation provides coherence and fills a world that has been amputated by an enormous blackout.

The elderly often first have trouble with the working memory. This is the memory that enables actions to be planned in advance: 'Where have I put my glasses?' But as they have conserved the memory of the early shaping, they do not need to make stories up: 'I can't remember what we did yesterday, but I can tell you what I did at school and give you the names of my classmates when I was ten.' At the early stages of Alzheimer's disease, on the other hand, when words become more and more elusive, the patient goes back to the finger-pointing of their infancy and uses gestures to indicate the things they can no longer call by their name. When access to vocabulary becomes difficult, gestures thus take over and paraverbal skills can continue to be used for communication for a long time yet.[40]

9.6   The Use of Words Modifies the Word-Making Machine

A healthy memory is evolutive. When a person has suffered trauma and has never been able to speak about it, when they have denied it or been forced to keep it to themselves, when with age the short-term memory (e.g., the ability to repeat a list of words or numbers) and the working memory (e.g., giving one's

---

[38] Anosognosia is the inability or refusal to recognize a defect or disorder that is clinically ostensible.
[39] The Korsakoff syndrome is a chronic memory disorder most commonly caused by alcohol abuse. Anterograde amnesia refers to a decrease in the ability to retain new information.
[40] Jean-Pierre Polydor, *Alzheimer, mode d'emploi : Le livre des aidants* (Bordeaux: L'Esprit du Temps, 2014).

phone number backwards) become impaired, the memory imprint of the trauma rushes back 'as if it had just happened to me'. But when sufferers have been able to speak of their trauma, they will have added to their memory images of horror, the memory of the words that gave verbal shape to the horror of the trauma. Through this work with words, they have been able to reshape not the horror, but the representation of the horror in their memory.

The impact of a language on the brain, its trace, varies according to the level of construction of the brain. When plurilingual subjects suffer from aphasia, the languages are erased in the reverse order of learning them, and when recovery begins, the first language to return is the Mother tongue, the first and most deeply imprinted language. With dementia, in which the deterioration is gradual, it is not rare to see an Italian immigrant who has spent his life speaking French say in Italian what he has forgotten in French. Language recovery does not always take place in chronological order because each brain circuitry is the result of its own existence, and because the most deeply imprinted language is the one that is the most emotionally charged. This is often the Mother tongue, provided the words are laden with attachment, but when socio-historical events have made it a language of misery, such as the language of the occupier or the language of persecution, as was the case with Yiddish for Jews in the 1950s, this language, albeit the Mother tongue, is difficult to learn because it conveys distress and, in aphasic patients, will be difficult to recover.[41]

The language imprint in the brain combines with its emotional power to produce a language that provides the pleasure of relationship or the unpleasantness of inhabiting a language that conveys distress and evokes wretchedness.

The imprint is evidenced by alexia and agraphia in Asians.[42] When Asians suffer from thrombosis in the middle cerebral artery, they become aphasic, alexic, and agraphic in our sign system but can continue to read in their own system, which, more ideographic than ours, has developed circuitry in a brain area closer to the occipital visual zones.[43]

The fact that brain circuits are developed by language does not exclude emotional pressure: 'Forget your Mother tongue, German, the language of the genocide'.[44] Yet when there is a change of culture, the meaning of a language changes its emotional connotations. Young Jews take pleasure in learning Yiddish and Klezmer songs: today, seventy years after the genocide, they

---

[41] Claude Cervini, *Contribution à l'étude des facteurs de la récupération de l'aphasie*, Unpublished PhD thesis, (Strasburg, 1988), 40–47.

[42] Alexia is the loss of the ability to read, agraphia is the loss of the ability to write.

[43] Sumiko Sasanuma, 'Kana and kanji processing in Japanese aphasics', *Brain and language*, 2 (1975), 369–83. See also 'Impairment of written language in Japanese aphasics: Kana versus kanji processing'. *Journal of Chinese Linguistics*, 2.2 (1974), 141–58.

[44] Aharon Appelfeld, *Histoire d'une vie*, translated by Valérie Zenatti (Paris: L'Olivier, 2004).

connote the pleasure of rediscovering the language of their grandparents so as to lay claim to their ascendancy. In the groups learning this language, the young people develop strong emotional bonds; for them, Yiddish has become the language of family ties.[45]

The simple fact of being able to make words alters the sense of self. The frequent transient ischemic attacks (TIA) that people are sometimes afflicted with help us to understand what it feels like to be unable to produce language for forty-eight to seventy-two hours.[46] When these patients are questioned just as they are recovering speech, they speak about how, in a world without words, they were living in glass coffins with leaden bodies, along with a surprising obligation to adhere closely to the stimuli they perceived.[47] As soon as circulation in the planum temporale is back in place, the patients use metaphors of lightness, such as 'an ice-skater eddying round and round', 'a bird flying in the sky', or 'I had seven-league boots on'.

It is frequently said that words are the tools of thought. This is true of rational thinking, but it is only relatively true of rationalisation, and it is false where chanting slogans is concerned. These rhythmic and graphic verbal catchphrases give rise to a collective psittacism that triggers a delicious feeling of belonging by stalling all divergent thought. Those who have experienced transient aphasia explain that 'thought survives language impairment', and that 'concepts outlive words'.[48] It is possible to understand and solve numerous problems thanks to a form of cognitive thought that precedes speech.

Neuroimaging shows how a speech act can modify the way the brain functions. It would suffice to invite a Muslim friend to dinner and offer him a dish, saying, 'It's top-quality pork'. If you were to use functional magnetic resonance imaging on him at the same moment, you would observe the sudden release of a large amount of energy in certain brain areas: the front part of the insula, the front swelling of the anterior cingulate zone, and especially the rhinencephalon amygdala.[49] When a tumour or an infection aggravates these zones, the patient cannot stop vomiting, even if they have had nothing to eat. In my example, a speech act has stimulated this zone and you would obtain the

---

[45] Anne-Marie Houdebine-Gravaud, *L'imaginaire linguistique* (Paris: L'harmattan, 2005).

[46] A transient ischemic attack is a brief episode of cerebral ischemia generally characterised by temporary blurring of vision, slurring of speech, paralysis, numbness, or syncope, and often precedes a serious stroke.

[47] Serge Zlatine, 'Praxis de l'aphasie: Au moment de répondre', *Ornicar? Revue du champ freudien*, 33 (1985), 65–68.

[48] Dominique Laplane, 'Langage et pensée', *La Revue du praticien*, 41.2 (1991), 143–49.

[49] The insula is a small region of the cerebral cortex, and the anterior cingulate zone or cortex is the frontal part of the cingulate cortex. Cf. Leonardo F. Fontenelle, Ricardo de Oliveira-Souza, and Jorge Moll. 'The rise of moral emotion in neuropsychiatry', *Dialogues in Clinical Neurosciences*, 17.4 (2015), 413.

same modification of the brain's functioning if you offered beef while saying, 'it's pork'.

Spoken words and written words trace neural circuits akin to repeated stimuli in what is known as 'the language area'. In this case, it is not the word that acts on the receptor neurons but the speech act, which, in producing an emotion of repulsion, stimulates the brain zone that triggers a sensation of disgust. This is comparable with the athlete who, by imagining himself throwing a heavy weight, increases the consumption of energy in area F5 of the left ascending frontal gyrus.[50] And it is just like the person who is asked to relate a memory and who first 'turns on' their two prefrontal lobes, the neural anticipation base, thereby revealing that they are anticipating their past and that they are about to look for the right images and words to use to relate a memory.[51]

It is this effort of elaboration that stimulates and modifies the way certain cerebral circuits function. The best-known example is that of London taxicab drivers. Before obtaining their licence, they have to train to be able to prepare mentally the circuits they'll need to be familiar with. Magnetic resonance imaging was offered to them before they began, then again three months later, and a third time after a year of professional cab rides. The result was crystal clear: hypertrophy of the grey matter at the back of the hippocampus (the neurological base for the effort of memorising), whereas the front of the limbic circuitry was diminishing in size. The same neuroimaging carried out on bus drivers indicated no impact on any neural circuit since the routine bus trajectory required no representational effort.[52]

These data have been verified during the emotional and verbal work of psychotherapy. Twenty-four people suffering from severe depression agreed to submit to neuroimaging when they began and then again after several months of psychotherapy. In the depths of depression, a bifrontal hypofunctioning was observed, an atrophied limbic dentate gyrus, and a hyperreactivity of the amygdala.[53] After three months of psychic work, these dysfunctions had disappeared. Another group of severely depressed patients agreed to neuroimaging but refused any kind of psychotherapy. Three months later, the dysfunction was the same or worse.[54]

[50] Area F5 is involved in different aspects of motor control and cognitive functions.

[51] Daniel L. Schacter, *À la recherche de la mémoire* (Bruxelles: De Boeck, 1999), 90–91.

[52] Eleanor A. Maguire, Katherine Woolett, and Hugo J. Spiers, 'London taxi drivers and bus drivers: A structural MRI and neuropsychological study', *Hippocampus*, 16 (2006), 1091–1101.

[53] The dentate gyrus is part of the hippocampus, itself part of the subcortical structures of the limbic system.

[54] Mario Beauregard, 'Functional neuroimaging studies of the effect of psychotherapy', *Dialogues in Clinical Neuroscience*, 16.1 (2014), 75–81.

9.7   Conclusion

Speech therefore does not fall from the sky like an incarnation of the soul and does not spurt forth from the brain as bile does from the liver. It takes shape in the interaction between two people in which each seeks to represent to themselves the other's representations. Numerous animals are capable of empathy and cooperation, but only humankind possesses the genes of that cluster of neurons capable of being organised into circuitry by that mental effort and that will go on to form the areas of human language.

This neurological conception of speech brings into focus the force of the emotional and cultural environment in sculpting the brain. But since we can influence the environment that influences our mental world, this degree of freedom gives us a huge responsibility.

Bibliography

Appelfeld, Aharon. *Histoire d'une vie*. Translated by Valérie Zenatti. Paris: L'Olivier, 2004.
Beauregard, Mario. 'Functional neuroimaging studies of the effect of psychotherapy'. *Dialogues in Clinical Neuroscience*, Vol. 16, n° 1, 2014, pp. 75–81.
Bergounioux, Gabriel. 'L'origine du langage: Mythes et théories'. In Jean-Marie Hombert (ed.), *Aux origines des langues et du langage*. Paris: Fayard, 2005.
Bustany, Pierre, Mélanie Laurent, Boris Cyrulnik, and Claude de Tichey. 'Les déterminants neurologiques de la résilience'. In Claude de Tichey (ed.), *Violence subie et résilience*. Toulouse: Érès, 2015.
Cervini, Claude. *Contribution à l'étude des facteurs de la récupération de l'aphasie*. Unpublished PhD thesis. Strasburg, 1988.
Cyrulnik, Boris (chairperson). *The First Thousand Days Report on Families and Children*. A Governmental Commission. Report submitted to the French Government 8 September 2020.
Decasper, Anthony J., Jean-Pierre Lecanuet, Marie-Claire Busnel, Carolyn Granier-Deferre, and Roselyne Maugeais. 'Fetal reactions to recurrent maternal speech'. *Infant Behavior and Development*, Vol. 17, n° 2, 1994, pp. 159–64.
Dehaene-Lambertz, Ghislaine. 'Bases cérébrales de l'acquisition du langage: Apport de la neuro-imagerie'. *Neuropsychiatrie de l'enfance et de l'adolescence*, n° 52, 2004, pp. 452–9.
Fivaz-Depeursinge, Elisabeth, and Antoinette Corboz-Warnery. *The Primary Triangle: A Developmental Systems View of Mothers, Fathers and Infants*. New York: Basic Books, 1999.
Fontenelle, Leonardo F., Ricardo de Oliveira-Souza, and Jorge Moll. 'The rise of moral emotion in neuropsychiatry'. *Dialogues in Clinical Neurosciences*, Vol. 17, n° 4, 2015, pp. 411–20.
Garralda, M. Elena, and Jean-Philippe Raynaud (eds). 'The Developmental Being'. In *Brain, Mind and Developmental Psychopathology in Childhood*. New York: Jason Aronson, 2012.
Granier-Deferre, Carolyn, and Benoist Schaal. 'Aux sources fœtales des réponses sensorielles et émotionnelles du nouveau-né'. *Spirale*, n° 33/1. 2005, pp. 21–40.

Grobon, Sebastien, Lidia Panico, and Anne Solaz. 'Inégalités socioéconomiques dans le développement langagier et moteur des enfants à 2 ans'. *Bulletin Épidémiologique Hebdomadaire*, n° 1, 2019. invs.santepubliquefrance.fr/beh/2019/1/2019_1_1.html.

Houdebine-Gravaud, Anne-Marie. *L'imaginaire linguistique*. Paris: L'harmattan, 2005.

Hubel, David H., and Torstel N. Wiesel. *Brain and Visual Perception: The Story of a 25-Year Collaboration*. Oxford: Oxford University Press, 2004.

Joras, Marine. 'CrossDoc: La solution de téléexpertise labellisée adaptée à vos questions en hépatologie, gastroentérologie et nutrition pédiatriques'. *Medecine et Enfance*, n° 4, 2020. www.edimark.fr/medecine-enfance/crossdoc-solution-teleexpertise-labellisee-adaptee-a-vos-questions-hepatologie-gastroenterologie-nutrition-pediatriques.

Laplane, Dominique. 'Langage et pensée'. *La Revue du praticien*, Vol. 41, n° 2, 1991. pp. 143–9.

Maguire, Eleanor A., Katherine Woollett, and Hugo J. Spiers. 'London taxi drivers and bus drivers: A structural MRI and neuropsychological study'. *Hippocampus*, n° 16, 2006, pp. 1091–1101.

Mehta, Mitul A., and Nicole I. Golembo, et al. 'Amygdale, hippocampal and corpus cellosum size following severe early institutional deprivation: the English and Romanian adopted study pilot'. *Journal of Child Psychology and Psychiatry*, Vol. 50, n° 8, 2009, pp. 943–51.

Noirot, Éliane. 'Réflexion sur la stratégie de recherche du développement humain précoce'. *Enfance: La première année de la vie*, n° 36, 1983, pp. 169–97, www.persee.fr/doc/enfan_0013-7545_1983_num_36_1_2810.

Polydor, Jean-Pierre. *Alzheimer, mode d'emploi: Le livre des aidants*. Bordeaux: L'Esprit du Temps, 2014.

Robichez-Dispa, Anne, and Boris Cyrulnik. 'Observation éthologique du pointer du doigt chez des enfants normaux et des enfants psychotiques'. *Neuropsychiatrie de l'enfance et de l'adolescence*, n° 5–6, 1992.

Rousseau, Pierre, Florence Matton, Renaud Lécuyer, and Willie Lahaye. 'Étude éthologique des premières interactions enfants-parents lors de la naissance'. *Devenir*, Vol. 31, n° 1, 2019, pp. 5–54.

Sasanuma, Sumiko. 'Kana and kanji processing in Japanese aphasics'. *Brain and language*, Vol. 2, 1975, pp. 369–83.

'Impairment of written language in Japanese aphasics: Kana versus kanji processing'. *Journal of Chinese Linguistics*, Vol. 2, n° 2, 1974, pp. 141–58.

Schacter, Daniel L. *À la recherche de la mémoire*. Bruxelles: De Boeck, 1999.

Soulé, Michel, and Boris Cyrulnik. *L'intelligence avant la parole*. Paris: Éditions sociales françaises, ESF Éditeur, 1998.

Tamminent, Tuula, and Kaija Puura. 'Infant/early years mental health'. In Anita Thapar and Daniel S. Pine, et al. (eds.), *Rutter's Child and Adolescent Psychiatry*, 6th ed. Oxford: Wiley-Blackwell, [2015] 2018.

Tardif, Carole, and Bruno Gepner. *L'autisme*. Paris: Armand Colin, 2007.

Vauclair, Jacques. *La cognition animale*. Paris: Presses Universitaires de France/Que sais-je?, 1996.

Zlatine, Serge. 'Praxis de l'aphasie: Au moment de répondre'. *Ornicar? Revue du champ freudien*, n° 33, 1985.

Subject Index

accents, 8, 39, 113, 120
accident at birth, 17
acting out, 148
affectivity
  depressive affects, 165
  emotional legitimacy, 23
affiliation, process of, 7, 96
aggressive impulses, 158, 165
agraphia, 182
alexia, 182
alternity, 61
Alzheimer's disease, 181
Aneignung, 46, 49, 55
anti-destiny, 25
aphasia, 11, 19, 23
  optical, 180
aporia of transmission, 7, 99
appropriation, 4, 20, 46, 49, 99, 107
articulated language, 17, 20, 22, 140
assessment, 62, 77–8
autism, 150, 178

Babel, 8–9, 40, 140
beyond the bounds of the mother, 4, 12, 20, 27,
  34–5
beyond the verb, 11
beyond the word, 163, 168
biculturalism, 73
birth, preterm, 17
black hole, 150
blackout, 181
body, the, 2, 9, 121, 127
  bodily capture, 44
  body oriented, 2, 19, 23, 26, 30
  body words, 139
border tax, 8–9, 120
breast milk speech, 139

catchphrases, 183
chora, 6, 69
circuitry, 11, 174, 179–80
class, social, 26, 32

code switching, 53, 64
cognitive thought, 183
conflict
  between languages, 23, 26, 30, 32, 97
  of loyalty, 18, 32, 65
  between parents, 177
  psychic, 147
corporeality, 12
cortisol, 173
creative writing, 3, 5, 12, 69
  plurilingual workshops, 6, 60, 65, 72, 79

decentring, 67
degeneration, 18
delusion, 127, 177
dementia, 182
dialect, 32, 51–2, 54–5, 73, 87
  family, 39, 47
  of French, 40
  the mother tongue as, local, 44
diglossia, 54
dissertation, 73, 145
dissolution, filial, 18
distancing, 31, 67, 128
divide, 30, 32, 45, 96
dyslalia, 113

ethnopsychiatry, 7
ethology, 11
exile (etymology), 25
exile within exile, 11
exiles, 17, 19, 24, 43, 70, 152
exophonic, 10, 63, 76
explication de texte, 73

Father tongue, 139
fatherland, 54
filiation
  linguistics of, 6
  process of, 96
finger-pointing, 177, 181
foetus, 139, 174–5

Author Index

For EU product safety concerns, contact us at Calle de José Abascal, 56–1°, 28003 Madrid, Spain or eugpsr@cambridge.org.

www.ingramcontent.com/pod-product-compliance
Ingram Content Group UK Ltd.
Pitfield, Milton Keynes, MK11 3LW, UK
UKHW020351140625
459647UK00020B/2407

* 9 7 8 1 0 0 9 0 1 4 2 4 3 *